A BIRD'S-EYE VIEW OF
OUR CIVIL WAR

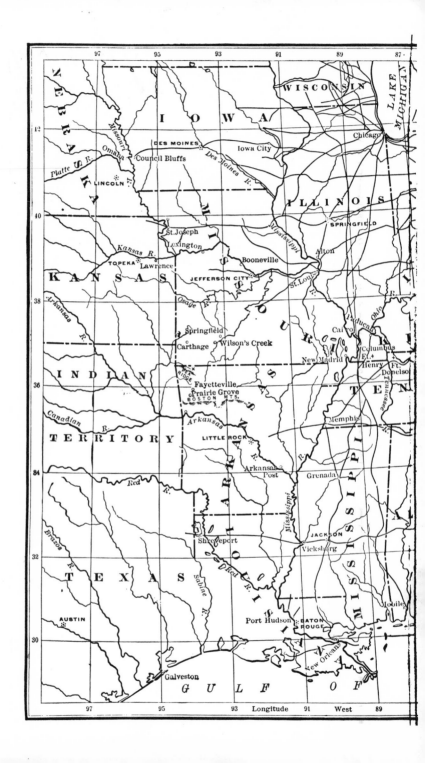

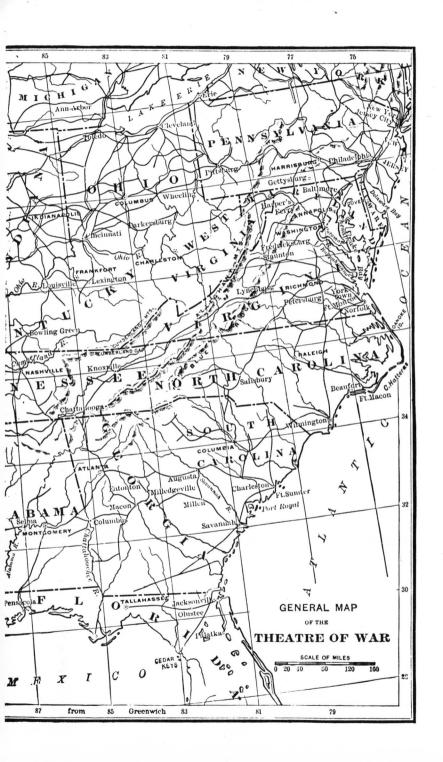

GENERAL MAP

OF THE

THEATRE OF WAR

SCALE OF MILES

A BIRD'S-EYE VIEW OF
OUR CIVIL WAR

THEODORE AYRAULT DODGE

BREVET LIEUTENANT-COLONEL UNITED STATES ARMY, RETIRED LIST; AUTHOR OF
"THE CAMPAIGN OF CHANCELLORSVILLE," "PATROCLUS AND PENELOPE,"
"A CHAT IN THE SADDLE," "GREAT CAPTAINS," "ALEXANDER,"
"HANNIBAL," "CAESAR," "GUSTAVUS ADOLPHUS,"
ETC., ETC.

DA CAPO PRESS • NEW YORK

Library of Congress Cataloging-in-Publication Data

Dodge, Theodore Ayrault, 1842–1909.
  A bird's eye view of our Civil War / Theodore Ayrault
Dodge.
      p.   cm.
  Originally published: Boston: Houghton, Mifflin and Co., 1897.
  Includes index.
  ISBN 0-306-80845-5 (alk. paper)
  1. United States—History—Civil War, 1861–1865—Campaigns.
I. Title.
E470.D64   1998
973.7′3—dc21   97-32938
                                                              CIP

First Da Capo Press edition 1998

This Da Capo Press paperback edition of *A Bird's-Eye View of
Our Civil War* is an unabridged republication of the revised
edition published in Cambridge, Massachusetts in 1897.

Published by Da Capo Press, Inc.
A Subsidiary of Plenum Publishing Corporation
233 Spring Street, New York, N.Y. 10013

Manufactured in the United States of America

CONTENTS.

MAPS AND CHARTS.

MAPS SPECIALLY PREPARED FOR THIS WORK.

DEDICATORY LETTER.

To ROBERT ELKIN NEIL DODGE:—

MY DEAR NEIL,—Few of the generation to which you belong will ever become familiar with the details of the gigantic struggle through which your father's generation fought. But every young American should know its outlines. The following pages are what I long ago promised you, when you should be of an age to take an interest in the subject. They are too few to make any pretence to being a history of the war; nor have they anything to do with its political aspect.

A soldier can discuss calmly victory or defeat. Politics do not seem to be treated with equal good-temper. Each side in our great Civil War believed itself in the right, and fought with the courage so engendered. You need not busy yourself with the asperities of the political field of twenty years ago. The causes which brought about the war have been stated in the briefest manner only.

The principal military events are herein grouped in such sequence that a careful reading, *with the maps before you*, will yield you a fair knowledge of what modern war is, and what our Civil War was. Many interesting minor operations have been barely mentioned; some altogether omitted. All important ones have due space allotted to them as even-handedly as the matter and the general purpose of the work will allow. Many of the manœuvres about Petersburg in the last year of the war were on a scale so vast that they rank almost as separate campaigns. But although they called for endurance and skill of the highest order and for enormous sacrifices, as they were really parts of one great whole, less space has in some instances been devoted to these than to other lesser but independent conflicts. The skeleton thus presented, can readily be clothed from the standard histories.

To know this subject well requires the diligent study of many volumes. I have tried to give you a good general idea in one.

No claim to originality is made for this book. The facts, and many of the opinions, have been gleaned from the pages of numerous authors. Their patient labors have made the history of our Civil Strife the property of the public; and to all of them my thanks are due.

The maps are accurate enough for the purposes of the book. To convey a rapid general idea of the various battle-fields is their aim rather than the greater exactness which may be found in more extended works. The small rectangles, representing troops, indicate general position only. Too great detail has been purposely avoided.

The few technical terms, which for convenience and greater conciseness have been used in the book, all but explain themselves. And few, indeed, are the firesides in this country which have not at least one member who can interpret the ordinary manœuvres of grand-tactics or strategy. A short glossary is appended.

Though but twenty years have elapsed since these events were enacted, the authorities on our Civil War constantly disagree as to numbers and localities; frequently even as to dates. Errors have probably crept into this volume. But they will be found, it is hoped, neither many nor grave.

The intelligent treatment of military operations necessitates more or less criticism. That which has here been indulged in is meant to be temperate as well as honest. It is made with a full appreciation of the unusual difficulties which beset our generals, with a sincere admiration of their qualities and services, and in that spirit of diffidence which should become a soldier who bore but a modest part in the great struggle which they conducted to a successful issue.

Our Civil War was full of dramatic incident. Every war is. But the narrow limits of this work forbid the devotion of any space to what others have sufficiently painted. My aim has been to give the layman a clear idea of the war as a military whole, paying no heed to individual heroism nor dwelling upon the war as a spectacle. Regimental histories have already done, and will continue to do, this. Names are given only to elucidate operations.

While holding the conviction that the cause of the North was right, I yield to no Southerner in my admiration of the splendid gallantry of our old enemy, now our brother ; and I believe that no one will accuse me of intentional partiality in my narration of events.

I need not ask you, my dear Neil, to study these pages, for you are now old enough to desire an intelligent knowledge of our great war.

Your affectionate father,

THEODORE AYRAULT DODGE.

Brookline, Mass., 1883.

PREFACE.

IN correcting the figures given in this new edition, the latest War Department publications, the invaluable work of Colonel Fox, and other well-known sources have been consulted. It must be remembered that no war statistics can be absolutely accurate. Records were not kept in the same manner in the Northern and Southern armies; many have been lost; some were never made. Should two equally competent and honest men figure up, from the material at hand and by the same rules, the combatants and casualties of half-a-dozen battles, they would vary more or less. Even the War Department has, from time to time, altered the figures in many of its tables. But reasonable accuracy can be attained; and the author desires, among other sources of information, to express his peculiar indebtedness to the valuable work of Col. Thomas L. Livermore, whose tables of forces and casualties have been laid under free contribution. Colonel Livermore has figured out the numbers for the Northern and Southern armies on the same basis. His studies are intended to enrich the archives of the Military Historical Society of Massachusetts; and his tabulation of figures of the Civil War is singularly accurate and suggestive.

The facts stated have been diligently compared with the Official Records of the Rebellion by Capt. Edward B. Robins, for many years Secretary of the same Society; and, owing to his valuable labor, for which my earnest thanks are due, every such fact can now be substantiated from the record.

The author alone is responsible for the opinions expressed.

New maps have been prepared from the Government surveys and charts. These have equally passed under the scrutiny of Captain Robins. They are all north and south.

The author hopes that, in its new dress, the work may continue to give the same satisfaction which, from its constant sale in a more expensive form, he is assured that it has so far done.

BROOKLINE, October, 1896.

I.

THE CASUS BELLI.

FOR many years a great political strife had been gradually undermining the ties of tradition and mutual
interest betwixt North and South. The rival sections had
fought side by side in conquering our independence and in
maintaining it. Every reason, commercial and national,
should have held us together. The slighter differences of
opinion had been mainly about tariff protection to the
Northern manufacturers, and kindred financial subjects.
Differences like these could scarcely have involved serious
results. The real cause of the growing animosity was
associated with the questions attending slavery.

With whatever unanimity servile labor may now be condemned as a social and commercial mistake, — leaving its
moral aspect entirely out of the question, — the institution
of slavery, in the decade preceding the war, was asserted
by the Southern States to be the keystone of their success
in the same measure that paid labor was held in the North
to have built up the wealth of its manufacturing communities and to have opened the wheat fields of the West.
The difference in climate and products yielded each section
abundant sources of argument for its own peculiar views.

But the matter did not stop at discussion. The South, to acquire additional political power, desired to extend the institution into the rapidly growing Territories of the Union; the North, for similar reasons, desired to have it excluded from all but those States where it had taken such firm root that it could not be extirpated without too great upheaval. There was of course in each section a minority of very bitter opponents and favorers of slavery, whose extreme utterances and acts bred more or less ill-feeling. But the general question was confined to the territorial extension or restriction of slave labor.

For many years the pro-slavery men North and South had held possession of the reins of government. But the party of free labor, owing to immigration, which preferably sought the Northern and Western States, was thought to be on the point of dispossessing them. The Republican party, which desired to restrict slavery to the limits it already occupied, existed mostly in the North. The Democrats of the South wished to extend slavery; their political allies in the Northern States aimed to prevent rupture by concessions to the Southern idea.

In 1860 a new President had to be chosen. The Democrats North and South outnumbered the Republicans. If they worked together, they could scarcely fail to elect their candidate. But the Southern Democrats demanded a platform which should recognize both slavery as a national institution, and the right of secession. This latter was no new doctrine. Secession had been threatened before, and the abstract right of a State to rupture its relations with the Union had been stoutly maintained and denied on the one and the other side. The demands of the Southern wing led to a breach in the Democratic party, the result of which was that four presidential candidates came into the field, — two Democrats, Douglas representing the North and Breckenridge the South; a Whig, Bell, representing the party of concession; and a Republican, Lincoln.

Out of nearly 4,700,000 votes, Mr. Lincoln received 1,900,000. This fell short of an actual majority, but was much more than any other candidate received, and the usual machinery of election gave the Republican candidate the suffrages of the electoral college. He was legally chosen President.

Still, despite their defeat, the Democrats would retain a majority in Congress, and could assert their rights in ample measure. But this power was not ample enough. The ultra men among the Southern leaders determined upon actual secession as a remedy, hoping to retrieve by threats of force what they had lost by their political rupture with the Northern Democracy. Many opposed this course. But in vain. The passions of the Southern people were at fever heat. Secession measures were at once put in play. And as the National administration, until the succeeding March, was still Democratic, the South reaped many advantages from the weakness, and in some instances outright dishonesty of United States officials.

Compromises were attempted. But matters had gone too far. Before New Year of 1861 had dawned, South Carolina had set up as an independent power. The other Southern States in turn passed ordinances of secession, a

Confederacy was formed, and North and South were openly arrayed against each other.

But it must be remembered that while slavery had been at the root of the trouble, the actual *casus belli* was the act of secession, to maintain and to prevent which our Civil War was really waged. As the struggle grew in intensity, the final extirpation of slavery became an element in the calculations of the North, and even a means of encouraging its people. But at the outset the contest was solely a War for the Union.

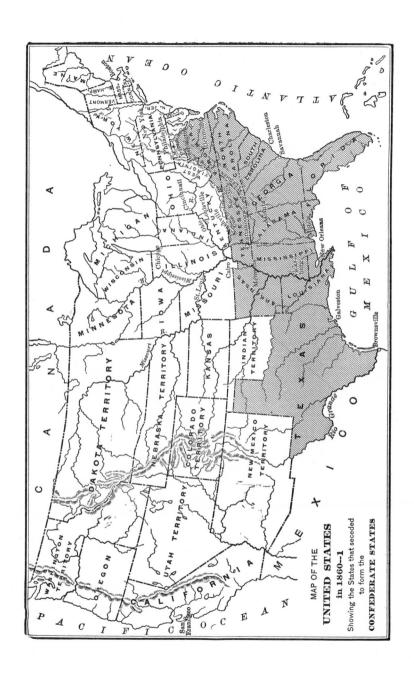

MAP OF THE
UNITED STATES
in 1860–1
Showing the States that seceded
to form the
CONFEDERATE STATES

II.

THE OPENING SITUATION.

A BIRD'S-EYE view of Our Civil War shows a
threefold division of military operations. The
mightier conflicts had their scene in the States bordering
on the East or on the West of the Alleghany Mountains.
Most minor hostilities were waged on the outskirts of the
Confederacy. Many of the latter had so little, if any,
bearing upon the general result, that they may be briefly
dismissed from sight without affecting an intelligent view of
the whole. Some bore a weighty share in our eventual
success.

It will be remembered that, in a general way, the offensive was ours, the defensive the Confederate share of the
struggle. But as the best defense is often a vigorous attack, so the Confederates waged sometimes an offensive-
defensive warfare, as in the case of Lee's incursions across
the Potomac in 1862 and 1863, or Bragg's march to the
Ohio river in 1862. But the general policy pursued by
the Confederates was formulated by Jefferson Davis when
he said that "all we ask is to be let alone."

In the East the two rival capitals faced each other at no
great interval. and were hungrily fought for over the nar-

row territory lying between them. Here, too, was the great Confederate captain, and under him served the *élite* of the Southern legions. In the West there was no such topographical limitation. The possession of the Mississippi river was our primary objective, both as a base for operations into the interior and to cut off from the enemy the supplies he gathered from beyond. The outskirt operations consisted mostly of lodgments on the coast, which were not utilized to any greater extent than to keep the blockade of the Southern ports intact.

Munitions of war were the prime necessity of the Secessionists. Within the boundaries of each State there had at various times been granted to the National Government certain small tracts of land for forts, arsenals, and navy-yards. These had been kept more or less liberally supplied with arms, ammunition, and stores of all kinds. A large part of this material fell into the hands of the seceding States. It was claimed that the act of secession revested in each State the title to the land so granted to the Government; and, wherever possible, the claim was made good by taking possession of this national property. In some instances the garrisons of the forts held their own, and preserved these coigns of vantage to the United States.

South Carolina had been the most prominent State in warlike activity. But the forts in Charleston harbor were still in possession of the National Government and under command of Major Anderson. Without these citadels the new-born power of South Carolina would be unable to control the entrance to its only seaport. After the act of secession, therefore, negotiations were opened with Presi-

dent Buchanan for yielding up their posses-
sion.   Vacillating   though   he   was,   the   _{December, 1860.}
President could not consent to this.   He prolonged the
discussion.   Anderson, with soldierly decision, cut the knot
of the difficulty by abandoning the shore fortresses and
transferring his small force of one hundred
and twenty-eight men to Fort Sumter, in   _{December 26.}
the centre of the harbor, prepared to hold it to the last.
Months elapsed in inaction.   Anderson's commissariat
began to fail.   Attempts were made by the
President to revictual the fort, but they were   _{Jan., Apl., 1861.}
unsuccessful.

Finally South Carolina struck the blow.   Always a
leader in the South, she now had at her back the moral
support of the other seceding States.   After summoning
Fort Sumter to surrender, fire was opened
upon it from the rehabilitated United States   _{April 12.}
forts, and from shore batteries erected during the inter-
regnum of three months.   A bloodless bombardment of
two days resulted in a conflagration which, added to the exhaustion of his ammunition, obliged Anderson to capitulate.
This he did, and, marching out with all the honors of war,
he embarked his troops for the North.   This
first act of war was, however, more a politi-   _{April 14.}
cal than a military combat.

The Northern people had until this moment disbelieved
in a final rupture.   But their eyes were now opened, and
Fort Sumter was the signal for an universal uprising to
avenge the insult to the National flag.   President Lincoln
at once issued a call for volunteers.   The response was

unmistakable in its intensity. The busy merchant, the
plodding farmer, the mechanic and the professional man,
each dropped his avocation to enter the ranks, and, as if by
magic, the peaceful North became one vast camp.

In the South preparations were much further advanced,
but recruitment was no more speedy. Both sides donned
their armor for the now inevitable fray.

The navy-yard at Norfolk contained much material of
war sadly needed at the South. By a series of blunders
this valuable possession was allowed to fall into the hands
of the new Confederacy, much to our dis-
April 20.
comfiture and eventual danger. Harper's
Ferry, too, an arsenal containing the most necessary machinery for producing arms and ammunition
April 18.
owned by the United States, was evacuated
and destroyed by its garrison.

The city of Washington stood in no little peril. A
vigorous raid from Virginia could readily have seized
the capital at any time during the first month of hostilities. But gradually troops from the North arrived
and rescued the seat of government from danger. In
Baltimore sentiment was strongly for secession. The
government of Maryland was on the point of leading the
State in the wake of her erring sisters. The passage
through Baltimore of the first Northern regiment occasioned
a serious riot, and the regiments that followed had to be
transported by way of Annapolis, until Bal-
April 19.
timore was occupied by a sufficient force to
control its unruly population.

All these events, and many other minor circumstances,

were mere incidents to the opening of hostilities, and neéd
but a casual reference.   They scarcely belong to the military history of the war.

The new belligerents proposed to make their primary
line of defense along the Ohio river and the northern
boundary of Maryland.   A glance at the map shows how
large is the territory so covered, as compared with the
loyal States, and quells our wonder at the opinion which
foreigners at first held as to the probable issue of our
struggle, although the census of 1860 shows nearly two
thirds of the population to be in the North.

But the conditions under which the Southern people
lived were doubtless such as to enable it to organize an
efficient army with more celerity.   And this fact was overestimated abroad, while the knowledge of where resided
the sinews of war was naturally more limited than at
present.   For be it remembered that, thirty-five years
ago, we occupied no more important place in the eyes of
even intelligent Europeans than do at present the South
American States in ours.

There lurked no doubt in the minds of the Southern
leaders that Maryland, Kentucky, and Missouri would join
the Confederacy, while Virginia was considered one body
indivisible.   But they were as early destined to disappointment as they were to eventual miscarriage of the
bitterest.   In the seething of political uncertainties, Kentucky was saved to the Union.   Even the western half
of Virginia followed her water-courses and affiliated with
Ohio rather than with her slave-holding twin ; while the
troubles in Baltimore culminated in the half-willing re-

demption of Maryland. The Potomac thus became a Northern barrier instead of a Southern base. The Confederates were driven to substitute for it the Rappahannock, in Virginia; while west of the Alleghanies, as the Ohio river remained in our control, they were forced to adopt an irregular line across the State of Kentucky, on which to make their first defense.

This line was, however, weak, because it is tapped by the Mississippi, the Cumberland, and the Tennessee rivers; and these became at once available to our armies as lines of operation and supply. And the early control by us of both banks of the Ohio river, together with the rescue of Missouri from secession government by Blair and gallant Lyon, enabled us to keep the war off loyal territory.

April and May.

Confederate General Pillow had occupied New Madrid on the Mississippi. The intention of the Confederates had been to seize upon all important points about the mouth of the Ohio river, and shortly a move was made from New Madrid to Columbus by fifteen thousand men, under Polk, who from thence attempted to grasp Paducah, where the Tennessee empties into the Ohio. This and Cairo were two points of great military value.

July.

August.

General John C. Fremont was at this time in command in the West. His ancient reputation, beyond his abilities, at least in regular warfare, had placed him where he was. Under orders from him, Grant, early appointed a brigadier-general, anticipated Polk by seizing Cairo, and a day or two later Paducah. He had a

September 2 and 6.

force of about fourteen thousand men; Polk some five
thousand more. This move on Grant's part checkmated
the Confederate plans, and saved this important strategic
centre to the Union.

The Confederates were, however, reluctant to yield up
control of Kentucky, and were equally anxious to forestall
our use of the, to them, all-important rivers above-named.
They speedily fortified Columbus, New Madrid, and Island
No. 10 on the Mississippi, erected Fort Henry on the Tennessee, and Fort Donelson on the Cumberland, and established a strong camp of observation at the railroad centre
of Bowling Green as an outpost to their main position at
Nashville, while Zollicoffer was sent through Cumberland
Gap to form a flying right wing. This was the first Confederate line of defense in the West, after the Ohio river
had been lost beyond hope of recovery.

It will be borne in mind that in a country whose sparse
population prevents its sustaining large armies, and where
each contestant has to be victualled from his own base,
lines of operation must follow navigable rivers or railroads.
These will always be observed in our war to play a larger
part than in European campaigns, where provisions and
forage are abundant enough for an army to live upon the
country through which it is operating, and roads are such
as to allow supplies to be readily collected and troops
moved.

Upon our side, preparations were at once entered into
for piercing the Confederate line in Kentucky. A river
flotilla was built. It consisted of Eads' "turtle" gun-boats,
which were stern-wheelers of some five hundred tons bur-

den, light draught, and with hull barely a foot out of water, carrying an iron-plated casemate eight feet high armed with a dozen guns; of remodelled river steamboats; of flat-boats carrying heavy mortars and towed by tugs, and of a motley assortment of other vessels.

On their side, the Confederates were not behind us in vigor, though they lacked our mechanical appliances, and their fleet was supplemented with several cigar-shaped rams.

While in the West weapons are being wrought for conflict, let us turn to the East.

III.

THE FIRST CLASH OF ARMS.

HOSTILITIES were initiated in the East by General Geo. B. McClellan's campaign in West Virginia. It was essential to preserve intact the new-born State from the aggression of her ancient partner, and to organize her forces. A movement culminating in a small success at Philippi gave a happy inspiration to our arms, and did something to save the Baltimore and Ohio Railroad to the Federals. To recover possession of or interrupt this great highway, of imperative necessity to us, was the cause of constant Southern raids thereafter. Following upon Philippi, early in the summer, McClellan, with Rosecrans as his second, won an easy triumph over Garnett and Pegram at the battle of Rich Mountain, and definitely rescued West Virginia from the control of Confederate troops. This first success, though obtained by simple means, was lauded as a great strategic feat. It gave both McClellan and Rosecrans a reputation which did them eventual injustice, inasmuch as it thrust them into prominent positions which no officer in the country was equal to without the experience of many months and frequent fail-

June 3.

July 11.

ures.   The nation was utterly uneducated in war.   General Winfield Scott, our Commander-in-Chief, whose native ability was unquestioned, had outlived his powers.   Few of our officers had commanded even a regiment.   Our only recent training had been in the Mexican War, a distinctly fine campaign, but of limited scope.   The work now to be done required armies such as none since Napoleon had seen under his control.   Unlucky they who were early placed in high command.   The conditions of failure were strong in both themselves and the people for whom they fought.

Inspired by McClellan's success, General Patterson, appointed to command Pennsylvania forces, projected a plan for recapturing Harper's Ferry, now held by General Jos. E.

June 15.

Johnston.   This proved easy of accomplishment, for Johnston evacuated the place as untenable, destroyed the works, and retired upon Winchester.   Not far away, Patterson, after sundry counter-marchings, sat down before his opponent, under explicit instructions from General Scott to bring him to battle, or in any event to stand athwart his path and prevent his reinforcing the main body of the enemy, in the movement now being projected toward Centreville.

Encouraged by certain logistic successes at Annapolis and Baltimore, General Butler, who had been transferred to

June 10.

Fortress Monroe, managed to make his first military *fiasco* at Big Bethel.   This affair, which was an attempt to break up a Confederate camp at that place, amounted to no more than to display incompetency in conception and conduct.   But it greatly elated the South, as did also Schenck's quasi-picnic reconnoissance on railroad cars to Vienna, Va., about the same time, in which he was preceded by June 17. neither vanguard nor flankers, and was surprised and routed by a party of the enemy who concealed themselves in the woods for the purpose

IV.

BULL RUN.

IT was between the rival capitals that public opinion first
worried our army into serious operations. The forces
in the field at this time had grown to unusual proportions.
On the Union side close upon two hundred thousand men
bore arms; on the Confederate, all but one hundred
thousand. The Union fleet consisted of sixty-nine vessels,
carrying one thousand three hundred and forty-six guns.
There lay along the Potomac a full one hundred thousand
men. But the eager champions of either belligerent were
yet far from being soldiers.

June. McDowell, who commanded the army in
the field in front of Washington, though he
had little confidence in the discipline of his troops, was
constrained into action by pressure from the War Department and the President, who in their turn responded only
to the clamor of the impatient North. He accordingly set

July. a column of about thirty thousand men
in motion against the Confederate general,
Beauregard, who withdrew behind Bull Run with a somewhat inferior force. Each was determined to measure
swords with his ancient comrade.

When the armies have been brought into tactical contact,
each commander plans a manœuvre by which to turn the
other's left.   The Federals are earlier in the
execution of theirs, crossing Bull Run above   July 21.
the Stone Bridge, and come very near to crushing the Con-

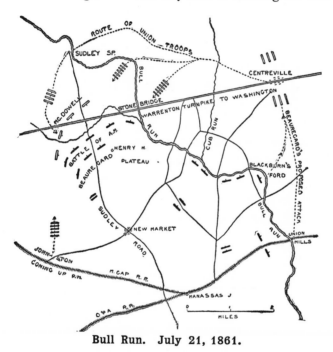

Bull Run.   July 21, 1861.

federate left, which has been depleted by Beauregard in
order to strengthen his right; for with the latter wing he
proposes to cross the stream at Blackburn's Ford and
Union Mills, and to fall upon McDowell's left at Centreville.   A small force of the enemy has gallantly held the
Manassas plateau against our advance, but only with

grievous loss. It is here that Thomas J. Jackson well earns the soubriquet of " Stonewall " by his solid defense.

Victory seems to declare for McDowell. It is almost within his grasp. The Southern outlook is desperate. But Beauregard recalls his scattered forces from the right. The plateau is secured. The conflict is again renewed and with vigor. The raw troops on both sides have fought with a gallantry premonitory of bloodier contests. Officers have fallen in great numbers. Both contestants have been quickly exhausted, and on either side there is wanting but a trifling cause to incline towards victory or defeat.

But Patterson's senility works our ruin. In lieu of barring Johnston's passage, his one obvious duty, he has left an open road for this wily soldier to escape him in the Valley and to march to the assistance of Beauregard. Johnston, with a portion of his troops, is already present. The rest are coming up by the railroad.

It is 2.30 P.M. The dust of an approaching column is seen on the horizon. Is it Patterson? Or is it Kirby Smith, with the balance of the Army of the Shenandoah? Beauregard prepares for retreat, for he fears it is the Federal column. But the stars and bars are finally descried. The Confederate hour of triumph has come. The arrival on the field of this last detachment throws eight thousand fresh troops upon the Union flank and rear, and turns the tide. The laurels which McDowell should have added to his always solid reputation are lost in a confused retreat, and this, before the vicinity of Washington is reached, becomes utter rout. The enemy is, however, in a similar strait, and no idea of pursuit is entertained. The losses, twenty-seven hundred on ours and nearly as much on the enemy's side, show that the field has been neither won nor lost without stubborn contest. Patterson, after this disgraceful lapse, retires to Harper's Ferry, where he is superseded by Banks.

After Bull Run, McClellan, fresh from his too quickly won laurels in West Virginia, was placed in supreme command, and sat down to the giant's task of making a mob an army. The South, lulled into the exultant belief that this one victory would suffice to close the war, really suffered worse than the consequences of a defeat in allowing self-applause to take the place of a vigorous course of discipline. Bull Run worked benefit to the Union in as great measure as it damaged the Confederate cause. The minds of all in the Northern States were cemented by this disaster into the one purpose of crushing out the heresy of secession.

Generals Rosecrans and R. E. Lee lay facing each other in West Virginia, with August. some ten thousand men apiece. There are but three roads across the Alleghanies in this State. One, near the Potomac, the Federals had kept; one, further south, at Great Pass, McClellan's campaign had secured; the third, by way of Sewell's Mountain, was still open. While Rosecrans had moved south, against Floyd, September 10. at Gauley river, who retired after a combat at Carnifex Ferry, Lee sought to overcome J. J. Reynolds' brigade, which alone was left in his front at Great Pass. But his method showed none September 12. of the wonderful vigor he later on exhibited, and, after fairly surrounding Reynolds, he failed to attack him, and returned to make head against Rosecrans. He thus enabled Reynolds to assume the offensive against his lieutenant. But Reynolds' attack at Green-

October 3.

brier River had no results. Meanwhile Rosecrans, though with a weaker force, had succeeded in shutting Lee up in the defiles of Sewell's Mountain, but lacked numbers sufficient to warrant attack. Lee was recalled to other duties. After a couple

October.

of minor engagements on the Greenbrier, New, and Gauley Rivers, which had small importance, winter put an end to operations in this barren region.

This disjointed campaign proved of value in that it enabled us to maintain our hold on the new State of West Virginia. But the tools of war were in raw hands, and the operations were as incomplete as the country was rugged, and the means of transportation difficult.

We must now turn to what the active West has accomplished.

V.

THE MIGHTY WEST MOVES.

THE operations in Missouri command but a passing notice, as all trans-Mississippi manœuvres bore small relation to the general strategy of the more important fields. Yet, as the possession of any part of that State by the enemy would have made the opening of the Mississippi river a much more onerous task for us, the work of rescuing its entire territory from Confederate control deserves its due credit among the efforts of the war.

General Lyon had assumed control of affairs in Missouri, and had dispersed the forces of seceding Governor Jackson at Booneville, while   June 17.
Sigel, an ancient German officer, had been very active in raising a small force of volunteers in the lower counties, and had crossed swords with the enemy at
Carthage ; but, meeting with a reverse, he   July 5.
was fain to retire to Springfield under the ægis of his chief. The effect of these and other lesser operations had narrowed the control of the Confederates to the south-west corner of the State, whither Lyon had pushed his little army. It was not long, however, before Lyon, unsupported by his superior, Fremont, found

that the advance of the Confederates Price and McCulloch upon his position at Springfield with a large force was seriously compromising his safety.

To rescue himself he boldly assailed the. enemy at Wilson's Creek. Sigel was sent by a circuit to fall upon the enemy's rear, but his men, largely three months' volunteers, whose time was nearly up, fought half-heartedly, and his own lack of conduct resulted in defeat. Lyon was outnumbered two to one. The battle fought here was one of the most stubborn minor contests of the war. The Federals lost the field, and gallant Lyon his life, while heading a charge to retrieve the disasters of the day. The little army was barely rescued from destruction by a summary retreat, happily without pursuit, to Springfield, under command of Major Sturgis. Out of six thousand men our casualties were twelve hundred. The enemy lost a less number out of twelve thousand. The Southerners have named this victory "Oak Hills."

The Confederates were soon able to score an additional triumph in Missouri by the capture of Lexington, of which place Colonel Mulligan was in command. Price advanced from Wilson's Creek. With some three thousand men, Mulligan bravely held the town against Price with twenty thousand, until his water supply was cut off, when he surrendered what remained of his force. The enemy had thus recovered for a time a substantial part of the State.

After many delays Fremont finally took the field

with forty thousand men, and advanced to Springfield, the Confederates having already retired. He seems to have expected to fight a battle here, though the enemy was actually some sixty miles away; but on the eve of this hypothetical combat he was superseded by Hunter, and retired to St. Louis.

November 2.

Fremont undoubtedly possessed ability, and had in former days exhibited brilliant qualities in irregular warfare; but his conduct in the Civil War lacked every element of usefulness.

Meanwhile, in July, General Pope took command in Northern Missouri, which, by a few vigorous blows with sword and pen, he cleared from open and secret rebels. He later rescued the region between the
Osage and the Missouri rivers from Con-

July–December.

federate control. He was building for himself the reputation which soon placed him in command beyond his powers.

All these stirring events in Missouri evinced the greatest activity; but their only effect on the general struggle lay in the moral weight the possession of this State gave to our arms.

In the shifting of commanders, so constant in the first years of the war, General Halleck early became chief player on the chess-board west of the Appalachians, while his subordinates accomplished, in
great part, the results attributed to his

November.

strategic ability. Halleck was a most scholarly soldier. In the cabinet none was more astute. But his action was slow. In the field he personally brought to pass nothing. Subsequently, as Commander-in-Chief at Washington, his peculiar methods more than once induced disaster.

General Sherman had succeeded Anderson in Kentucky. General Grant began to display his activity, and enabled the troops under

October.

his orders to learn something of warfare, in an expedition against Belmont. With a force of three thousand men he moved from Cairo against

November 7.

the Confederate camp at that place, and, though obliged after a day's skirmishing to retire with a loss of five hundred men, he nevertheless broke up the insurgents' stronghold. The Confederates may lay such claim to victory as the possession of the field of battle always gives. No permanent gain was accomplished by Grant, and he was forced to retire to Cairo.

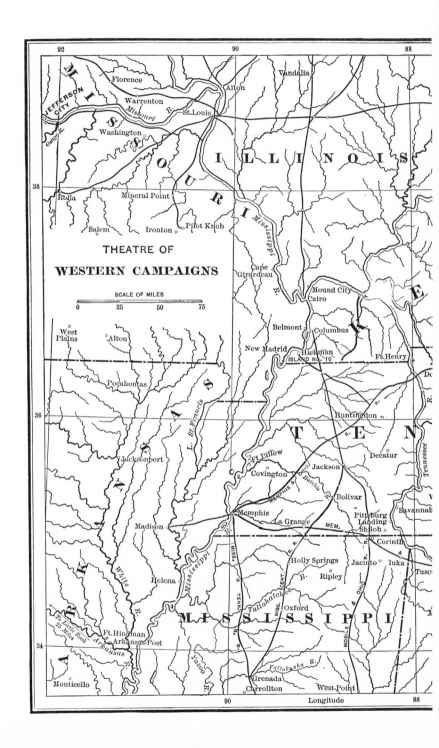

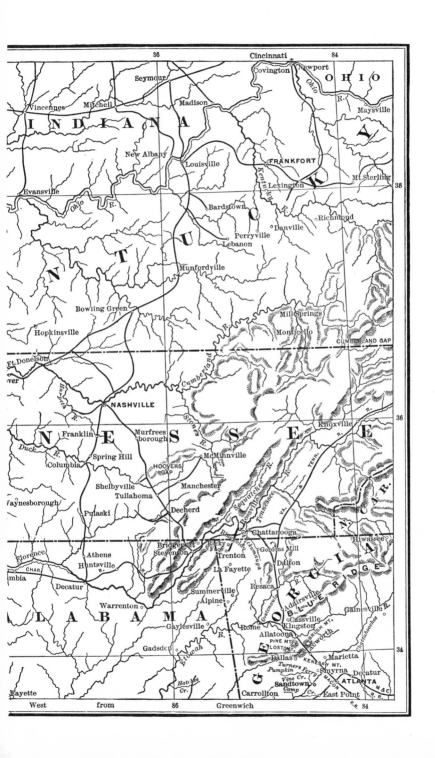

VI.

THE FIRST CONFEDERATE LINE BROKEN.

A T the beginning of the new year the Union armies
were five hundred and seventy-six
thousand strong, backed by a fleet of two
January, 1862.
hundred and twelve vessels. McClellan lay quiet upon
the Potomac all winter, drilling, organizing, disciplining
the Army of the Potomac. In his front was Joe Johnston, with a much smaller force, pushing forward with
equal energy the schooling of his soldiers.

The Western generals were more active. Albert Sidney Johnston, perhaps the most promising Southern officer, was in command in the West, with head-quarters at
Bowling Green. Buell lay in Johnston's
November.
(1861.)
front, having superseded Sherman, whose
"crazy" suggestion that two hundred and fifty thousand
men would be required for operations on the Western field
had lost him the confidence of his superiors. There was
abundant method in his madness, as time all too fully
showed.

In Eastern Kentucky the Confederate Humphrey Marshall had been creating more or less political trouble, and
General Garfield was sent against him with some two

thousand men. Marshall somewhat outnumbered Garfield; but in a vigorous January campaign,

January 10.

culminating at Prestonburg, Garfield quite
dispersed his forces, and drove him into the mountains.

About the same time, Zollicoffer, who had held the
extreme right of the Confederate line in advance of Cumberland Gap, had retired from his post and joined Crittenden near Mill Springs, in Central Kentucky; and to
General George H. Thomas was committed the duty of
disposing of them. With a somewhat superior force
Thomas moved upon the enemy, and in a sharp engagement at Logan's Cross Roads, utterly broke

January 19.

up their army. Zollicoffer was killed. This
first of our substantial Western victories (called "Fish-
ing Creek" by the enemy) was a great encouragement
to our arms. Our loss was two hundred and fifty, to
the enemy's five hundred. Crittenden withdrew his troops
across the Cumberland, abandoning his

January 20.

artillery and trains. Eastern Kentucky
was thus freed from the Confederates.

Halleck's first task as commander of the Western armies
was to penetrate the Confederate line of defense. This
could be done by breaking its centre or by turning one of
its flanks. The former appeared most feasible to Grant
and Commodore Foote, who commanded the naval forces.

Under instructions from Halleck, seven of

February.

the gun-boat flotilla, with Grant's seventeen
thousand men in reserve, moved up the Tennessee river to
attack Fort Henry and essay the value of gun-boats in am-
phibious warfare. Grant landed below the fort, and Foote

then opened fire upon it. Tilghman, in command, foreseeing its capture, was shrewd enough to send off the bulk
of his force to Fort Donelson. He himself
made a mock defense with a handful of men, February 6.
surrendering the fort after the garrison was well on its way.

Without the twin citadel of Donelson, however, Fort
Henry was but a barren triumph, for no column could advance up the Tennessee river while this garrison threatened its flank. It was here that Grant earned his first
laurels as a stanch soldier, by compelling, after a stubborn
fight, the surrender of this second fortress with its entire
garrison.

Every effort had been made by Johnston to hold the
place. He must here fight for the possession of Nashville.
Fort Donelson was strongly fortified and garrisoned.

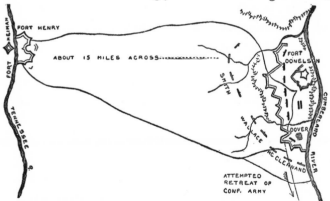

Forts Henry and Donelson. Feb. 6 and 16, 1862.

Grant moved against it from Fort Henry with fifteen thousand men, six thousand less than the enemy.

The ground is difficult; the troops are green. But heavy

reinforcements and the fleet come to Grant's aid. The fort is fully invested, under great difficulties from severity of weather and the inexperience of the men. Happily there is not much ability in the defence. Floyd, the senior officer, determines to cut his way out. He falls heavily upon Grant's right, held by McClernand and backed by Wallace, thinking to thrust them aside from the river and to escape over the road so won. A stubborn resistance defeats this sortie, though but narrowly. A general assault is ordered, which effects a lodgment in the works. Divided responsibilities between Floyd, Buckner, and Pillow weaken the defense so as to oper-

February 16.

ate a surrender.

Our loss was two thousand eight hundred. The Confederates captured were nearly fifteen thousand men.

These successes broke through the centre of the Confederate line, established with so much pains, and compromised its flanks. Johnston found that he must retire to a new line. This lay naturally along the Memphis and Charleston Railroad. He had retreated from Bowling Green on receipt of the news of the fall of

February 14.

Fort Henry, and was forced thereby to cede to Buell possession of Nashville, and practically of Kentucky. The advanced flank on the Mississippi at Columbus was likewise compromised, and with the bulk of the armament was withdrawn to Island No. 10, some sixty miles below Cairo. We could congratulate ourselves upon a very substantial gain.

VII.

NEW MADRID AND ISLAND NO. 10.

THE left flank of the Confederate line, thus entrenched at New Madrid and Island No. 10, is still too far advanced to be safely held more than a short time. Pope receives orders to reduce the place, and in less than two weeks puts in an appearance March 3. at New Madrid. He has some twenty thousand men, well equipped and officered. The enemy is under command of General McCown, later replaced by General Mackall, with a much inferior force.

The Mississippi here makes one of its gigantic double loops. Island No. 10 lies at the bottom of the southerly loop, and New Madrid at the bottom of the northerly. Across the isthmus of the upper loop is about three miles; across the lower, four. In rear of Island No. 10 on the mainland to the south is swampy ground, making exit possible only by the river, by New Madrid, or by a single road at Tiptonville. Pope's first effort is devoted to rendering New Madrid untenable, by effecting a lodgment at Point Pleasant below the town, and by erecting siege batteries near New Madrid so as to cut it March 6. off from its source of supply. By this action he compels its

March 14. surrender.   Commodore Foote now comes
upon the scene from above, and supplements
Pope's efforts, by attacking the defenses of Island No. 10

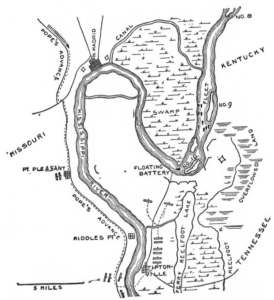

New Madrid and Island No. 10.   March, 1862.

with his heavy guns.   The river is exceptionally high;
gun-boats can fire across country.   The possession of
the river and of New Madrid has left the enemy only
the Tiptonville road to escape upon.   To secure this,
Pope must procure transports to get his men across the
river.   The transports are all above Island No. 10 and
cannot be run past the batteries.   With gigantic labor a
canal is cut across the isthmus, through heavily wooded
country, from a point opposite New Madrid to that place,

and the transports are floated through, thus
escaping Island No. 10.   Two gun-boats   April 1–8.
run the batteries.   Pope transfers Paine's division to the
Tennessee shore, and Foote again attacks with his flotilla.
Entirely cut off from succor or retreat, the whole force
surrenders, consisting of seven thousand men.

Pope received hearty congratulations for this brilliant
exploit, which had lasted but thirty days, and accomplished
such excellent results.

In Missouri General Curtis still held all the ground
which had been gained, against Price and Van Dorn,
defeated the insurgents, and drove them into the Bos-

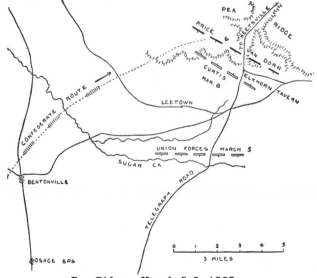

Pea Ridge.   March 5-8, 1862.

ton Mountains in the north-western part of Arkansas.
They here accumulated a motley force of not far

from thirty thousand men. Curtis had but eleven thousand. But in a two days' conflict at Pea Ridge (Confederate "Elk Horn") in which Van Dorn commanded the enemy, Curtis defeated him with a loss of three thousand men. Ours was much less.

March 7–8.

Price, before the commencement of the battle, had managed to get into Curtis' rear, and stood across the post-road, his only line of retreat. This obliged Curtis to change front to rear. The first day's combat was disadvantageous to the Federals; they were placed where they must beat the enemy or surrender. The Confederates had met with heavy losses, and on the second day did not exhibit the discipline of the first. Sigel was thrown upon their flank, and after brilliant conduct on both sides, Curtis wrested victory from a desperate strait.

This good fortune definitely relieved the Federals of any anxiety regarding Missouri, and did great credit to Curtis' endurance and capacity.

After this campaign the enemy never made his appearance in force in that State. Curtis shortly undertook a march across country to the Mississippi river, and arrived in due time at Helena, Ark.

July 9.

During the spring and summer of this year the Department of Missouri was under command of General Schofield. But there were no larger operations, though numerous bodies of guerillas, and some organized forces, were dispersed, and the State was brought to a condition of greater quiet under his sensible and vigorous administration.

June to September.

VIII.

THE BLOCKADE.

WITHIN the territory of the Southern Confederacy there was an abundance of corn and cotton. The former sufficed to feed the people and the armies. The latter was useless unless it could be marketed; for there were no cotton factories in the South. If the Confederacy could sell its cotton at its vastly appreciated price in the English marts, it could buy materials of war which might help it indefinitely to prolong the contest. Cost was the last thing thought of in the manufacturing towns abroad, which must have the raw material, or starve; and the exceptional profit to be made in this traffic induced numberless vessels to ply from European ports, or from Nassau, Havana, and Bermuda, to the Southern outlets, laden with all manner of goods, from Armstrong guns to quinine, which they could exchange for cotton.

The United States adopted the usual military means of preventing this trade by employing its abundant naval resources to blockade the Southern ports; and the embargo was more or less effective during the whole war. Still, many merchantmen did manage to run in and out of

Southern ports, and yet other vessels, built and armed in the Confederacy and abroad, preyed upon our commerce under letters of marque from the Confederate Government. By the latter these cruisers were regarded as men-of-war. We called them pirates, because we denied the validity of their commissions. These vessels captured all merchantmen sailing under American colors, and sold or destroyed them and their cargoes. We kept a fleet on all the great highways of commerce to prevent this depredation, but only partially succeeded. The eventual result was that our merchant marine was ruined. In 1861 we were the great ocean-carriers of the world; by 1865 nearly all freight was carried in English bottoms.

Our navy at the outbreak of the war was in very poor condition; but with the greatest vigor it was at once taken in hand, and the gaps filled temporarily, until more substantial vessels could be constructed. Craft of all kinds were pressed into service; even ferry-boats made up into effective men-of-war. A converted Fulton ferryboat captured the "Circassian" off Havana, — an exceedingly valuable prize. The types of vessel which came mostly into use were converted merchantmen, sloops, gunboats, double-enders, and iron-clads.

To declare the Southern ports blockaded was a bold step with the limited means at our command. The recent Declaration of Paris had been to the effect that, to be binding, a blockade must be a substantial danger to the passers in and out. Still, with our national

April 27, 1861.

adaptiveness to circumstances, we managed, after announcing the blockade in the spring, to make it

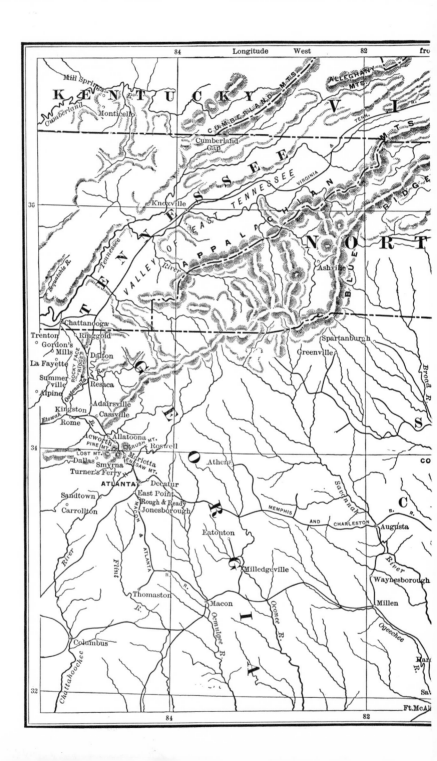

THEATRE OF

GEORGIA AND

THE

CAROLINAS CAMPAIGNS

SCALE OF MILES

0   25   50   75   100

de facto during the summer, and at the most important points within a month.

The theory of the United States was, of course, that the Southern hostilities were an insurrection, and not a war. But the enormous extent of the uprising obliged us to construe this theory very liberally, and to do many things on a war scale. The position was often inconsistent, but was fairly well maintained. By 1864 we were blockading a coast three thousand miles in extent, — a thing utterly unprecedented.

The blockade was naturally not heard as much of as the land operations, nor had it the same effect in suppressing insurrection; but it necessitated a vast amount of hardship and danger. Nor must its services be underrated. There were often naval fights of importance with vessels built in the blockaded ports to run out and break up the embargo. A typical combat was that between the Atlanta and Weehawken. The former left Savannah to attack the blockading fleet. June 17, 1863. Much was expected from her efforts. But she fell foul of the Weehawken, whose heavy ordnance proved quickly too much for her. In fifteen minutes, and with but five shots from the 15-inch guns, she was disabled and captured.

It must not be forgotten that this was still the day of the old naval *régime*. To-day a navy cannot be created in less than a dozen years; then, the wooden ship was still the type of fighting craft, and a few weeks sufficed to convert a merchantman into a very useful man-of-war.

IX.

EARLY OUTSKIRT OPERATIONS.

THE briefest mention of the principal outskirt operations must suffice.

Hatteras Inlet had become a place of much resort for Confederate cruisers and blockade runners. To break up this rendezvous, General Butler, whose military reputation was then still reasonably intact, and Commodore Stringham, with a land force and small fleet, were despatched thither from Fort Monroe. After a bombardment of two days, the forts protecting the Inlet were captured and garrisoned by our troops. Beyond this nothing was undertaken.

Aug. 28–29, 1861.

Fort Pickens, near Pensacola, had at the outbreak of the war been preserved to the Union, and was held by a small force of troops. Some interchange of hostilities took place at this point, with no result beyond giving us a yet firmer foothold, which was not, however, utilized to push operations into the interior.

October 9, November 22–23.

In this same month fifteen thousand men, under command of General T. W. Sherman, and in convoy of Admiral Dupont, were sent to Port Royal, S.C. Fort Walker, on Hilton Head, was capt-

October and November.

ured by the fleet, and Beaufort, S.C., abandoned by the enemy. Sherman fortified Hilton Head, and Dupont took Tybee Island at the entrance to Savannah. But no orders were issued for following up these successes, and whatever could have been accomplished was forfeited. General Parke captured Fort Macon, defending Beaufort, N.C., while Reno made a April 26, 1862. barren expedition towards the rear of Norfolk.

Early in the new year Burnside and Goldsborough, with twelve thousand men and a fleet of light- draught gun boats, set sail for Pamlico and January, 1862. Albemarle Sounds, N.C., with a purpose similar to the Port Royal expedition. General Wise commanded the Confederates at this point. After much danger from storms, and delay from the difficulty of passage into the Sound, Roanoke Island was captured, and a portion of the fleet took possession of Elizabeth City. February and Later New Berne was taken by Foster, as March. well as the town of Washington near by. But again no sensible demonstration into the interior was attempted.

About the same time Capt. C. H. Davis made a recon- noissance of Fort Pulaski, the main defense of the city of Savannah. As a consequence, January, 1862. some works were erected on adjacent islands, for the pur- pose of isolating Pulaski; and, two months after, Wright and Dupont visited and garrisoned several points on the coast of Florida. March, 1862.

General Hunter succeeded Sherman. Gilmore was the engineer officer in immediate charge of the operations against Fort Pulaski. After March, 1862.

some time spent in preparation he got ready
April 10–11, 1862. to begin his bombardment from Tybee Island,
and two days sufficed to reduce the place. Thenceforth
Savannah was isolated from the outside world.

The fight between the Merrimac and the Monitor —
the first combat of iron-clads — opened a new era in naval
warfare. The Merrimac had been built in Norfolk. She
was a huge, iron-plated, casemated hulk, whose armor could
resist all artillery then known. She was probably not
seaworthy enough for a cruise; but she could make her-
self mistress of the Chesapeake; she would have prevented
troops from landing on the Peninsula; and she might have
approached and bombarded Washington. Great apprehen-
sion was felt about her. The only worthy antagonist of
this terrible vessel was the Monitor, — a low-decked craft
with a turret, " a raft with a cheese-box on it," as she was
laughingly called, — which was building at the same time
in Brooklyn. The contest was as much a race between
mechanics at the start, as between seamen at the close.
The earliest constructed vessel should win the laurels.

The Merrimac made her appearance first. Leaving Norfolk she steamed for Newport News, near
March 8, 1862. Fort Monroe, destroyed the United States
frigates Cumberland and Congress, and forced the Min-
nesota aground, before the Monitor came up. The latter
reached the scene of action during the night. Next day a
gallant struggle ended in what has been called a drawn
battle; but the Merrimac put back into Norfolk disabled.
She had been "neutralized," and the class of iron-clads, of
which the Monitor was the first, became the type from

which grew a large fleet. We could fairly claim the victory, as the Monitor had nipped the career of the Merrimac in the bud.

The blockade at New Orleans had been peculiarly difficult to keep intact, and several privateers, as well as many merchantmen, had been able to break through. Among these the ram Manassas steamed down the river, and made a sudden diversion among the blockading squadron; but it was of no great duration, and quite without result. Towards the close of the year Ship Island, near New Orleans, had been occupied by Union troops. General Butler had charge of this department, but had brought nothing to a head. Admiral Farragut, with Porter second in command, reached the place in the early spring to see what could be done. The capture of New Orleans would not only exert a very depressing effect upon the Confederates, but the city would also serve as a base for operations up the Mississippi, in connection with those already moving down.

Oct.-Dec., 1861.

December.

February, 1862.

The approaches to New Orleans by the main channel were held by two strong works, Forts Jackson and St. Philip, and the river was patrolled by a flotilla. Farragut moored his mortar-boats below the forts, back of a bend in the river, and for six days bombarded Fort Jackson; but, impatient to secure the city, he determined to try the experiment of running his fleet past the forts, and thus to isolate them. This was a feat never before attempted and of questionable result. But, to

April 18.

the utter astonishment of the Confederates, it was successfully accomplished, and the next day Farra-

April 25.

gut took possession of New Orleans, evacuated by General Lovell on his approach.

Porter shortly afterwards received the surrender of the
forts, — it is claimed, on account of a mutiny

April 28.

of the garrison of Fort Jackson, — and they
were duly occupied. Butler then took possession of the
city with his troops.

It must be said in praise of Butler, that in provost-marshal work, such as he was called upon to perform in New
Orleans, he showed remarkable capacity. The city was
never healthier or in finer condition than under his *régime*.
There was, however, just complaint against him in matters
connected with trade ; nor did he make the least attempt
to mix suavity of method with strength of action in his
government of the city.

This long series of coast operations, none of which,
except Farragut's, had any immediate effect upon the war,
was yet not without its uses. It was essential to keep up
a strict blockade, for, by the law of nations, none but an
effective one is a blockade at all ; and it was a *sine qua non*
to forestall any disposition on the part of foreign nations to
aid the enemy. All these ends were subserved to a considerable extent. And as the only enlightened military
policy is to concentrate against and destroy the large armies
in the field, it is perhaps well that no greater numbers
were taken from the all-important work, to be frittered
away on minor operations on the coast. Still some of the
expeditions were in such force that they really drained

the large armies; and it seems as if they might have annoyed the enemy by frequent incursions on a large scale into the country, thus drawing troops from the armies in front of those of their comrades who were fighting the more sanguinary battles of the war, but often to no good purpose.

In the early part of 1862 the Confederate general, Sibley, undertook a campaign against the Union forces, occupying the forts in New **February.** Mexico under command of Canby. He advanced up the Rio Grande, with considerable physical labor, but met with brilliant success in several combats where his hardy Texans proved more than a match for Canby's regulars. The conduct of the regulars did on this occasion no justice to the splendid record they made for themselves during the war.

But Sibley's triumphs were resultless. He found that he could not maintain himself in that territory, and he was eventually forced to abandon it to the Federal forces and make a disastrous retreat.

X.

THE ADVANCE OF THE WESTERN ARMIES. — SHILOH.

NO sooner had untiring Grant ruptured the Confederate line at Donelson, than he proposed to ascend the Tennessee and essay to break their new defence along the Memphis and Charleston Railroad. The key points of this line were Memphis on one flank, with Fort Pillow up the river as an outpost; Chattanooga on the other flank, and Corinth as a centre. While McClellan was making vast preparations for his Peninsular campaign, Grant quietly transported his army to Pittsburgh Landing, on the Tennessee, and Halleck despatched Buell, with thirty-seven thousand men, from Nashville across the country to join him. General Mitchel, with a division, was sent out as a flying left flank to seize and hold some point on the Memphis and Charleston Railroad, where the Confederates were not in force. This railroad was the great central east and west artery of the Confederacy. South of it all railroad transportation had to go by way of Mobile. And it was of the last importance to the enemy.

March, 1862.

Mitchel, with great celerity, proceeded upon his task,

captured Huntsville, and despatched parties
along the road east and west to hold bridges   April 11.
and destroy material of war.   Alarmed at his movements,
Beauregard sent a cavalry detachment to operate against
him, while Halleck, apparently unable to handle two
simultaneous problems, afforded him no support.   His
position was precarious; but, burning the bridge at
Decatur, he moved eastward, and occupied Bridgeport.
With proper reinforcements Mitchel could have seized
Chattanooga, and have even raided on Rome and Atlanta,
and there destroyed the foundries and arsenals, — an interruption which would have been of grave consequence to
the insurgents; but his operations were neglected by
Halleck, as of secondary importance.

Beauregard, who held a species of second command
under A. S. Johnston, had formed certain ambitious plans
for an advance on Cairo and St. Louis.   Not so Johnston,
whose soldier's wit told him that the armies in the field
must be first beaten before conquest could follow, and who
preferred to make solid preparation for a decisive struggle
near Corinth.

These movements lead to the first of those desperately
contested battles in which Americans have shown themselves preëminent.   While McClellan is laboriously dig-
ging his way into Yorktown, Johnston ad-
vances from Corinth, purposing a descent   April.
upon Grant's army at Pittsburgh Landing, before the
arrival of Buell.   Grant has under his command forty-
five thousand effectives.   Buell is yet two marches distant.   Johnston's force is forty thousand men.   With a

suddenness we had in those early days not learned to
guard against, Johnston falls upon our
army. The onslaught bears our lines back.
We have been taken unawares. The troops are not
well in hand. Grant is, for the moment, absent. Wal-

April 6.

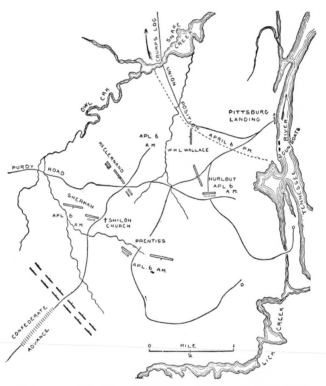

Shiloh (or Pittsburg Landing).   April 6 and 7, 1862.

lace is at Crump's Landing, with seventy-five hundred
men, useless for the emergency.

Johnston's plan is simple. Attack constantly by the right and drive the Federals from the Landing and into the angle made by Snake Creek and the river. Beauregard, Hardee, Bragg, his lieutenants, are well able to second him. The onset is full of fire. Sherman, on our right, struggles manfully to hold Shiloh Church; but it is wrenched from his grip. Prentiss is surrounded and captured. The left is almost crushed. Recognizing the serious emergency, Sherman, with McClernand to back him up, fights desperately to hold the road across Snake Creek, by which Wallace can join them. At this juncture Johnston is killed. His place there is no one to fill. The Confederate lines begin to show huge gaps from casualties, and yet greater ones from stragglers, tempted by the prizes in the abandoned Federal camps. But the army, still in line, strikes lustily for its goal almost won, — Pittsburgh Landing.

Happily for us, success itself has disorganized the enemy's ranks. A number of heavy guns have been massed at the Landing. The ground is favorable. The advance brigade of Buell's army puts in an appearance. All is not yet lost. And Beauregard, who succeeds to the command, under the impression that Buell is still distant, and wishing to reform his troops and complete the victory on the morrow, suspends the battle.

But the situation yet is critical. Buell is near at hand, but he must be got across the river and on the field. Sherman, on the right, is in much disorder. The rest of the Union Army is fairly huddled into a narrow space near the Landing. Our fortunes still bear a questionable aspect, but faint-heartedness possesses no one.   Happily, transports can be procured for Buell; and by early dawn on the morrow he is able to put twenty-four thousand fresh soldiers in array against the wearied Confederates.

April 7.   The second day dawns.   Beauregard struggles hard to keep what has already been fairly won; and his troops, though decimated, second his purpose nobly.   At one moment, though greatly outnumbered, he succeeds in all but turning the Union left by the same tactics which won so much on yesterday. But Buell's men have profited by their rigid discipline. Their ranks are adamant.   They will not be denied.   An order for a general advance is given.   Wallace comes up on the right.   Victory shifts to the stars and stripes. The exhausted Confederates are forced in confusion from the field.

The losses at Shiloh were thirteen thousand on our side, two thousand less on the Confederate; but this does not count the grievous loss by the death of Johnston.   With a reputation for skill which experience in the Black Hawk and Mexican Wars, and the expedition to Utah, had fully warranted, he was deemed by the South the choicest of her soldiers; and better could the enemy have spared thousands of her sons than this one.

Returning to Corinth, unpursued by Grant, Beauregard heavily fortifies the place.   He is leisurely followed up by Halleck, who has assumed personal command of the forces

May 1.   under Grant, Buell, and Pope, the latter having joined from a projected attack on Fort Pillow.   Halleck very deliberately opens the siege, with his forces recruited up to one hundred thousand men, while Beauregard numbers fifty thousand effectives. Operations would have sooner culminated had Halleck left their direction to his more energetic second in command, Grant.

Corinth was naturally strong, and easily victualled. By very slow degrees the several divisions worked their way nearer the town. Beauregard contested every inch, while preparing constantly for evacuation. Finally our troops had reached a position from which assault was feasible. But Beauregard, who had har-   May 30. bored no idea of permanent defense, abandoned the place as untenable.

This was alleged to be a strategic manœuvre on his part; but in what manner is not clear, for, beyond detaining Halleck some weeks, he can scarcely claim to have accomplished any good end by the defense of Corinth, and the Confederacy lost with Corinth its main line of communication east and west. Its voluntary evacuation seems to be without purpose. A stubborn defense might as well have been made here as at any other point; and to yield the Memphis and Charleston Railroad without a struggle was surely a lame military proceeding.

The natural result of these successes fol-   June 5. lowed. Fort Pillow was evacuated, and Memphis surrendered to Davis and the flotilla, after a smart battle with the Confederate fleet. The   June 6. Mississippi river was now open down to Vicksburg.

In little more than a year the western armies had accomplished a task to which they could point with just pride. The public could see the result of their labors, and naturally yielded to them the palm.   In the East apparently no gain had been made.   The different conditions under which each army worked were not fully considered.   As in all human affairs, the victor wore the crown.

XI.

McCLELLAN MOVES TO THE PENINSULA.

OUR attention is now due to the Army of the Potomac.
Since McClellan had been in command the army
had grown rapidly in discipline and efficiency. As an
organizer McClellan was in his element. Few have ever
done more substantial work than he; and well did the
Army of the Potomac testify to his ability in its subsequent
campaigns. Little memorable had occurred for months,
save the Ball's Bluff disaster narrated below. The
enemy had lain encamped at Manassas and Centreville.
Geary's brigade had obtained a slight success at Harper's
Ferry. Every one was impatient to cross swords in earnest.
Seven strong divisions garrisoned the fortifications of
Washington, or occupied the banks of the Potomac from
Alexandria up, in all some one hundred and fifty thousand
men.

McClellan has seventy-five thousand effec-
tives who can be spared for the field. He October 16, 1861.
reconnoitres with his right wing across the Potomac. No
enemy is found north of Centreville. Stone is ordered to
patrol his front, to ascertain the whereabouts of the enemy
and develop his strength. He sends a regiment across the

river at Ball's Bluff, with Baker's brigade in support, to
capture Leesburg.   But with singular blindness he fails to
provide a sufficient means of recrossing in an emergency.
The river is high and the current strong.   The advance
regiment feels the enemy near Leesburg and falls back.

October 21.   Stone insanely crosses more men, two thousand in all, to follow up what he deems a
success.   Without means of retreat, these troops are
attacked by the enemy in force, driven back to the
Potomac, and, before they can cross or scatter, are crowded
upon the narrow banks of the river, below a bluff on
which stand the Confederates.   After a gallant attempt at
defense barely one-half the force are able to save themselves from this slaughter-pen, — a success which greatly
inspirited the South.   General Stone is imprisoned to
appease the Northern public.

December 20.   A handsome combat and victory by Ord,
at Dranesville, a few weeks later, where
about an equal number on each side came in collision, com-
pensated partly for this defeat.

After a variety of plans discussed, and manifold delays in
March 8, 1862.   arriving at one satisfactory to the President
and himself, McClellan had concluded to
transfer his forces to the Peninsula between the York and
James rivers, and had received the President's sanction to
the scheme.   No sooner was this decision reached than Joe
Johnston, who had been in command of all the troops in
front of Washington since Bull Run, evacuated Manassas,
March 9.   and anticipated McClellan in his march.
Secrecy was not one of our then virtues.

The newspapers were able to publish all prospective movements with scandalous accuracy; and what these were
unable to learn, secession sympathizers at the capital
appeared constantly to unearth for the benefit of their
Southern friends.

Stonewall Jackson, now in command in
the Shenandoah, had essayed a winter
January, 1862.
campaign against our General Lander, but when Manassas
was evacuated he fell back up the Valley. General
Shields succeeded Lander, and, desiring to engage Jackson, devised a plan to lure him back by a simulated retreat.
Followed up by Ashby's cavalry, a stand is made at Kernstown. Jackson arrives, expecting to crush a small
detachment. Banks is absent, Shields has been wounded;
but our troops, well led by subordinates, invite attack, and
inflict on Jackson a smart defeat, with a loss
of five hundred men on each side. Jackson
March 23.
again retires up the Valley. Even the Confederates
admitted that this eminent soldier had for once been
entrapped, — a thing of rare occurrence.

Vigor half equal to his ability should months ago have
enabled McClellan to crush his enemy at Centreville; for,
with sixty thousand men, Johnston had for eight months
bidden defiance to our capital, surrounded with one hundred
and eighty thousand armed men. Such vigor should have
cleared the Potomac of the impertinent blockade. It
should have captured Norfolk, — that nest of Merrimacs
and gun-boats. It should have brought him to the very
gates of Richmond. Had but a part of these results been
accomplished, McClellan would have enjoyed the full con-

fidence and support of all in power. But now other
influences were beginning to work. Fremont, for whom
some harmless place must be made, was put in command
of the "Mountain Department," in West Virginia, and
furnished with an army to confront an imaginary enemy.
Banks kept twenty odd thousand men to defend the Valley
against Jackson's eight thousand; and the President wanted
at lowest fifty thousand men in the immediate vicinity of
Washington, heedless of the fact recognized by all military
minds that to keep the enemy busy was the only sure
defense of the capital.

In consequence of all this no sooner had McClellan
fairly embarked on his expedition than he found a large
part of his available force taken from him. He had
planned a "rapid movement," and had been led to expect
the coöperation of the navy on the York river, as well as
that of McDowell's forty thousand men on the Fredericksburg route. Both these were to fail him.

With early spring McClellan embarked his troops,
transferred them to the vicinity of Fort
Monroe, and began to move up the Peninsula. But no sooner was he on the way
than his progress was arrested by some twelve thousand
men, under Magruder, on the banks of the Warwick river.

March and
April.

The position could have been forced without
great effort. In fact, a small body did cross
and effect a lodgment on the other side, and, if supported,
could have held it. But the conduct of affairs was weak,
and this slight check enabled the enemy to arrest the
progress of the entire Army of the Potomac, and cul-

April 5.

minated in the defence and siege of Yorktown. Indeed,
McClellan seems to have anticipated such an event, for he
was accompanied by siege artillery, which in a "rapid
movement" would seem superfluous.

But, being checked, he sat down to capture Yorktown by
regular investment, all of which was done with scientific
accuracy. Still, no sooner had he completed his parallels
and got ready to bombard the place, than the
enemy evacuated it. They had detained us
May 3.
a precious month. Our columns followed on in pursuit,
McClellan remaining in Yorktown, busy with questions
of transportation.

Williamsburg. May 5, 1862.

The enemy under Longstreet had awaited our approach
at Williamsburg. Hooker first attacked, having been
brought to a stand by a work known as Fort Magruder,
and kept up a heavy pounding all the forenoon. Kearny came to his rescue when
May 5.
Hooker's men were all but spent. Hancock moved

around the enemy's left, seized some abandoned redoubts, and made a brilliant diversion.   But there was no coöperation in our attack; no one on the field was in supreme command, and the day was fruitlessly spent in partial blows. The enemy retreated at night.   Our loss was two thousand two hundred; theirs some six hundred less.   McClellan then leisurely moved up the Peninsula on the east side of the Chickahominy.   Franklin moved as a separate body up the York river, intending a demonstration from White House.

May 7. None was made, the enemy having passed this vicinity in his retreat before the Federals were ready to attack.

XII.

THE PENINSULAR CAMPAIGN IN JEOPARDY. — FAIR OAKS.

WHILE all this is taking place, Jackson, who seems to have been created especially to become the unknown quantity in the problem

April.

of the Army of the Potomac, again begins, with twenty-five thousand men, his restless manœuvring in the Valley.

A glance at the map will show the peculiar relation of the Shenandoah Valley to the Virginia campaigns. Lying between the two ranges of the Alleghanies, and running down in a north-easterly direction towards the Potomac, this valley not only afforded the enemy a hidden and secure means of marching from their base at the upper end down towards Maryland and Pennsylvania, at the mere expense of watching the eastern gaps to hold in check detachments from the Army of the Potomac, but led their column for every day's march closer to the rear of Washington; while a march up the Valley, on the contrary, was taking a Federal army further away from the vicinity of Richmond. To the Confederates the Valley was a sally-port which we must be constant in watching. Its strategic value to the Confederates was often great; but this was

not all.   The Valley was also the granary of Virginia;
for no portion of her soil yielded such abundant harvests
as the smiling plains along the Shenandoah.   No wonder
the Confederates clung tenaciously to its possession.

As usual in the Valley, our forces were on this occasion,
also, scattered about in detachments which could not sustain one another.   Moving the Army of the Shenandoah
sharply upon Milroy and Schenck, Jackson
May 8.
inflicted upon them near the town of
McDowell, despite four hours' resistance, a defeat which
forced them sharply back.   He then turned upon Banks,
who prudently and promptly retired.   Following him up,
Jackson fell upon one of his detachments at
May 23.
Front Royal, destroyed it, and sent Banks,
May 25.
after a stinging defeat at Winchester, whirling back to the Potomac.

Bred of unreasoning fears for the safety of Washington, action was immediately taken by the President,
upon receipt of the news of Banks' defeat, to deprive
McClellan of the assistance of McDowell, against the
protest of both.   The latter, who with his forty
thousand men was to have reinforced McClellan's
right as a flying wing, and would have added moral
strength far beyond the actual assistance, was hurried to
the Valley to assist in "trapping Jackson."   This blow to
the *morale* of the army, or rather of its commander, weakened still more the conduct of this campaign.
May 20.
McClellan had reached the Chickahominy,
and crossed with his left wing.   He had been building all
his hopes upon McDowell's aid on his right.

Nor was McDowell's march to the Valley of any avail. Jackson was the last man to be trapped. Fremont moved upon him from the west; Shields from the east. But the bold raider, determined to complete the scare at Washington, which was so rapidly spoiling the prospects of the Peninsular campaign, made a diversion on Harper's Ferry, paused but to make capture of abundant stores, and reached Strasburg in advance of Fremont, who was to have closed that outlet as Shields actually did the one at Front Royal. Jackson amused Fremont by a few demonstrations, while he got his columns and trains beyond reach, and started up the Valley. Pursuit was made; but Jackson's marching capacity was beyond theirs, as it was beyond that of any other soldier during the war, and, though harassed by our cavalry, he reached in due time Port Republic. Here he was anticipated by Carroll's brigade, and had this officer destroyed the bridge across the Shenandoah at that point, Jackson's safety would have been seriously compromised. But in war no man's judgment is infallible, and the situation at other points is rarely known. The bridge was left standing. This mistake gave Jackson the opportunity to drive Carroll away and occupy it.

June 7.

Jackson was now beyond danger, his means of retreat being assured. But, like himself, he could not leave without dealing a final blow. While his lieutenant, Ewell, defeated Fremont at Cross Keys, with a loss of seven hundred men, Jackson crossed the Shenandoah river at Port Republic, burned the bridge behind him, and attacked Tyler and Carroll, who

June 8 and 9.

had a bare quarter of Jackson's twelve thousand men. These brigades held him in check many hours, but were finally driven into retreat.

In this short passage of arms Jackson had lost but six hundred men, and had kept three armies playing at hide-and-seek, the presence of but one of which might have turned the tide of victory towards the banners of the Army of the Potomac. So soon as the enemy had left the Valley, Fremont, Banks, and McDowell, each retraced his steps, disheartened and decimated by useless countermarching.

The effect, meanwhile, of this brilliant campaign was to sink McClellan's offensive on the Peninsula to the rank of mere self-protection; and the Battle of Fair Oaks, which occurred at this time, was but the prelude to the Seven Days' Retreat.

Following the thunderclap of McDowell's detachment, McClellan sent Fitz John Porter to clear away a Confederate force threatening his right at Hanover Court House, under command of Branch. This was accomplished in Porter's usual good style; the road to our forces at Fredericksburg was opened, and some bridges over the Pamunky and South Anna rivers, by which the enemy could approach our rear, were destroyed.

McClellan had thrown Keyes' corps across the Chickahominy, followed by Heintzelman's, leaving Sumner's, Franklin's, and Porter's on the left bank. Unless the means of crossing the river were reliable, and so ample that the wings could have mutual support in any emergency, this was a dangerous division of the army. The

reports showed a total of one hundred and twenty-five
thousand men and two hundred and eighty guns.

Johnston, whose forces had been recruited from every
section of the Confederacy to help him meet the imminent
danger to its capital, found himself in command of about
ninety thousand men. For the defense of Richmond this
was a fair match for the Army of the Potomac. Johnston
wisely determined to take summary advantage of McClellan's perilous situation astride the river, and to attack the
isolated left wing. He had just received information that

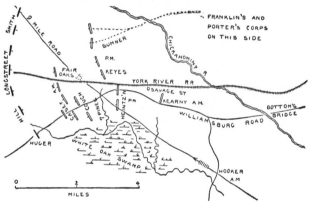

Fair Oaks. May 31-June 1, 1862.

McDowell had been arrested in his movement to McClellan's aid, and sent to the Valley. He ordered the bulk of
his force to fall upon Keyes and Heintzelman, while a
small body watched the crossings of the Chickahominy
above to prevent a junction by the other three corps. Our
left wing had entrenched at Seven Pines, just beyond Fair
Oaks, and had daily indulged in picket skirmishing with
the enemy.

In pursuance of these orders Longstreet
and Hill fell heavily upon Casey, whose divi-

May 31.

sion was in the advance. Huger was to have attacked the
left flank of Casey, by a circuit; but his progress was arrested at streams swollen by a heavy storm of the previous
day. It is now well proven that Casey's men fought stanchly;
but they were overmatched and soon driven in; sad confusion took possession of their ranks; destruction seemed
imminent; and only by heavy reinforcements from Heintzelman were we able by nightfall to reform and hold a line
near Savage Station. We had been driven back more
than a mile. The enemy could claim a brilliant victory.
Had he been more vigorous, the two corps, so largely
outnumbered, might have been driven into the Chickahominy. Happily, at the outbreak of the action, McClellan had ordered Sumner across the river to sustain the
right of Keyes and Heintzelman, and the brave old
sabreur, after many difficulties and a heavy fight, managed to join his line to that formed of the relics of the two
defeated corps, and held Smith in check.

The following morning the battle was
renewed. Longstreet soon comprehended

June 1.

that the chance of completing his triumph had been forfeited, and did not attempt much; the Federals not only
held their own, but drove the enemy from the ground
occupied the day before. Had Franklin and Porter
crossed on this day, a vigorous push might have carried
us into Richmond; but a rise in the river prevented
their so doing. Our loss had been five thousand out of
forty-five thousand engaged; the enemy's in excess of six

thousand out of an equal force ; three thousand men on
each side was the loss of the first day.   General Johnston
was wounded.   G. W. Smith, who had commanded the
Confederate left, replaced him.

For a term of three weeks' bad weather, McClellan now
waited for the again promised reinforcement of McDowell.
During this period great excitement was created by a bold
cavalry raid of Stuart's, during which he
rode entirely around our lines, and escaped   June 13–15.
unharmed after doing some damage to our supplies.   Mc-
Clellan was still pressing forward his lines toward Richmond inch by inch, and every day promising himself an
assault for the morrow.   And the last heavy
picket fight enabled him to gain ground to   June 25.
within four miles of the Confederate capital.   To the un-
initiated, success seemed already within our grasp.   To
those in a situation to know, the outlook appeared far
from promising.

XIII.

THE SEVEN DAYS.

GENERAL Lee, who had succeeded wounded Johnston, took advantage of the lull following Fair Oaks,
and not intending to afford McClellan breathing-time to
recover from the weakness engendered of McDowell's
removal, called upon Jackson to rejoin him from the
Valley; but at the same time he actually sent him reinforcements as a blind. Troops were put on the cars in full
view of some of our prisoners in Libby, who were just
about to be exchanged, and these, on reaching our lines,
spread the story of a new operation by Jackson in the
Valley.

The corps of the Army of the Potomac lay as follows:
Porter, north of the river at Gaines' Mill, Franklin joining
him on the south, with Sumner on his left as far as Fair
Oaks; then Heintzelman, on to White Oak Swamp, and
Keyes in reserve. This line was in the arc of a circle,
whose centre was at Bottom's Bridge. The five corps
numbered some one hundred thousand men.

Lee had the divisions of Longstreet, A. P. Hill, Huger,
Magruder, and D. H. Hill, about seventy thousand, not
counting Jackson, who was to join with twenty-five thou-

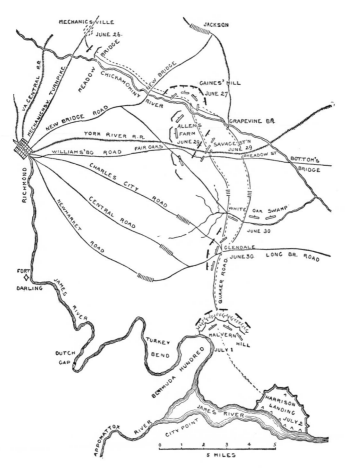

Seven Days. June 26-July 2, 1862.

sand more. Huger and Magruder were opposite Sumner and Heintzelman. A. P. Hill confronted Franklin, while Longstreet and D. H. Hill lay in reserve. Jackson, never loth to be afoot, leaving a simple rear-guard at

Harrisonburg, to keep up appearances and deceive some
sixty or seventy thousand men who were watching him, put
his men aboard the cars, joined the Richmond

June 26.

forces, and marched around McClellan's right
at Mechanicsville, ready to further Lee's plan of crushing
his opponent's flank.

Meanwhile A. P. Hill fell upon our right at Meadow
Bridge. McCall made a stubborn resistance, inflicting
grievous loss upon the enemy, but at night he was withdrawn to Gaines' Mill. Next day McClellan received the
enemy's assault at the latter place. The blow lit on
Porter, whose task was to prevent the Confederates from
crossing the river. Lee was manifestly in earnest. He
intended no child's play. Porter was reinforced by
Slocum's division, and had nearly thirty thousand men,
including a body of regulars. Longstreet, A. P. Hill,
D. H. Hill, and Jackson were twice as

June 27.

many. Porter had the advantage of posi-
tion on heights in front of Grapevine Bridge; but was
isolated, and with a defile in his rear, — a critical
situation in case of disaster. The enemy's attacks
were furious to the last degree, but Porter's line was
tempered steel. Not until nightfall was any

June 27.

breach made in his ranks; nor could the
enemy penetrate the one they made. His loss was seven
thousand men; Lee's, seven hundred more. Stancher
defence to more brilliant assault was never made.

While this was going on beyond the river, Magruder
hammered away at the force south of the Chickahominy, to
engage McClellan's attention, and prevent his sending

reinforcements to sore-pressed Porter. In this he was successful. Porter withdrew during the night and burned the bridges.

While the battle of Gaines' Mill was in progress McClellan might have swung his left into Richmond, whose defences were sparsely held while the bulk of Lee's army was in action north of the Chickahominy; and it was for this object that gallant Porter believed that he was fighting his single corps against Lee's army. But, still again, McClellan was misled by his secret-service chief as to the number of the enemy, as he had been often before; and believing that he had one hundred thousand men between himself and the Southern capital instead of Magruder's mere handful, he sat down to figure out the itinerary of the predetermined retreat to the James river, in lieu of pushing through this film of troops and into Richmond.

It is true that McClellan always contemplated as a possibility a change of base to the James; but he surely never dreamed of making it under such immense pressure. Lee had based all his estimates upon McClellan's retreating by his right over the road he had come. But McClellan's manœuvre was by his left, thus frustrating his opponent's calculations and robbing his pursuit of two days' initiative. This was a great, but very natural, error on Lee's part. His intuitions were, as a rule, singularly near the truth.

The base at White House was abandoned; supplies were sent round to the James by transports, and all unremovable stores were burned. Eight days' rations and a large drove of beeves were sent on ahead. The hospital at Savage Station had to be abandoned.   It contained some twenty-five hundred sick and wounded, with surgeons and attendants, who had not yet been transported to White House.   The enemy behaved with humanity to these men.

Keyes led the advance, protecting the right flank of the

June 28.

interminable line of wagon-trains.   The first day passed without any serious action. To the enemy it was a wasted day, owing to Lee's error. He had put his forces still further down the left bank of the Chickahominy in imaginary pursuit.

June 29.

Porter followed Keyes.   Next morning these two corps, with McCall and Slocum, stood at Glendale.   Huger alone was in their front, and throughout the day no shot was fired.   Huger was kept

June 29.

diverted by a curtain of horse.   But Longstreet and Hill, as soon as Lee had discovered his mistake, retraced their steps by forced marches, crossed the Chickahominy by New Bridge and took post in rear of Huger ; while Jackson still remained at work, rebuilding Grapevine Bridge.

Sumner and Smith, of Franklin's Corps, could not escape a heavy combat with Magruder at Allen's Farm, and another at Savage Station.   They must fight to secure the retreat.   Heintzelman, who was on Sumner's left, extending down to White Oak Swamp, in lieu of sustaining them, left his two brother-officers to bear the brunt of the action, and began, before he was so ordered, to move his corps through the swamp, along a second road which had been happily discovered by Kearny.   As good luck would have it, Jackson

had not reached the ground. Rebuilding Grapevine
Bridge was an all day's job. At night-
fall, Franklin crossed the swamp, and, last   June 29.
of all, old Sumner, loth to leave.

Lee's cavalry was absent at White House, — a circum-
stance which saved us much complication. As soon as the
other corps began to arrive at Glendale, Keyes was moved
down to Turkey Bend. Porter edged to the left, making
room for the third corps. Franklin defended White Oak
Bridge against Jackson. Lee now hurled Longstreet and
Hill, with Huger and Magruder in support, down the
three avenues which tapped our line, massed along the
Quaker Road. Foreseeing the imperative
need of securing Malvern Hill, McClellan   June 30.
moved Porter down to that point.

Our line, well posted at Glendale (Confederate
" Frazier's Farm "), stoutly resisted the attacks of the
enemy, which fell particularly upon McCall. But once
during the day was a break effected by the Confederates,
and Kearny promptly filled the gap. Thus Franklin was
holding Jackson at bay at White Oak Swamp, while
Sumner and Heintzelman repulsed the vigorous onslaught
of Longstreet and Hill.

At night all the corps retreated to Malvern Hill. The
seven bloody days were to end here. Our
troops occupied a high plateau, and were   July 1.
disposed in convex order, with the flanks resting on the
river. We were warmly sustained by the fire of the gun-
boats in our rear, whose heavy shell passed over our heads
and exploded far beyond in the enemy's columns. It was

here that the Army of the Potomac received the parting
onsets of the enemy.   These were delivered in an isolated
manner, though full of Southern *élan*.   But, desperate as
were these assaults, repeated at intervals during the entire
day, and hardy as was the courage of the assailants, no
impression could be made upon our ranks.   Lee retired,
weary and in confusion, from the field.   The Army of
the Potomac had been saved.

During the seven days' operations the enemy, who had
been the attacking party, lost over twenty thousand men.
Our loss was under sixteen thousand.   Brilliant as had
been the conduct of the Confederate army, its performance
fell short of satisfying the Richmond public, which
demanded the annihilation or capture of the Army of the
Potomac.   The insatiability of nations for the results of
military skill and endurance is hard to be explained.
The impossible alone appears to equal the anticipations of
laymen;   and, were the impossible accomplished, more
would be apt to be demanded.   Even old soldiers, familiar with the difficulties which hedge about all military
exploits, will often join in this unreasoning clamor, when
not themselves engaged.

In this retreat McClellan showed undoubted ability.
But it was not the ability which accomplishes results.
He could fight for existence, and fight stanchly; but not
for conquest.   And when Halleck, wearing the laurels of his
Western lieutenants, became general-in-chief, it was all
over with the Peninsular campaign.   Lee quickly appreciated this fact, and at once set on foot a new campaign
towards the old battle-ground of Bull Run.

XIV.

POPE'S CAMPAIGN.

THE Army of Virginia, under Pope, is now to bear the brunt of Lee's assault, while the Army of the Potomac is dismembered and sent back whence it came, to add in driblets to Pope's effective. To the provoking changeableness of the President and his advisers, during McClellan's campaign, may be largely ascribed its failure. Who does not recognize Mr. Lincoln's keen perception of the general bearing politics should have on the operations in the field, as well as his military obtuseness? Harassed by a people at his back which demanded action, he was naturally unable to preserve his confidence in a general who would not act. And before McClellan did act, the confidence had ebbed away. "General McClellan did not give to the will of the President and the demands of the people that weight in the formation of his plans of campaign to which they were entitled." (Webb.)

The Western armies are resting on their laurels, well earned by the recovery of Kentucky, Tennessee, Missouri, and so material a part of the Mississippi river. General Pope's overestimated if brilliant success at Island No. 10 has persuaded Halleck to call him to the command of the

Virginia forces. A new army is created for him, and he
is unfortunate enough to open his Eastern

July 14.

career by a general order so ill-judged as to
rob him from the start of the confidence as well as sympathy
of his subordinates. The new Army of Virginia consists
of the corps of McDowell, Banks, and Sigel — the latter
having been Fremont's — which are all assembled from
their several departments.

McClellan has under his command ninety thousand men.
They are in a position which must compel Lee

July.

to stay in Richmond. He urges the capture of
Petersburg, at the portals of which two years later so much
blood will be spilled, and is allowed to believe that his
operations are to be continued from his present base. But
Halleck's will is now law, and Pope is his favorite. The
sacrifices and labors of the Army of the Potomac are
abandoned, and the troops put in motion for Acquia Creek.

Gordonsville is the key to the southern entrances of the
Shenandoah Valley. Anticipating a new march by Jackson
towards his favorite campaigning ground,

July 14-27.

Pope directs his scattered forces on this
town. But Jackson gets ahead of him. Lee has been
filling up his attenuated ranks ; he has got together eighty
thousand men. He sends A. P. Hill to reinforce Jackson.
So soon as Lee ascertains that McClellan's forces are
certainly to leave the James, he orders Jackson to assail
Pope's van, at Culpeper, without further delay. Jackson
advances with twenty-eight thousand men.

August 9.

Banks meets him near Cedar Mountain
(Confederate " Cedar Run ") with less than half this

force, and, attacking without discretion but with much
vigor, he almost compasses a victory.   Jackson retires
across the Rapidan.   Our losses are twenty-four hundred,
against thirteen hundred of the enemy's.

Lee now moves Longstreet to the new field of operations,
while one-third of the Army of the Potomac is on the march
to sustain Pope.   Overrating the numerical
superiority of Lee, Pope follows up the   August 17–18.

Pope's Campaign.   (1.)   August 24, 1862.

opening boast of his campaign by a retreat to the Rappahannock.   Here, under Halleck's orders, he is committed
to the very hazardous policy of protecting two divergent

lines in his rear, — one to Washington, whence come his supplies ; one to Acquia Creek, whence are to come his reinforcements from the Army of the Potomac ; and he is promised immediate and large accessions of troops. If from defeat, or for good tactical or strategic reasons, he is constrained to abandon the position so taken up, it need not be pointed out that he thus uncovers either one or both of these lines. Such a scheme is full of disadvantages if not positive dangers. It is rarely permissible.

Lee, with Jackson on the left and Longstreet on the right, advances upon him. Seeing no chance of forcing the river to advantage, Lee orders Jackson far around the Bull Run range to the left, to fall upon Pope's flank through Thoroughfare Gap.

August 21.

It must be remembered that Halleck was keeping both McClellan and Pope ignorant of the true state of affairs, while promising the latter reinforcements beyond his power to send. Pope had partially divined Lee's tactics, but believed Jackson's destination to be the Shenandoah Valley, and proposed to counter this manœuvre and attack Lee by crossing the river while he was isolated from his lieutenant. But the river rose, — as rivers can rise only in Virginia, — by a heavy storm, and Pope had again to change his plan. This was done under the excitement of a swoop by Stuart on Catlett's Station, which carried off Pope's head-quarter papers, spread alarm among the whole body of camp followers, and set the War Department in a panic.

August 22.
August 23.

McDowell had arrived at Warrenton. Porter was marching along up the Rappahannock from Acquia Creek.

Sigel was at Waterloo ; Banks at Sulphur
Springs. Heintzelman sent part of his corps
on from Alexandria. The men were already leg-weary
and disheartened.

August 24.

Lee meanwhile had given his troops a long rest while
waiting for Jackson to complete his flank march, and the
rise in the river had enforced some quiet upon Jackson near
Waterloo, before he could safely get his
corps across.

August 25.

Pope had it in his power to neutralize Jackson's march
by occupying Thoroughfare Gap. But again he was
slower than the Confederate general. Anticipating a
crossing by Lee, as the waters were subsiding, he began
a new movement to place himself on the Orange and Alexandria Railroad facing westerly to protect his communications with Acquia Creek. While thus manœuvring,
new advices as to Jackson being on the march reached him
and almost induced him to make another attempt on Lee
across the river. But his forces were happily too much
scattered to be got in hand.

Meanwhile Jackson, with Stuart protecting his right and
front, after a march of fifty miles in thirty-six hours, debouches from Thoroughfare Gap and descends upon Bristoe
and Manassas Stations. Here are Pope's supplies and
munitions of war. Jackson makes an utter wreck of them
all. Up to this moment Pope has appar-
ently never thought of Thoroughfare Gap.

August 26.

His consternation is complete, while Washington is at the
end of its wits.

Jackson had placed himself in extreme peril. In all the

campaigns he conducted under the orders of Lee, he showed himself peculiarly fond of manœuvres which can not but be condemned by the logic of warfare, and which an opponent who was his equal in audacity and skill could repeatedly have turned to his all but destruction. But the celerity of Jackson's manœuvres, and the fact that he was never pitted against any antagonist ready to take summary advantage of his breach of the rules of strategy, saved him and his reputation harmless. His genius was as eccentric as he himself was daring; his soldierly qualities were of the highest, and brilliant success stamped him the ablest lieutenant of the war. And after all must not the strictest methods of strategy subordinate themselves to the one rule of doing the most apt thing at the proper moment? This Stonewall Jackson invariably did.

But if Jackson was in danger, so was Pope cut off from his base. Halleck, aghast, was utterly ignorant as to what force was in Pope's rear. Franklin had arrived at Alexandria and a brigade was sent out to Bull Run to reconnoitre. Here these troops were waylaid by Jackson and fell back to Centreville, spreading consternation on every side.

This flank march accomplished in his usual splendid style, Jackson occupies the old Bull Run battle ground and gives his men an ample rest August 27. while he awaits the arrival of his chief. His corps is in the highest spirits, and each man's haversack is filled with rare good provender. Pope hurries hither and yon in the hope of striking the, to him, invisible foe. The two armies are about to close and wrestle over the familiar ground.

Pope has had good reason to rely on Halleck to pro-

tect his right and rear. The capture of Manassas unde-
ceives him. But he can now make Jackson pay dearly for
his venture by striking him before his chief comes up to
his aid; for Longstreet has set out to march towards him by
the same long circuit. But he goes to work in the wrong
way. Pope should evidently plant himself between Jackson and Thoroughfare Gap. This is the one thing needful
to be done, and Gainesville is the strategic key of the op-

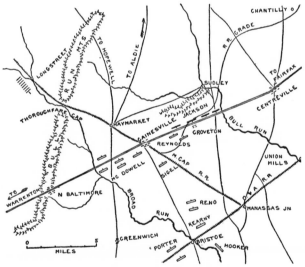

Pope's Campaign. (2.) August 28, A.M.

eration. McDowell appreciates the fact and does occupy
both Gainesville and Haymarket. He then proposes to
demonstrate on Jackson and develop his position. All this
is well to the purpose and shows foresight and activity.

Longstreet is thus cut off from Jackson. The Army of

Northern Virginia is actually in bad case.
August 28. Pope only needs to advance his left to compass absolute success. But a strange infatuation makes him again conceive a fear for his right flank and robs him of the power of gauging his advantage. He withdraws McDow-

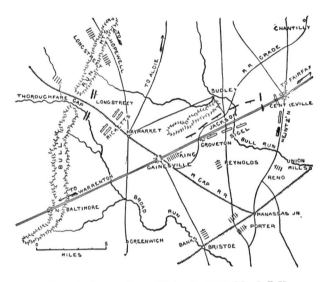

Pope's Campaign. (3.) August 28, 6 P.M.

ell with other troops from Gainesville to the vicinity of Manassas. Exhausted, confused, and dispirited, this new and puzzling march is made by the divisions concerned. Only Ricketts remains at the key-point, McDowell having left him to observe Thoroughfare Gap.

Jackson could ask no better treatment. He has taken position from Sudley Springs to Groveton, and utilizing a new railroad grade as defence, he sends Hill towards Cen-

treville as a *ruse* to draw Pope away. Ricketts is driven
from Thoroughfare Gap at the same moment
he is recalled.   King, of McDowell's corps,   August 28.
has a sharp battle with Jackson's right, but retires at night.
The Federals have lost all they possessed the day before.
Jackson and Lee can now shake hands, while
Pope scarcely knows what has become of all   August 29.
his troops.

   Having blundered away his advantage, the thing for Pope
to do now is to take position north of Bull Run and receive

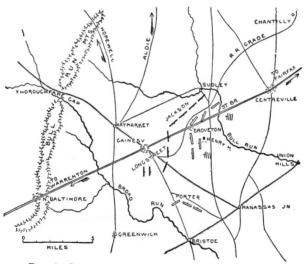

Pope's Campaign. (4.) August 29, Noon.

the enemy on strong ground, where he can be securely
joined by the balance of the Army of the Potomac, and can
rest and victual his men.   But he now, at this late hour,

endeavors to reoccupy Gainesville, so as to separate Lee and Jackson. Heintzelman and Reno are to pass the stone bridge. McDowell and Porter are to go to Gainesville. Sigel and Reynolds will be the centre. All this is too late. Pope is already tactically defeated.

August 29.   Sigel arrives and attacks Jackson's right. Starke holds him off; reinforcements come up, but the combat is not heavy. Longstreet puts in his appearance. Groveton becomes the centre of the Confederate line, while Longstreet works gradually around our left.

McDowell and Porter are barred from the road Pope has ordered them to pursue. Porter faces Longstreet astride the railroad. McDowell gets his corps together and marches towards the booming of the guns at Groveton. Pope still hugs the delusion that Longstreet is far away, and that McDowell and Porter can turn Jackson's right. Assuming that they have actually got at this work, Hooker and Kearny are thrown upon Jackson's railroad defences, but repulsed by Hill and Early. Pope again sends an order to Porter to attack Jackson's right, and again assuming that he has received and acted on it, once more hurls Kearny and Reno on the embankment. These divisions capture it, but being without reserves, must fall back with useless slaughter. McDowell appears at Groveton and attacks, but he falls foul of Longstreet's veterans and can make no impression. Porter remains inactive. He might create a diversion in Pope's favor by attack, but the operation is delicate. His orders are nullified by the facts which Pope ignores.

While our troops have had the advantage of the fighting

on this day, they are now out of rations and
should be withdrawn. But Pope determines to   August 29.
fight again on the morrow, with the fifty odd thousand men
left him. He strengthens his right wing by de-
pleting his left, and attacks at noon. Porter is   August 30.
brought to the centre and launched upon the enemy. His
gallantry, which no one has ever questioned, can effect
nothing. Lee assumes the offensive. Despite hard blows
the Unionists are forced back all along the line. Had not
a successful stand been made by a hurriedly assembled force
massed on the Henry House Hill, the disaster would have
been fatal to the Army of the Potomac.

Pope retires to Centreville.   August 30.

Here Jackson again outflanks him. By a   August 31.
march around his right to Chantilly, he is nearer Fair-
fax than Pope. A still more hurried retreat towards
Alexandria follows. Pope is barely saved from this new
destruction by the successful head made against Jackson at
the battle of Chantilly by the divisions of Kearny (in
making which this *preux chevalier's* life   September 1.
is lost) and Reno.

During this campaign we lost fourteen out of eighty
thousand men; the enemy nine out of fifty-four thousand.

Thus, despite the gallantry of the troops, the Federals
have been sent whirling back towards the capital, having
fought half-a-dozen battles to no purpose whatsoever. Lee
can not further follow Pope. He must also revictual his
army, and give his gallant men time for recuperation.

Pope should not be held alone to blame for the issue of
this campaign. He was brave, light-hearted under adver-

sity, and sanguine. That he was unable to cope with Lee's steady purpose and Jackson's splendid marching capacity must not rob him of what he fairly deserves. He was utterly outgeneralled ; he never knew where his enemy was ; he fought to no purpose. But when he did fight, it was with a will beyond his discretion ; and he would have cheerfully marched out again to meet his late antagonists so soon as he had reached the protection of the defences of Washington. It was Halleck's secretiveness, and his illusory promises of reinforcements, dangerous because he kept the actual facts both from Pope and McClellan so that neither could sustain the other, that were the actual causes of failure ; while Pope's lack of power to divine Lee's manœuvres and his exhausting energy in parrying the thrusts he vainly imagined to be aimed at him, were immediately at fault. But from Cedar Mountain to Chantilly, the conduct of our troops stands out in brilliant relief from the tactics of their commander ; while we cannot sufficiently wonder at the courage, patience, and muscular legs of the Southern veterans. Mere words cannot do them justice.

Pope attributed his overthrow to the failure of Fitz John Porter to obey orders to attack Longstreet on August 29. Facts now well known exonerate this officer, and his splendid service whenever called upon has deserved better of the nation. That Porter should have more definitely developed, by a reconnoissance in force, the fact, which he knew by scouts, of Longstreet's presence in his front, or perhaps have attacked him as a diversion, is almost the only criticism that can be honestly and intelligently brought home to him by his opponents. And, confronting as he

did, half of Lee's army, unknown to Pope, such a course
might have proved highly disastrous.   What other citizen,
during our entire history, ever suffered for so slight an
error?   Moreover every corps commander in the army was
at that time in utter daze at the eccentric tactical combinations of Pope; while the troops were exhausted, hungry,
and without confidence in their chief.

XV.

BUELL AND BRAGG.

AGAIN to return to the West, where we left the Union Army to recruit from the fatigues of their successes against Beauregard. After the fall of Corinth the Confederates dispersed their forces over a considerable area. As Halleck made no effort to follow up his advantages by a forward movement, this necessitated a similar disposition on his part.

It is altogether probable that, starting from Corinth, a column of ten thousand or fifteen thousand men could have captured Vicksburg. But enterprise in the field was not one of Halleck's virtues, and the enemy was able to erect defences both there and at Port Hudson which checked our operations for at least a year.

When summer opened Halleck stood at the head of one hundred and seventy-five thousand men, of which one hundred and ten thousand were carried on his Morning Report as "for duty." In addition to this Mitchel was at Huntsville on the Memphis and Charleston Railroad with seven thousand; Morgan at Cumberland Gap with nine thousand; and Curtis with ten thousand more was, after the battle of Pea Ridge, ap-

June, 1862.

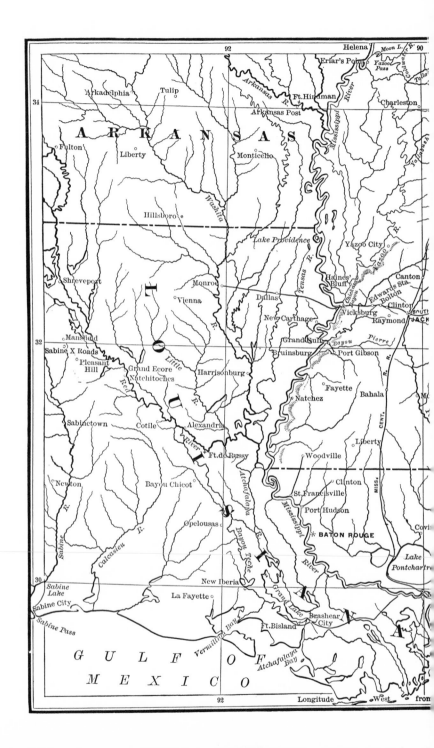

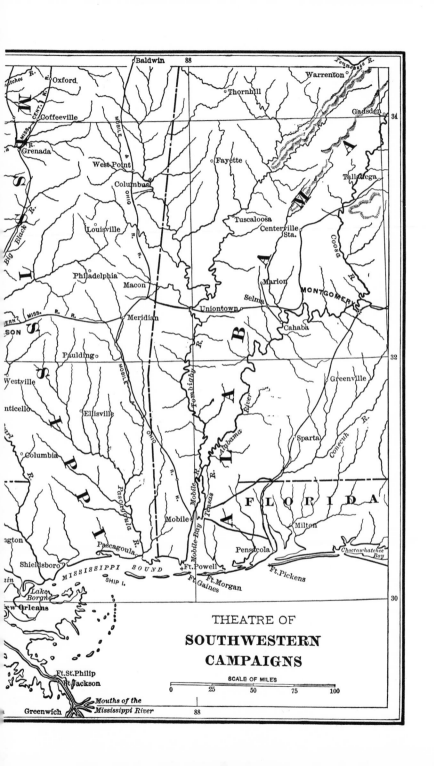

THEATRE OF

SOUTHWESTERN

CAMPAIGNS

SCALE OF MILES

0   25   50   75   100

proaching the Mississippi river.   Our forces were much elated by recent victories, which had a correspondingly depressing effect upon the enemy.   With this force at his command, it seems as if Halleck might have marched at will to Mobile and neutralized the entire belt of country for a hundred miles east of the Mississippi.

Beauregard was south of Corinth with one hundred and twelve thousand men, fifty-three thousand "for duty," and in addition eleven thousand in East Tennessee, with head-quarters in Knoxville, and ten thousand in Jackson and Vicksburg.   The Arkansas forces had been ordered to Corinth against the protest of the governor of that state.

There were two roads open to Halleck by which to pierce the heart of the Confederacy ; one down the great river, one from Chattanooga to Atlanta and beyond.   He had the numerical ability to control both, and each being a highway to the North, it behooved him to protect both. The Memphis and Charleston Railroad was in his hands. His army was strong enough to divide and yet hold the keys to each of these strategic routes.   The bulk of his force was still disposable for whichever route he might choose to advance upon.

But Halleck was feeble in movement.   Buell could well have been despatched towards Chattanooga to secure what Mitchel had already seized.   This would have left Halleck plenty of force with which to attack Beauregard.   But Halleck's whole scheme is formulated in his own words : "I think the enemy will continue his retreat, which is all I desire."

Not so the Confederates.   While Halleck, with his

forces disjointedly strung out, was losing precious time in repairs on the railroad and in contemplating his past triumphs, Bragg sent his thirty-five thousand men by rail *via* Mobile to Chattanooga.   This foresight pro-

July 21-30.

longed the Western contest indefinitely, and enabled Bragg to control events until Grant, more than a year later, had freed the Mississippi and could devote his active energies to the interior.

The cards are again shuffled, during which operation every one is without definite instructions ; there is no one head, and the Western armies are practically put on the defensive.   Pope is transferred to Virginia,

June 26-27.

and Rosecrans is given the Army of the Mississippi ; Buell retains the Army of the Ohio ; Halleck's questionable strategy in the field is rewarded by the supreme control of the Union forces in the War De-

July 16-17.

partment—work for which he is better fitted. To Grant's lot falls the Army of the Mississippi in addition to the Army of the Tennessee, forty-two thousand effectives, with which to keep open his communications with Buell and guard the railroad from Memphis to Decatur. While Grant and Sherman devote their energies to the line of the Mississippi, Buell is ordered to regain East Tennessee, where the loyal population is in extreme suffering.

Mitchel's capture of Huntsville and of some hundred miles of the Memphis and Charleston Railroad, which he had held, together with all territory north of the Tennessee River, had been full of possibilities.   Had he but received the authority, he might readily have anticipated Bragg in taking possession of Chattanooga, and have saved much subsequent blood and treasure. For this town is the key to that entire strategic field.

Buell desired to establish his base of supplies at Nashville and to make an immediate advance upon Chattanooga from thence. Halleck insisted on his advancing along the Memphis and Charleston June 15 to Aug. 1. Railroad and putting it in thorough repair as he went. This he did; but it was the delay so caused which enabled Bragg to seize the coveted prize, and A. S. Johnston had well filled the place with stores when he had found himself obliged to abandon Nashville months before.

Buell had barely reached a position in which he could confront Bragg, when the Confederate partisans Forrest and Morgan began their equally brilliant and troublesome raids against his communications. These Buell was unable to meet for entire lack of horse. But he took up a line calculated to protect Nashville as well as to threaten Bragg, who lay in advance of the Tennessee.

Buell supposed that Bragg would attempt to turn his right in order to obtain possession of Nashville. He therefore concentrated the bulk of his force at Murfreesborough. Thomas, then command- August. ing a wing of the Army of the Ohio, whose military intuitions were as keen as his judgment was reliable, and who was always the safest adviser either Buell, Rosecrans or Sherman ever had, was shrewd enough to recognize Bragg's crossing of the Tennessee river as a threat to invade Kentucky. Not so Buell, to his sorrow.

By a sudden movement, Bragg steals a march around Buell's left through the Sequatchie Valley August 28.

and marches straight toward Louisville,
while Kirby Smith turns Cumberland Gap,
August 30.
defeats Nelson at Richmond and makes for Cincinnati.
This is all in pursuance of the plan of A. S. Johnston,
which he had purposed to put into execution, when, as he
confidently believed, he should have beaten our army at
Shiloh.

Thoroughly alarmed, as is also the country, Buell at
once swings his left in pursuit of Bragg, while he endeavors
to retain his grasp on Nashville with his right.   Bragg has
the shorter line and the start.   But he is
delayed a day or two by the capture of
Sept. 14–17.
Munfordville, and by scattering his forces instead of
pushing home.   This is a serious fault on Bragg's part.
He fairly holds success in his hand, but forfeits it by
this delay.   After some rapid marching and manœuvring,
Buell enters Louisville just ahead of his opponent.

The authorities in Washington have lost all confidence
in Buell.   He is summarily relieved from
command and Thomas appointed to succeed
September 29.
him.   But this magnanimous soldier, though far from
always agreeing with the methods of his chief, declines the
proffered honor, and, at his earnest solicitation, Buell is
reinstated.   The Army of the Ohio marches out to meet
Bragg, with Thomas second in command.

Bragg expects to defend the line of the Kentucky and
Duck rivers, but divides his forces, leaving Kirby Smith
near Frankfort.   Buell makes a demonstration upon
Bragg's communications.   After some cautious feeling,
Buell comes upon Hardee with only sixteen thousand

men, at Perry-
ville, where, had
he at once at-
tacked he could
h a v e punished
B r a g g severely
for this division.
But, owing to
lack of w a t e r,
one-half of Buell's
army is distant
from the field,
and he in turn
pays the penalty
of lack of con-
centration. Polk

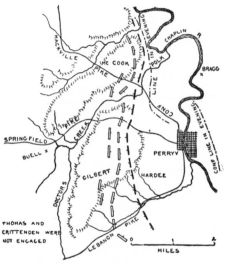

Perryville. October 8, 1862.

joins Hardee and they both fall heavily upon McCook,
who holds Buell's left, and bear him back.

October 8.

But they cannot break the Union centre;
and after a stubborn conflict Bragg retires, leaving
to our forces the field. Our right has not been engaged. The loss is: Buell, forty-two hundred; Bragg
thirty-four hundred; a fifth of the men actually engaged. On being followed up, Bragg re-

October 13.

treats through Cumberland Gap, and leaves
Kentucky and Tennessee once more in our possession.
His retreat ends only at Chattanooga.

What Bragg expected to obtain in Kentucky was a vast
accession of recruits and horses, as did Lee in Maryland.
Both fell short of their calculations, though Bragg carried
off a goodly train of supplies. Forgetful of what he had

really done, the South was bitter in its criticism of Bragg's failure to hold Eastern Tennessee and Kentucky. But his campaign had really placed him in a position in Buell's front far superior to the one he had occupied before he marched for the Ohio, morally and materially. And it was beyond reason to anticipate his holding any considerable part of these States in permanency.

Halleck now insists that Buell shall undertake a campaign in East Tennessee, still occupied by the enemy. But Buell alleges the utter impossibility of subsisting his troops so far from the railroad, and again concentrates at Nashville. Here he is relieved and Gen. Rosecrans is appointed to the command.

October 30.

During this campaign every one lost confidence in Buell except his stanch lieutenant, Thomas, who, though he could have had the command, allowed his sense of justice as well as his very singular distrust of the great powers he possessed to stand in his own light. Thomas desired nothing less than to have an independent charge. A rare union indeed of ability and modesty.

Buell was a thorough soldier and a fine disciplinarian. The effectiveness of the divisions he had led was due to his care and skill in organization in as full measure as that of the Army of the Potomac to McClellan. More than one soldier of our war acquired fame and achieved success on a basis less sound than his. But he had served in the bureau more than with troops, and the marshal's baton was bestowed upon him too early. Had he possessed the experience of moderate field command before he worked in so large a sphere, he might have compassed final success of much more enduring character.

XVI.

IUKA AND CORINTH.

WHEN Bragg had confronted Buell in Tennessee with the purpose of operating towards the Ohio, as just narrated; it became necessary for him to adopt measures to prevent Rosecrans or Grant from detaching reinforcements to, or indeed from making a junction in force with, their associate. He therefore sent orders to Price, whom he had left south of Corinth, to advance upon the Federals and divert their attention. Price, deeming himself too weak to cope single-handed with the Army of the Mississippi, requested Van Dorn to lend his assistance to the enterprise.

Grant is meanwhile anticipating that the enemy will make an attack upon Corinth, where the bulk of our force is stationed, while we have heavy detachments at Memphis and Bolivar. But Rosecrans' cavalry discovers Price's vanguard in Iuka. Well aware that Van Dorn is at least four marches distant, Grant determines to crush Price singly, and feels that he has numerical strength enough to divide his forces. He sends Rosecrans to make an attack upon Price along roads reaching Iuka from the south, while another column from the north shall intercept him and if possible drive him back

September 15.

upon the Tennessee river.   Grant accompanies the latter
body under command of Ord.

September 19.   Bad roads and worse maps of the country
delay Rosecrans.   And when he finally does

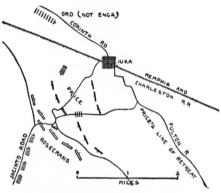

attack, it is in so
disjointed a way
that only a por-
tion of his force
can engage the
enemy.   Rose-
crans' task is to
seize both roads
running south
from Iuka; but
he manages only
to reach one.   On

Iuka. September 19, 1862.

the other Price escapes unharmed.   The loss on either
side is not far from eight hundred men.

October 1.   Grant has, all told, some forty-eight thousand men, seven thousand being under Sher-
man at Memphis, twelve thousand under Ord at Bolivar,
twenty-three thousand under Rosecrans at Corinth, and
six thousand at head-quarters at Jackson.

Price and Van Dorn in due time join their forces, twenty-
September 28.   two thousand men, at Ripley, the latter as
senior taking command.   He is wise enough
to see that a successful attack upon isolated Corinth will
thrust Grant back, as Bragg has served Buell, and neutralize
all his victories.   Full of his purpose Van Dorn with his wonted
energy moves upon Corinth and marshals his army on the

north-west of the town. His position sev-
ers Rosecrans' force from Grant's. Van   September 30.
Dorn's plan is to feint upon Rosecrans' left, thereby drawing
troops from his right, and then to throw Price upon the
depleted wing and crush it. He attacks. At an early
stage of the battle a gap is opened in Rosecrans' line. Into
this breach Van Dorn is not slow to press. Our left and
centre is borne back, but the right remaining
intact, wheels and threatens Van Dorn's ex-   October 3.
posed flanks. Darkness brings the combat to a close.

The forces of each are about equal. The night is spent
in reforming the troops for the morrow. Van Dorn pur-

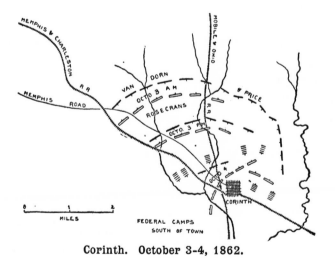

Corinth. October 3-4, 1862.

poses to assault at dawn, but is belated by subordinates.
When, however, he does attack, it is with characteristic
vigor. Part of his troops actually enter the city, and for

about an hour cannot be ejected.   But Rosecrans holds his own ; Van Dorn finds that he cannot worst him, and, fearing an attack upon his rear, determines on retreat.   This he skilfully effects, under cover of renewed attack.

October 4.

Rosecrans makes no motion to follow.   In falling back Van Dorn runs across Ord at the fords of the Hatchie river, and had Rosecrans been at his heels, Van Dorn might have been badly used up.   But by ably manœuvring his rear-guard, Van Dorn manages to elude Ord, crosses the Hatchie a trifle to the east and escapes.

The Confederate loss and ours were not far from two thousand five hundred each.   We took two thousand prisoners.

Shortly after, Van Dorn was displaced by Pemberton, while Rosecrans was promoted to Buell's command.   In subordinate positions Van Dorn rendered excellent service to the Confederacy until the close of the war.   It is not saying much to assert that had he remained in command of the Vicksburg forces, Grant's task would have proved a harder one than with Pemberton in his front.

October 30.

XVII.

GRANT'S FAILURE AGAINST VICKSBURG.

SOON after Farragut had passed into New Orleans, he moved up the river to Baton Rouge and Natchez. In connection with this movement a land force had made its way to Vicksburg, under command of General Williams, hoping to capture the place by a *coup de main;* but its batteries, during the weeks just elapsed, had been completed, and General M. L. Smith made show of so good a defense that Williams deemed it unwise to attack. Farragut having run the batteries, then incomplete, both up and down river, returned to New Orleans. The next month the importance of the new fortress was the occasion of putting Van Dorn in command.

May 8, 1862.

May 18.

June.

Subsequently Admiral Porter was ordered up the river by Farragut, and Williams began to dig the afterwards famous canal, which its projectors imagined would make Vicksburg an inland town by diverting the current of the Mississippi. At this time Farragut again ran the batteries with his fleet up river, at a loss of some sixty men, satisfying himself that he could at any time perform this feat.

June 25.

June 28.

But he was by no means strong enough to successfully engage the forts without coöperation of a land force.

The ram Arkansas had been building in the Yazoo river, above Vicksburg. Farragut had hoped for a chance to destroy the vessel; but the ram eluded his watchfulness, and sought refuge under the Vicksburg guns, much to Farragut's disgust. He again ran down past the batteries, intending to destroy the ram, but vainly. Later he was ordered back to New Orleans; Williams returned to Baton Rouge, and Admiral Davis moved up the river, leaving Vicksburg mistress of the situation.

July 25.

This invited Van Dorn to make a raid from Vicksburg on Baton Rouge, which he entrusted to Breckenridge. A stubborn resistance succeeded in holding the city, though Williams was killed in the defense. But Breckenridge actually accomplished his purpose by securing an available point for another fortress below the mouth of the Red river, to wit, Port Hudson. Baton Rouge was, in consequence, shortly abandoned by us, as at the time comparatively of no value.

August 5.

While Rosecrans was planning a campaign against Chattanooga, Grant, in immediate command of the Thirteenth Army Corps, as it was now called, suggested the capture of Vicksburg to the general-in-chief. There was a force of not far from fifty thousand men in this vicinity. With Halleck's half-approval Grant made a forward move; but was no sooner under way than he stopped and decided to wait for some twenty thousand reinforcements promised him. Hereupon Halleck placed all

November 2.

the forces in the Department under his orders, and told
him " to fight the enemy where he pleased."

November 11.

Grant's fifty-seven thousand men still lay
substantially as they had, with Pemberton in their front.

A threatened complication of serious nature arose in a
half promise extorted from Mr. Lincoln and the Secretary
of War by General McClernand, that the latter should have
a separate command to operate down the Mississippi;
and while Grant and Halleck were planning one thing,
Secretary Stanton and McClernand were secretly confer-
ring about another.   These cross-purposes were, however,
for the time being, arrested by Grant's mov-

Nov. 26–27.

ing on Holly Springs, Sherman at the same
time starting from Memphis, and Hovey crossing from
Helena to threaten Grenada on Pemberton's flank and rear.
Some skirmishing was had with the enemy's outposts, but
without results.   Pemberton had established his head-quarters at Jackson, Miss., with Van Dorn out as vanguard at
Holly Springs.   All told, he had some forty thousand men
under his command.

Grant's line of operations was long and weak; he could
get no locomotives nor cars so as to utilize the railroad, nor
did support, moral or material, reach him from Halleck.
He had desired to bring Pemberton to battle, but the latter
retired behind the Tallahatchie.   And, lest McClernand
should actually receive the command of the Mississippi venture, while he himself was left to fight on the overland route
single handed, Grant devised a new plan.   This contemplated that Sherman should take the bulk of the forces at
Memphis, at once descend the river in transports, and, in

connection with Admiral Porter, assail the works at Vicksburg, while he himself would push the enemy down the line of the Mobile and Ohio Railroad, and if they retired to that fortress, endeavor to enter the city with them.

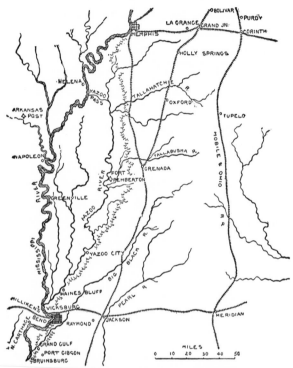

Memphis to Vicksburg. 1862-63.

This double attack was certainly not strategically sound. None of the attendant circumstances warranted such a division of forces. But, at that stage of the war, it was not deemed possible to subsist an army very far from its base, nor at all upon the country.   And McClernand was so very uncertain and disturbing a factor in Grant's calculations that the latter deemed any action preferable to delay.

McClernand meanwhile had received the sole command of the river expedition.   But, as it fell out, Sherman got under way before the news could reach him.   About the same time Joe Johnston was put in command of all Confederate forces between the Alleghanies and the Mississippi river.

While Sherman and Porter are moving down the river, with thirty thousand men and sixty guns, beside the flotilla of eight gun-boats, Grant pushes forward to Oxford, while Pemberton retires to the line of the Yallabusha at the town of Grenada.   Grant's line of operations is protected at various points along the railroad by strong detachments.   Van Dorn, now commanding a cavalry division, and Forrest, the noted Confederate raider, join forces to operate against Grant's communi- cations, and during the last ten days of the   December, 1862. year, while Forrest demonstrates against Jackson, Tenn., Van Dorn attacks, and with scarcely any opposition from its negligent commander, captures Holly Springs, with large stores of food, arms, and ammunition.   Several important bridges in Grant's rear are at the same time destroyed.

The whole scene is suddenly changed.   Grant's advance is made impossible, for starvation stares him in the face. He is obliged to fall back to reëstablish his base, while Pemberton in his turn retires to defend Vicksburg from Sherman and Porter.   This raid has not only destroyed

Grant's supplies, but also his ability to accumulate more for the moment. A courier is at once despatched to Sherman to notify him of this disaster, but does not overtake him with the news. Grant is ordered by Halleck to follow Sherman down the river. This he proceeds to do by way of Memphis.

It took all Grant's patience to bear up under this utter failure of his campaign, and especially to brook the appointment of McClernand. But his zeal and activity never flagged. Grant possessed the rare power of standing firm under the hardest conditions of disappointment or defeat.

XVIII.

SHERMAN'S FAILURE AGAINST VICKSBURG.

MEANWHILE Sherman, convoyed by Porter and his fleet on some sixty transports, had reached the mouth of the Yazoo river. Next day he moved up stream to effect a landing, expecting that Grant was near at hand or else was holding the enemy on the Yallabusha. Halleck had also promised Banks' coöperation from New Orleans; but fortunately no immediate reliance was placed upon this promise. December 25.

A line of bluffs runs for many hundred miles along the east bank of the Mississippi river. From Vicksburg north these bluffs leave the river to join it again at Memphis. The land between the river and the bluffs is low, much cut up by bayous, and like to an impenetrable morass. Its waters all flow into the Yazoo. Some fifteen miles above Vicksburg, where the bluff abuts on the Yazoo, Haines Bluff, as it is there called, is some two hundred feet high, and all but inaccessible. The ground in front is of the same low character, and is diversified by the presence of several small lakes connected by Chickasaw Bayou.

There were no maps of the ground in Sherman's possession. It was *terra incognita*. And it was equally un-

known to him that strong works had been erected all along
the bluffs, the few approaches to which were specially
defended.   Sherman had hoped to get in rear of Vicksburg
by this route ; to cut the railroad and to isolate Pemberton,
whom he imagined at the moment to be confronting Grant.
Our success depended entirely on a surprise.   But Pemberton was actually in Vicksburg and fully aware of Sherman's
every move.   We were already checkmated, but did not
know it.

December 28.   Sherman has with him four good divisions,
He makes a reconnoissance, to ascertain the
best point of attack.   It is thought that a lodgment can
be effected on the bluff.

December 29.   Two well-pushed attacks are made.   Some
of the enemy's defences come near to being
taken.   But after an all-day struggle to get a suitable force
across the open and up the perpendicular bluffs from which
the resistance of the enemy is steadily maintained, and with
absurd ease, our troops fall back with a loss of nearly two
thousand men.   The Confederate casualties are nominal.
Sherman then makes an attempt further up and nearer the
Yazoo, but as Porter can not coöperate with the flotilla he
is unable to accomplish material results.

This disheartening failure was not caused by want of
courageous effort or intelligent action.   Even had Sherman
taken the bluffs, as he thinks might have been done, it is
doubtful if he could have held them.

Grant's subsequent success goes far to show that a campaign overland with all forces in one body would have come
much nearer to compass the end than these two isolated

attempts by land and water. A division of forces requires a background of good luck. It can not face bad fortune or accidents.

McClernand now joined the army on the Yazoo and assumed command under his general orders to that effect.

January 4, 1863.

An attack on Arkansas Post had already been planned by Sherman and Porter, and McClernand as commanding officer having assented, they now proceeded to put it into effect. Fort Hindman, as the Confederates called it, lay some distance up the Arkansas river, and was a constant threat to the rear of any force operating against Vicksburg. It was at this time garrisoned by some seven thousand men, under command of General Churchill.

The troops embark and in a few days reach the scene of action. A landing is effected below, and next day the heavy guns of the fleet, after a few hours' bombardment, silence the artillery in the fort. An assault is in contemplation when (as it is afterwards claimed by the enemy, under a mistake) white flags are raised along the parapet, and the fort is surrendered with nearly five thousand prisoners. Our loss was about one thousand.

January 11.

This very brilliant and cheap success was in the nature of a compensation for the grievous failure at Chickasaw Bayou. McClernand arrogated its accomplishment to himself, and proceeded to project a visionary movement into the heart of Arkansas. But this expedition was nipped in the bud by Grant, who under authority from Halleck ordered the forces back to the Mississippi. McClernand sullenly obeyed.

XIX.

LEE'S FIRST INVASION. — ANTIETAM.

LEAVING Grant to profit by his failure, and to study up a new means of compassing the reduction of Vicksburg, we will see what is doing in Virginia.

The natural sequence of Pope's reverse was an incursion by Lee across the Potomac. Active Bragg had just marched around Buell's left flank and made his way into Kentucky. The Army of Northern Virginia had utterly worsted both McClellan and Pope. Confederate *prestige* was high. In Southern eyes "My Maryland" was groaning under the tyrant's heel. And were there not corn, and horses, and shoes, as well as perhaps recruits, to be had in exchange for liberation?

No sooner then had the *disjecta membra* of the short-lived Army of Virginia been gathered within the defences of Washington, than McClellan, informally reinstated by unspoken verdict of army and people alike, found it necessary to move up the left bank of the Potomac to encounter the divisions which a few weeks since he had fought within the suburbs of their own capital.

Rather than march on Baltimore, Lee had chosen a campaign in the mountainous region of Maryland. D. H. Hill was the first to cross the Potomac, and within three days the whole Confederate Army was put over, and occupied the line of the Monocacy.

The disenchantment of the Marylanders at the raggedness of the Southern chivalry was only equalled by the mortification of these gallant soldiers at their lukewarm reception, and Lee's campaign from the start wore the signs of failure.   Harper's Ferry barred his communication up the Valley with a garrison of eleven thousand men, and offered a tempting bait as well.   With reckless contempt of his foe, Lee once again divided his forces, sending Jackson back across the river to capture this position.

Harper's Ferry, with Lee in Maryland, was worse than useless to the Federals.   It was a mere key to gates already broken down.   Lee, of course, expected to see it evacuated.   But to Halleck's soul this position was always dear.   To lose it was to endanger the republic; he ordered it held at any sacrifice.

Meanwhile McClellan was moving from Washington into Maryland by his right, reorganizing the crestfallen but still resolute Army of the Potomac as he went.   The troops had received the return of "Little Mac" as a harbinger of success, though it was a bitter task to follow the enemy into loyal territory.

McClellan occupied Frederick, moving with more than his usual caution on account   September 12. of Halleck's absurd fears that he would uncover the capital.   Here unexampled good luck put into his possession a copy of Lee's order of march to   September 13. his division commanders.   To secure the

fruit of this good chance he had but to extend his hand.
An immediate march through the then undefended South
Mountain passes would have enabled him to crush Longstreet, separated from Jackson by the broad Potomac.
But McClellan was incapable of moving rapidly. He
loitered till the enemy occupied and he had to force
these passes, at equal sacrifice of men and opportunity.

Reno finds Hill in force in Turner's Gap. Reinforced
by Hooker, a heavy fight enables them to gain a domi-
nating foothold. Hill retires. On the
September 14. same day Franklin forces Cobb out of
Crampton's Gap. These two actions, known as the
Battle of South Mountain, cost us eighteen hundred men.
The enemy's loss was much larger, for we captured some
twelve hundred prisoners.

Meanwhile Jackson has cooped up eleven thousand
Federals in the *cul de sac* at Harper's Ferry. The
heights on both sides of the river are occupied. The
bombardment begins. But within an hour Colonel Miles,
the commander, who could have cut his way out, as did
his cavalry, surrenders. His death, by almost the last
shot fired, ill atones for this weakness. Jackson, with
a part of his force, at once starts to rejoin
September 16. his chief in Maryland. The rest follows
after completing the details of the capitulation.

McClellan's inertia had thus permitted Lee to capture
eleven thousand men and to reunite his separated corps.
The Army of Northern Virginia now takes up at Sharps-
burg a strong defensive position, covered by the Antietam.

Lee had over fifty thousand muskets, every one of

which was as usual put to use.   McClellan had eighty-seven
thousand, but he not only failed to deceive Lee as to his
tactical dispositions, but managed to use barely two-thirds
his men, while his successive instead of massed attacks
enabled Lee to fight what English roughs would call a

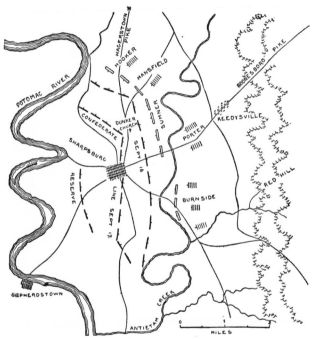

Antietam.   September 16 and 17, 1862.

"one down t'other come on" sort of battle.   Wherever
engaged, the Confederates were equal to the Federals in
number.

The main attack is by the Federal right.   Hooker crosses
the Antietam, and opens the battle by a sharp assault on

Lee's left.   Next morning the attack is re-
Sept. 16 and 17. newed, but is stopped by Jackson at Dunker
Church.   All day the tide ebbs and flows over this ground.
Meade and Sumner and Mansfield fight their men to the
best advantage, though in isolated columns.   The lack of
single purpose is manifest.   Lee heavily reinforces this
wing.

But hard fighting across the Antietam is neutralized by
Burnside's sluggish movement on the left flank.   Ordered
to cross at 7 A.M., he barely works out his task, against
feeble opposition, by 3 P.M., when our ex-
September 17. hausted right has ceased to struggle, and the
balance of Jackson's corps comes upon the field from the
Harper's Ferry triumph.   Both combatants need rest, and
Lee next day withdraws from a tactically drawn battle and
a strategic defeat.

Our loss in this battle of Antietam (Confederate " Sharps-
burg ") was twelve thousand five hundred ;   Lee's over ten
thousand.   Except Shiloh, no such sanguinary struggle had
stained the sod of the civilized New World.

McClellan's pursuit was feebler than his critics deem it
should have been.   But he had under him many raw troops,
and his best were the men who had been disheartened
by the Richmond failure and Manassas ; who scarcely now
felt the elation of victory, and were exhausted by labors
such as critics oftener impeach than perform.

Lee crossed into Virginia without losing a
Sept. 18–19. man.

The Confederates had, during the summer of 1862, assumed a bold offensive all along the line, at Corinth, into

Kentucky and into Maryland. Each campaign terminated in disaster about the same time; by Lee's withdrawal from Antietam; by Van Dorn's defeat at Corinth; by Bragg's check at Perryville. After this date, a strong offensive, with any chance of success, was never undertaken by the enemy.

September 17.

October 4.

October 8.

XX.

AGAIN TO THE RAPPAHANNOCK.

THE elation of the North was equalled by the bitter disappointment of the South at the failure of the Maryland campaign. McClellan moved to Harper's Ferry, but did not attempt to cross the army. As a shadow of the great struggle, Stuart made a sudden raid into Maryland and Pennsylvania with a couple of regiments of horse. He penetrated as far as Chambersburg, remounted his troopers and retired again across the river, making the entire circuit of the Army of the Potomac. Our cavalry was unable to follow or cope with him, though great efforts were made to head him off. For some weeks, McClellan paused to rest and reorganize.

Oct. 9–12.

The Potomac having risen so as to be in the nature of a protection to Maryland, McClellan began to cross the army, intending to move down the eastern slope of the Blue Ridge until he struck the Manassas Gap Railroad, where he would be in direct communication with Washington, and successively to occupy all the debouches of the mountains. Lee retired up the valley on

October 26.

the western side of the range.   Beyond a successful cavalry combat by Pleasonton against Stuart
in the valley, no blood was spilt.

November 5.

Six weeks after the close of the Maryland
campaign the Army of the Potomac was concentrated near Warrenton.   McClellan was ready to move
upon Culpeper.   There was good ground for thinking the
prospect brighter than ever before, when suddenly he was
relieved, and Burnside appointed to command.

November 6.

McClellan " was an excellent strategist, and in many
respects an excellent soldier.   He did not use his own
troops with sufficient promptness, thoroughness and vigor
to achieve great and decisive results, but he was oftenei
successful than unsuccessful with them, and he so conducted
affairs, that they never suffered heavily without inflicting
heavy loss upon their adversaries. . . . .   There are
strong grounds for believing that he was the best commander the Army of the Potomac ever had. . . .   While
the Confederacy was young, and fresh, and rich, and its
armies were numerous, McClellan fought a good, wary,
damaging, respectable fight against it. . . .   Not to mention such lamentable failures as Fredericksburg and Chancellorsville, it is easy to believe that with him in command,
the Army of the Potomac would never have seen such
dark days as those of the Wilderness and Cold Harbor."
(Palfrey.)

XXI.

THE HORROR OF FREDERICKSBURG.

FROM McClellan's hyper-caution, a quality from which he seemed to be gradually weaning himself, to Burnside's utter recklessness, is a disheartening step. McClellan had followed up Lee rather charily, but his position and plans were good.

Longstreet was but one day's march in our front. A sudden attack in force might have proven fatal to him, for Jackson was in the valley, beyond supporting distance.

The Army of the Potomac numbered one hundred and twenty-two thousand men. McClellan had purposed to cross the Rappahannock, drive the enemy to Gordonsville, and then, by a sudden movement to the east, anticipate him in a march on Richmond by way of Bowling Green. Later events proved the soundness of McClellan's method.

It is dangerous to shift commanders on the eve of battle, and our cavalry had already engaged the Confederates'; it is more dangerous to change the plans of troops moving in the vicinity of the enemy. But as if impelled to do some new thing, for no reason dictated a change of the movement already in course of execution (which was, by the way, the first of McClellan's ever approved by Hal-

leck), the new commander of the Army of
the Potomac determined upon a flank move-   November 14.
ment by his left on the *north* of the river towards Fredericksburg.

To be sure, the lines of operation and supply by way of
Acquia Creek were shorter, but this was the only advantage, and McClellan's plan embraced this factor when he
should march eastward.   Burnside was on the wrong side
of the Rappahannock, and was widening the one great
obstacle in his path for every mile of distance.   Only by
movements equally wary and rapid, as well as by sure
means of crossing the river, could Burnside's manœuvre
possibly succeed.   In this last element he counted on Halleck, and, of course, failed.   The promised pontoons did
not, and could scarcely have been expected to come.

Arrived at Fredericksburg, Burnside still   November 16–18.
might have crossed by the fords, for the water
was low.   And once in possession of the heights beyond the
city, he could afford to wait.   But slower than even his pre-
decessor, Burnside sat down at Falmouth, on the north
side of the river, while Lee, having learned of his movement, by forced marches concentrated his army on the
opposite bank, and prepared to erect impregnable defences
in his front.

Burnside had reorganized the Army of the Potomac into
three Grand Divisions, the Centre Grand Division under
Hooker, and the Right and Left under Sumner and Franklin respectively.   These were in their system of responsibility practically separate armies, and robbed the whole
body of elastic force and mobility.

Before Burnside got ready to take any active steps, Marye's Heights, back of Fredericksburg, had been crowned by a triple line of works, and Lee had brought together seventy-four thousand troops to man them. Two canals and a stone wall in front of the left, as well as open, sloping ground on both flanks, served to retain an attacking party for a long period under fire. To assault these works in front was simple madness. To turn them below necessitated the crossing of a wide and now swollen river, in the face of a powerful enemy in his immediate front, an operation always attended with the greatest risk, and considered one of the most delicate in war. To turn them above was practicable, but it was a confessed return to McClellan's plan. Burnside chose the first.

Preparations for crossing were begun. The better part of three days was consumed in throwing the bridges and putting over the two Grand Divisions of Franklin and Sumner, all of which was accomplished under fire.

December 10.

But Lee was by no means unwilling to meet the Army of the Potomac after this fashion. Such another happy prospect for him was not apt soon again to occur. He did not dispute the crossing in force.

Burnside's one chance in an hundred lay in a concentrated assault sharply pushed home before the enemy could oppose an equal force. But in lieu of one well-sustained attack or of two quite simultaneous, Burnside frittered away this single chance by putting in Franklin on the left and Sumner on the right, without concerted action. Nearly one hundred thousand men were in line.

Our artillery opens the affair and, as always, proves
superior to the enemy's.   From Franklin's
front Reynolds assaults with a well-massed

December 13.

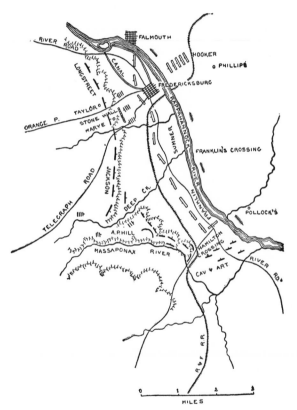

Fredericksburg.   December 13, 1862.

column.   Meade, who is in the lead, drives in A. P.
Hill, but being unsupported, Doubleday and Gibbon having

been delayed, is hurled back by Early, whose advance is
in turn balked by Birney's division.

In Sumner's front French is arrested at the stone wall.
Hancock comes up and makes a manful struggle to pass it.
Both attacks are easily repulsed.   Hunt with his artillery
on the north side essays to silence the guns on Marye's
heights.   It is too distant for his field ordnance.   Hooker
is ordered across.   Under protest, and yet Hooker lacked
not stomach for a fight, he obeys the useless order, and
leads his men into the slaughter-pen.   Humphreys again
assaults the stone wall with all the gallantry and coolness
which distinguish him.   All is in vain.   Even the Army
of the Potomac cannot do the impossible.   The defeated
troops are huddled into Fredericksburg, and gradually
withdrawn across the river.

Burnside was insane enough to wish to repeat the assault
next day.   But the counsels of his officers prevailed on him
to desist.

No such useless slaughter, with the exception, perhaps,
of Cold Harbor, occurred during our war, and thirteen
thousand men paid the penalty.   The enemy's loss was but
two in five of ours.   He had exulted in a fiery holiday.
Well were his pæans sung !   He had been obliged to put
in but a few divisions.

Lee was taken to task for not advancing from his defences,
and completing the destruction of the Army of the Potomac.
But he believed that the attack would be renewed, for he
did not know how heavy our losses had been, and was unwilling to risk the advantage of position which had already
gained him so much.   The Southern public was quite as

unreasonably critical of military events as our own, and Lee's splendid achievements were scarcely ever appreciated at a fraction of their true value.   In view of the difficulty to-day, with all the facts before us, of withholding from General Lee our sincere homage as the great soldier of our Civil War, of the difficulty we meet in passing any criticism upon his conduct as a soldier, it seems strange that, during the war, when it was he, whose unfailing equipoise and sturdy courage prolonged the life of the Confederacy from month to month, many of his fellow-citizens should have been bitterly arrayed against him.   And yet this was the case.   A dispassionate judgment places Robert E. Lee on the level of such captains as Turenne, Eugene, Marlborough, Wellington, and Moltke.

XXII.

THE SOLDIER OF NORTH AND SOUTH.

" THERE can be no doubt about the proposition that greater results were habitually achieved by a certain number of thousands or tens of thousands of Lee's army than by an equal number of the Army of the Potomac. The reason for this is not to be found in any difference in patriotic zeal in the two armies. The first reason probably was that the different modes of life at the South and at the North made the Southern soldiers more fond of fighting than the Northern men. Not to mention the intense and more passionate character of the Southerner as compared with that of the Northerner, the comparatively lawless (not to speak invidiously) life at the South, where the population was scattered and the gun came ready to the hand, made the Southern man an apter soldier than the peaceful, prosperous, steady-going recruit from the North. The Southerners showed that they felt the *gaudium certaminis.* With the Northerners it was different. They were ready to obey orders, they were ready to do the work to which they had set their hands, they were ready to die in their tracks if need be, but they did not go to battle as to a feast. They did not like fighting. Sheridan, Hancock,

Humphreys, Kearny, Custer, Barlow, and such as they, were exceptions; but the rule was otherwise." (Palfrey.)

Other reasons are alleged. The Confederate soldier was as a rule ill fed and clothed, worse shod and rarely had luxuries. And as a field won meant to him these sadly needed shoes and clothing and blankets and rations as well as arms and ammunition, — not indeed to mention money and other valuables, — this motive may fairly be said to have weighed also as an incentive to the fight. The very rags and starvation of the Southerner made him the better fighter and the quicker marcher. "'I can whip any army that is followed by a flock of cattle,' said Jackson, and it was a pregnant saying." (Ibid.) The Federal was embarrassed by his riches, and the difficulty of transporting all he had. The Confederate was always in light marching order, and all too often captured his rations on the field.

General Palfrey has struck the key-note of this interesting discussion. But there are still other reasons. The marked degrees of the Southern social scale as readily assigned to the enlisted man his musket as to the officer his side-arms. Wherever a regiment was raised, the men who had always been leaders at home were with rare exceptions chosen leaders for the field; they were uniformly the best men for the places, and the habit of command and obedience was instinctive. It must not be forgotten, moreover, that the early conscription laws kept under the Confederate colors the hardened men, making discipline more a matter of course than in our ranks where the individual soldiers were constantly changing.

That he accomplished more is true. But that the

Southerner was a better soldier cannot be claimed.   Even Friedrich's regiments at Leuthen showed devotion no greater than our own battalions at Marye's Heights ; and desperate as was the Prussians' task as they marched in parade order upon the Austrians' left flank, had they not Vater Fritz to lead them, and the pregnant threats of Friedrich the King to keep them to their work?   While every soldier in the ranks on that fatal thirteenth of December could see the hopeless nature of his struggle, and was far indeed from fighting for king and fatherland. In this most famous of Friedrich's victories he, the attacking party, lost six thousand two hundred men out of thirty thousand, all of whom were actually, and at the crisis simultaneously, engaged.   At Fredericksburg, without incentive, the Army of the Potomac laid at the foot of the heights ten thousand nine hundred dead and wounded, out of not much more than sixty thousand men actually in the assault.   Hancock lost two thousand and twenty-nine out of forty-eight hundred and thirty-four.

Not that the presumption is attempted of comparing the two battles *as such*.   Leuthen is the most splendid piece of grand-tactics of the last century, perhaps of modern times ; Fredericksburg was a tactical blunder of the purest water.   But Leuthen is often cited to show the grand fidelity of the Prussian infantry ; in this respect the comparison is not odious.

Nor is it hard to parallel Fredericksburg more than once during our war.   What shall be said of Grant's " hammering " campaign of 1864, in which the Army of the Potomac from May 5 to June 10 lost little short of sixty thousand men, killed and wounded, in front of Lee's intrenched lines, out of a total of one hundred and twenty thousand under arms? Or of the thirteen thousand out of forty-three thousand at Stone's River? Or of Chickamauga's sixteen thousand out of sixty-two thousand men on the field? Or of Porter's loss of seven thousand out of twenty-nine thousand at Gaines' Mill? Or of Sherman's loss of thirty thousand men out of one hundred thousand in his four months' campaign from Dalton to Atlanta? Shall further comparison be made? That the elation of the battle-field engendered of a sunny climate can be offset by the sturdier virtues of the patient North is the constant verdict of history.

Moreover, in Virginia, it was leadership which accomplished such results with so feeble resources. Look at other battle-fields, and, man for man, where commanders were of equal weight, what difference can be traced? The arithmetical value of the Southron as compared with the Yankee, which used to be so constantly rolled as a sweet morsel under the tongue by our ancient foemen, can to-day, I ween, be dismissed with a friendly shake of the hand as we shoulder our crutch for the rising generation, and show how fields were won.

It is a noteworthy fact that a list of the fifty most severe battles during the Civil War shows ten drawn and twenty victories to each side. At the point of fighting contact, in these fifty battles, the forces were within two per cent. of being equal.

In thirty-four battles the Union forces remained in possession of the field, and buried the enemy's dead; the Confederates did the like in twenty-nine. In eleven assaults by large forces, the Union troops won ; in eleven the Confederates drove them back; in eight the Federals repulsed such assaults.

The strongest reason for the acknowledged truth that the Southerner accomplished more with less means than we did lies in the fact that he was fighting for the preservation of his own soil.   It needs not history to teach us what this incentive can accomplish.   Every brave man carries it in the deepest recesses of his heart, and reads his willing duty in the eyes of the wife, the child, the mother, or the sweetheart, to preserve whose sacred right to a peaceful home his life stands always a ready sacrifice.

The North, thank God, was never called upon for the effort, the self-denial of the South.   That it is capable of yielding it when so called needs not to be asserted.   And there is sufficient to be proud of in American manhood not to draw lines of politics or climate in comparing either the intelligence or the hardihood of the men who marched and fought through our Civil War beside or against each other.

To attempt to give the American his proper place among the soldiers of other nations, ancient or modern, is an inquiry demanding a volume by itself.   But the stanchness of the American in battle may be measured to a fair extent by a few statistics.   Courage is only one of the necessary virtues of the soldier ; but it is an important one, and, if we take the average number of killed and wounded in the prominent battles of the past century and a half, we arrive at a conclusion reasonably secure.

Frederick and Napoleon are the two captains of modern

times who have fought their men *au fond*. Their losses are the heaviest; but ours follow hard upon.

The following percentages of men killed and wounded comprise the most noted battles since 1745. Only those whose full statistics are wanting are omitted : —

Up to Waterloo, the French, in nine battles (Napoleon's), lost in killed and wounded of the number engaged . .	22.38 per cent.
Since, in nine battles	8.86 "
Up to Waterloo, the Prussians, in eight battles (mostly Frederick's), lost	18.42 "
At Königgrätz they lost	3.86 "
Up to Waterloo, the Austrians, in seven battles, lost . .	11.17 "
Since, in two battles	8.56 "
The Germans, since 1745, in eight battles	11.53 "
The English, in four battles	10.36 "
During our Civil War, the Union forces lost in fourteen pitched battles, in which numbers and casualties are well ascertained	14.48 "
The Confederate forces, in twelve, ditto	18 "

Of very severe losses in small bodies, perhaps the most often quoted is that of the Light Brigade at Balaclava, viz. .	36.7 per cent.
At Metz the Gardeschützen battalion lost	46.1 "
At Mars La Tour, the Sixteenth Infantry (Westphalian) lost,	49.4 "
During our Civil War, there were lost, in some one action by one Union regiment, out of the men taken into action .	82 "
By three Union regiments . . between 70 per cent. and 80	"
By seventeen Union regiments, " 60 " " 70	"
By forty-one " " . " 50 " " 60	"

These numbers are all taken from the muster rolls on file in the War Department, where each man is accounted for by name.

The severest loss in the Civil War was by a Confederate regiment at Gettysburg, 720 out of 800 men	90 per cent.
Another lost in one battle	82 "
Three " " . . between 60 per cent. and 70	"
Nine " " . " .50 " " 60	"
Twenty-nine lost in one battle . . . . . . over 50	"

Longstreet's Division lost at Gaines' Mill and Glendale 4,438 out of 8,831 men . . . . over 50 per cent.	
Several divisions lost in some one action . . . " 40 "	

It thus appears that in ability to stand heavy pounding, since Napoleon's Waterloo campaign, the American has shown himself preëminent. Of course there are other factors in the problem. But these figures may surely be looked upon with pride — even if no absolute conclusion can be drawn from them.

XXIII.

ROSECRANS AND BRAGG. — STONE'S RIVER.

ROSECRANS was called to the command of the Department of the Cumberland in the place of Buell, as already stated. The forces operat-

October 30, 1862.

ing on this line were hereafter to be known as the Army of the Cumberland. The name of Army of the Ohio was to be borne by the troops in the East Tennessee Valley.

Much was expected of Rosecrans. His many friends claimed for him up to this date the only record of uniform success. His brilliant, if somewhat erratic, method was thought to embody the soldierly instinct, not so apparent in more quiet natures.

Rosecrans made many changes. He gave the command of his right wing to McCook; of his left to Crittenden; of his centre to sturdy Thomas. The position of the army about Nashville was not modified.

Towards the middle of November, Bragg, somewhat reinforced, advanced to Murfreesborough and laid distant siege to Nashville. Beyond this movement, except for some minor operations, — another notable

Nov.–Dec.

raid of J. H. Morgan among them, — there was no attempt to cross swords for two months.

Braxton Bragg's rank as a soldier is hard to gauge. He was put and kept in place by the personal favor of President Davis. Not lacking audacity or military skill, he was uniformly beaten, and, like all unsuccessful generals, he received no credit for what he did accomplish. It is easy to forgive errors to the eventually successful; hard to allow any credit for even good work which comes to nothing.

Rosecrans' objective was of course Chattanooga, as had been Buell's. But he must first clear the enemy from his front. In the last days of the year, in three columns, he advanced upon Bragg's posi-

December 26.

tion. Not intending active operations, Bragg had already put his army into winter-quarters over a considerable area; but no sooner aware of Rosecrans' intentions, than he concentrated his troops across the latter's path.

After some outpost skirmishing, the armies confronted each

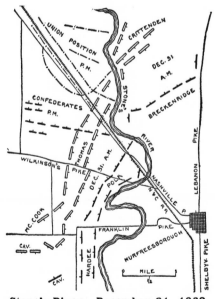

Stone's River. December 31, 1862.

other north of Murfreesborough, intent upon a prompt

struggle for mastery.   The Army of the Cumberland was in a position facing substantially south-east.   Stone's River, the turnpike, and the railroad, all near together, ran north-westerly from the town at right angles to the position of Rosecrans and near his left flank.   The river was fordable in places.   The country was alternate woods and clearing.

Rosecrans' plan of battle was to throw Crittenden across Stone's River upon Bragg's right in force, while McCook should hold our right where it lay.   Upon his strict performance of this duty depended success, and McCook protested his ability to hold his lines at least three hours against any odds.   Curiously enough, Bragg contemplated precisely the same field tactics, to wit : to crush *our* right. Under these conditions, other things being equal, whoever moved first upon his enemy with sufficient vigor would win the day.   Rosecrans ordered the men to breakfast and the movement to begin at 7 A.M.   Bragg ordered the attack to begin at daylight.

There was some carelessness in the disposition of the troops on McCook's wing, which Rosecrans should have personally known and rectified.   He placed too much reliance on this officer's assertion that he could hold his own.

December 31.

Bragg's left, under Hardee, overlapped our right.   His onset was made with true Southern *élan*, and immediately thrust back McCook, whose resistance ill bore out his boast.   Scarcely had Rosecrans crossed Stone's River and launched Crittenden's columns upon Breckenridge than he was forced to recall them to the assistance of his already routed right wing.   There was no let up to the Confederate attack. Hardee was in his element. Every success was quickly followed up, and McCook was driven in confusion upon the centre. The situation was grave.

But Thomas was of other stuff. He was not to be so easily disposed of. Forming his own divisions along the turnpike at right angles to our first line, he fought with his never flagging coolness and determination. Rosecrans' feverish activity served to reanimate the troops. Sheridan's division reflected the mettle of its commander. Young, and as yet unused to large commands, he seconded Thomas with the instinct of the soldier glowing in every fibre. Our lines struggled through the rest of the day against almost certain defeat. The success of the Confederates elated them, but in no sort demoralized the Federals. The fighting on either side was desperate.

Night fell. All we could claim was that we had not been driven from the field. A council of war was held. Neither Rosecrans nor Thomas would consider the question of retreat. A fresh conflict was settled for the morrow, the first day of the new year.

But Bragg's success had bred more disorganization than our defeat. He was in no condition to attack. His men and officers had exhausted themselves in the splendid efforts which had so nearly destroyed the Army of the Cumberland. New Year's passed without a demonstration on either side. Next day, Bragg essayed an attack on Rosecrans' left, but was thrown back. Unable to force defeat upon the stubborn battalions which Buell   January 2, 1863. had drilled, he withdrew into Murfreesborough, with a loss of ten out of thirty-eight thousand men against thirteen out of forty-three thousand on our side. Bragg could show as trophies some twenty-eight guns.

Both parties laid claim to victory. But Bragg retreated from Murfreesborough as a consequence of this battle, and it was occupied by our troops.

Bragg was apt to throw blame upon his subordinates for his own shortcomings. On this occasion he gave as the cause of his failure that Breckenridge did not promptly obey orders in reinforcing Hardee when sore pressed. But as the usual test of a general is success, or at least results, small attention can be given to the easily invented explanations of failure. Under equal conditions none but the victor may wear the laurel. Against overwhelming odds alone can defeat add honor to the soldier's name.

XXIV.

CHANCELLORSVILLE.

THE Army of the Potomac was never so demoralized as after the horror of December 13th, at Fredericksburg. Succeeding this battle a fine spell of weather invited a renewal of aggressive movements. But Burnside allowed the favorable time to pass. Just as the elements ceased to be propitious he began a manœuvre — it was on McClellan's plan — to turn Lee's left. But Virginia roads and rivers are treacherous. One day's down-pour of rain sufficed to destroy the possibility of success, and the farcical ending of the so-called Mud March gave the enthusiasm of the army its *coup de grâce*. A new commander became essential, and Hooker was promoted from his Grand Division, — Franklin and Sumner being overslaughed.

January 20 to 24

At this time, so lax had been its discipline, some eighty-five thousand officers and men appeared on the rolls of the Army of the Potomac as absent without leave. But "Fighting Joe" grasped the reins with firmness and in organization gave proof of great skill. A rare favorite among the men, and with solid record, it was only those who judged

January 26, 1863.

with exceptional insight and long knowledge of the man who mistrusted the result. And even their apprehensions were in part allayed by Hooker's steadiness.

By the beginning of April the recuperative power of the stanch old army had again made it equal to any effort. It lay in its cantonments about Falmouth, while Lee watched it from his ever strengthening heights back of Fredericksburg, with confidence bred of the knowledge that under him served sixty thousand of the hardiest troops which ever laughed at hunger, cold, or danger.

Hooker initiated the Chancellorsville campaign by a cavalry raid on Lee's communications intended to move about his left and far to his rear; but sheer blundering robbed this diversion of any good results. He followed up this raid by a feint under Sedgwick below Fredericksburg, while he himself so cleverly stole a march on Lee by the upper Rappahannock, that within four days he had massed forty thousand men on the enemy's left flank at Chancellorsville, before the latter had begun to divine his purpose.

April 30.

But here Hooker paused. Indecision seized his mind. He frittered away a precious day, and when he finally advanced on Lee, the latter had recovered himself and was prepared to meet him. After barely feeling his adversary, "Fighting Joe" retired into the Wilderness to invite attack, while Lee, with half his force but thrice his nerve, sharply followed him up. The *terrain* to which the Army of the Potomac had been thus withdrawn was well named. It was one vast entanglement of second growth timber

and chapparal, to the last degree unfitted for the manœuvres of an army.

With his wonted rashness, but relying on his adversary's vacillation, Lee divided his army and sent Jackson
around Hooker's right to take him in reverse and cut him
off from United States Ford, while his own constant feints
on the centre should cover the move. Meanwhile Hooker
weakened his right by blind demonstrations in his front,

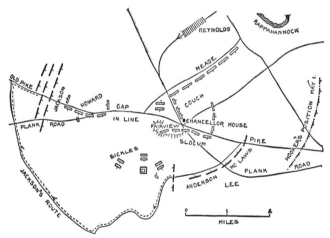

Chancellorsville. May 2, 1863.

and enabled Jackson to complete his manœuvre and to
crush at a blow the Eleventh corps, which held that flank,
and to throw the army into utter confusion.
                                                        May 2.
In this moment of his greatest triumph Jack-
son fell at the hand of his own men.

On the morrow, by dint of massed blows, with "Jackson" for a watchword, upon Hooker's lines, where but one
man in three was put under fire, Lee fairly drove our army

into a corner, from whence its dazed commander, with
eighty thousand men, cried aloud for succor to Sedgwick's
one corps fifteen miles away, still fronting the defenses at

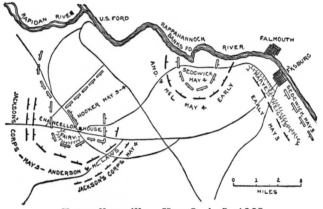

Chancellorsville.   May 3, 4, 5, 1863.

Fredericksburg.   Under quite impossible orders this gal-
lant soldier captured Marye's Heights, where
May 3.
Burnside had lost thirteen thousand men,
and advanced towards his chief.   But Lee, trusting to
Hooker's panic to keep him bottled up, turned upon Sedg-

May 4.   wick, drove him across the river after an all
May 5.   day's fight, and again confronted Hooker,
who, dizzy and nerveless, sought safety in retreat to his
old camps.

This ten days' passage at arms was glorious to the Confederate soldier's valor and to his leader's skill, while we
lost all save honor.   With an effective only half as great,
Lee had actually outnumbered Hooker whenever he

had struck him.   While a fraction of our forces were being decimated, the rest were held by Hooker in the leash at places where they were uselessly fretting to join their brothers in the fray.

It is true that Hooker was accidentally disabled May 3; but rather than turn over the command to his second, Couch, he chose to retain the responsibility.

Of this splendid campaign every American may make his boast.   Every Northerner must keenly deplore it.   Our losses were seventeen thousand out of one hundred and five thousand engaged, and the enemy's thirteen thousand out of sixty-one thousand.

Jackson's reputation as a soldier is national.   It is almost supererogatory to add anything to what has been narrated about this remarkable man.   Untried in large command, his powers as a captain can only be judged from his successes in the Valley.   But as a lieutenant he was far beyond any officer who fought on either side during our Civil War.

Hooker and Hooker's partisans have endeavored to shift the responsibility of this defeat on Howard, for allowing his corps to be surprised on the right; and on Sedgwick, for not fighting an impossible battle and making an impossible march in the middle of the night.   But neither can be so saddled.   Hooker himself must bear the load, however heavy, and however well he has otherwise deserved our admiration.   And this may be said with sincere appreciation of Hooker's services as a corps commander, and of his splendid gallantry on many a hard-fought field.

XXV.

LEE'S SECOND INVASION.

NOW supervenes another rest in the thrice-reoccupied Falmouth camps, while Lee plans with questionable political or strategic foresight a second raid into the Northern States. Still grasping with his right the old defenses at Fredericksburg, he covertly advances his left, under Ewell, to Culpeper, and thence into the Shenandoah Valley.

Hooker became aware of an impending movement, and threw his entire force of cavalry across the Rappahannock on a forced reconnoissance. At Beverly Ford

June 9.

a smart combat with Stuart, the loss on our side being some eight hundred men, on theirs half as many, revealed Lee's intentions.

Ewell, followed warily by the centre, pushed rapidly on down the Valley.

At one moment the line of the Army of

June 13.

Northern Virginia stretched from Fredericksburg to Winchester, — a distance of one hundred miles. This was a very dangerous extension, and Hooker suggested to his timid chief in Washington the obvious propriety of recalling Lee from his now evident objective by crushing his right wing, thus seriously compromised at Fredericksburg. But he was forbidden this safest of operations, for Mr. Lincoln's idea of fighting a divided army was that of " an ox jumped half over a fence and liable to be torn by dogs front and rear, without a fair chance to gore one way or to kick the other," while Halleck's one notion of defending Washington was by the presence of the entire army between it and the enemy.

Thus Hooker was chained to the hackneyed strategy of moving by his right towards the Potomac, while Ewell trapped Milroy at Winchester and captured some four thousand prisoners and much material. From here Ewell marched boldly into Pennsylvania, where his cavalry levied heavy contributions in stock and grain on the terrified farmers.

June 13-15.

So soon as Lee saw Hooker fairly started in pursuit of Ewell, he let go of Fredericksburg, and urged Longstreet and Hill to their utmost speed to rejoin him. Halleck had got the Union forces parcelled out in wretched driblets all over the map from West Virginia to the Peninsula, and could still not rise beyond his one idea of preserving Harper's Ferry. Within his restrictions Hooker's march had been conducted with logistic skill and discretion. He was simply hand-tied, while the enemy was free to ravage Pennsylvania. However fretted by Ewell's presence in the loyal States, Hooker could not cross the Potomac until he knew that none of Lee's three corps was left in Virginia.

The Army of the Potomac was put over a day after the Confederates and was concentrated at Frederick, from which point Hooker could

June 25-27.

debouch on Lee's rear through South Mountain, or else
move upon him on the line of the Susquehannah. For
intelligent concentration Halleck had substituted pitiful
fault-finding, all of which had resulted in the enemy's
reaching the vicinity of Harrisburg without opposition
worthy the name. And unable to control events within
his own reach, Hooker requested on the eve of engagement
to be relieved. This was an act scarcely to be condoned,
but for its happy outcome.

Few words sum up Hooker's military standing. As a
corps commander, or with orders to obey, unless jealousy
warped his powers, he was unsurpassed in bravery, devotion and skill. For the burden of supreme command he
had neither mental calibre nor equipoise. Self-sufficiency
stood in lieu of self-reliance.

Into Hooker's place quietly stepped business-like Meade,
and unhampered by Halleck, whose favorite
he was, continued to follow up the invaders.
Ewell was at York and Carlisle and might cross the Susquehannah and capture the capital of the State. Meade,
therefore, moved northward from Frederick, intent upon
loosening Lee's grip on that river. This he effected, and
Longstreet and Hill were ordered, not towards Harrisburg, but through the South Mountain passes. For Lee,
so soon as he knew of Meade's direction, became fearful for
his communications. And he was moreover troubled by
the naked defense of Richmond, which prize could have
been secured by a vigorous attack by General Dix from
Fort Monroe with more ease than at any time during the
war, had the attempt been made. Lee, therefore, deter-

June 28.

mined to draw back and make a diversion east of the South Mountain range to engage Meade's attention.

Lee's plan of invasion had been thwarted ; but his army must be defeated.

Having divined the purpose of his adversary, Meade selected the general line of Pipe Creek for his defense, and threw his left wing, preceded by cavalry, forward to Gettysburg as a mask. Lee also aimed to secure this point, for it controlled the roads towards the Potomac. The encounter was near at hand.

XXVI.

GETTYSBURG.

THE First and Eleventh corps met the van of Lee's Army under A. P. Hill, on the north of the now historic town. A severe engagement ensued, in which doughty Reynolds lost his life, and the Federals, after Ewell came upon the field, were driven

July 1.

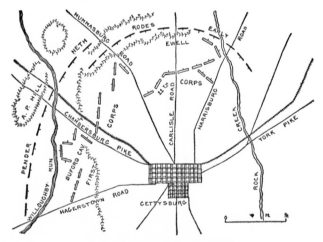

Gettysburg. July 1, 1863.

back through the town, with heavy loss, but unpursued. Hill and Ewell waited for Longstreet.

This check to the enemy's advance led to results worth all the sacrifice.

Few conflicts of modern times have become so familiar, in art and story, as the battle of Gettysburg. Only its chief features need be recalled. South of the quiet little town, covering the road to Baltimore, lies a chain of hillocks and bluffs shaped like a fish-hook. At the barb rises Culp's Hill, along the back what is known as Cemetery Hill, and the shank, running north and south, is formed by a hilly slope terminating in a rocky, wooded peak, called Round Top, having Little Round Top as a spur. For Hancock and Howard alike has been claimed the credit of selecting this ever memorable position. Perchance Reynolds' keen eye gauged its value as he hurried through the town to stem the approaching tide. On this eligible ground the retreating Unionists were rallied, and speedily reinforced, while Meade, at Hancock's suggestion, brought the army forward from Pipe Creek to secure it.

Meanwhile Lee cautiously advanced his own troops, and forgetting that he had promised his corps commanders that he would not in this campaign assume a tactical offensive, resolved to give battle. Longstreet's preference was to seize the Emmetsburg road beyond the Union left, and manœuvre Meade out of his position by compromising his communications with Washington. But there lurked in the healthy body of the Army of Northern Virginia a poisonous contempt of its adversary. This was the natural outcome of Manassas, Fredericksburg, and Chancellorsville. Lee was morally unable to decline battle. He could not imperil the high-strung confidence of his men.

As the second day dawned he must, however,
have watched with throbbing anxiety the
Federal line rapidly throwing up defences on just such a

July 2.

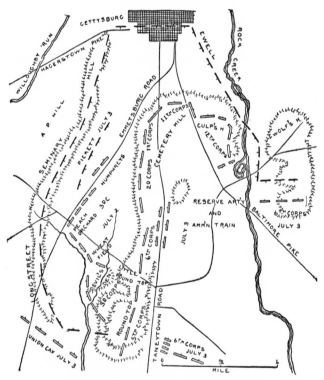

Gettysburg. July 2, 3, 4, 1863.

formidable crest as himself had held at Marye's Heights.
For Lee gauged better than his men the fighting qualities
of his foe.

His general line lay along Seminary Ridge, parallel to
Cemetery Hill, and about a mile distant, with his left
thrown round and through the town to a point opposite
Culp's, in order Longstreet, Hill, Ewell. He was thus
formed in concave order of battle, the Army of the
Potomac having been thrown by the lay of the land into
substantially the convex order.

By noon Lee had perfected his plans, and Longstreet
opened an attack on a weak salient thrown out by Sickles
from the general line of our left towards the Emmetsburg
road The possession of Round Top would take the
Federal line in reverse, and Sickles' position, an outward
angle, could be enfiladed in both directions, and if lost
would seriously compromise this point. Longstreet was
not slow to clutch at the advantage thus offered. But the
foresight of Warren, after a desperate struggle, secured
Round Top ; and though Longstreet wrested from Sickles
his salient, he secured only an apparent benefit not com-
mensurate with his loss.

On the Union extreme right, Ewell had meanwhile
gained a foothold on Culp's Hill, and, as night fell, Lee
was justified in feeling that the morrow would enable him
to carry the entire ridge. For he believed that he had
effected a breach in both flanks of the Army of the
Potomac. Indeed at the close of the second day the gravity
of the situation induced Meade to call a council of his corps
commanders. It was determined to abide the result at
that spot. Officers and men were in good spirits and
equal to any work.

Lee was tactically in error as to Longstreet's supposed

success on the left. It had in reality rectified Sickles' position. Our real line was undisturbed. And Meade at

July 3.

daylight attacked Ewell in force, and after a hard tussle wrenched from him the ground commanding Culp's. Thus Lee had failed to effect a permanent lodgment on our either flank, and we had thrown up strong field works to defend them. There was no resource for him but to break our centre.

He accordingly massed nearly one hundred and fifty guns along Seminary Ridge, and at 1 P.M. opened fire. Owing to the limited space for the batteries, barely eighty guns from our side could answer this spirited challenge. For two hours lasted the fiery duel, when Lee launched Pickett, "the Ney of the rebel army," with a column of thirteen thousand men, to drive a wedge into the centre of the Union line. A column charged with so desperate a duty — the forlornest of forlorn hopes — should contain none but picked troops. Pettigrew's division in the assaulting column was unable to hold its own. And though Pickett's Virginians actually ruptured Hancock's line and a few of the men penetrated some fifty yards beyond, he met an array in front and flank which rolled him back with fearful loss. Lee's last chance of success was wrecked.

The instinct of a great commander might have seized this moment for an advance in force upon the broken enemy. But Meade cautiously held what he had already won, rather than gain more at greater risk.

July 4.

Beaten but not dismayed, Lee spent all the morrow and until after daylight next day preparing for retreat, and yet in a mood to invite attack. And he would have met it stoutly. But Meade was content. He would adventure nothing. He had won the credit of defeating his enemy; he lost the chance of destroying him. He may be justified in this; but not in failing to follow up Lee's deliberate retreat with greater vigor. It must however be admitted that in almost all campaigns, a similar criticism may be passed, — after the event. There is always a term to the endurance and activity of armies and their commanders.

In this most stubborn battle of modern days we lost twenty-three thousand out of ninety-three thousand engaged; the Confederates twenty-two thousand five hundred out of eighty thousand men, beside fifty-four hundred prisoners. The loss in killed and wounded, twenty-two and a half per cent., is unexampled in so large a force.

Lee retreated by way of Williamsport, undisturbed save at a distance, and after some days was followed across the Potomac by Meade.

XXVII.

GRANT AGAIN MOVES ON VICKSBURG.

WHILE the old year closed with the tragedy of Fredericksburg and the drawn battle of Murfreesborough, the new year opened with Grant's second advance on Vicksburg, and with General Banks creating a base for operations at New Orleans.

1862 and 1863.

Grant was now in sole command of the forces operating down the Mississippi. His army consisted of the Thirteenth corps under McClernand, the Fifteenth under Sherman, the Sixteenth under Hurlbut, and the Seventeenth under McPherson, a body comprising the veterans of the West. We have seen how his overland march on Vicksburg was cut short by severed communications, and neutralized Sherman's efforts at Chickasaw Bayou. This only served however to whet his determination to capture the place, which, and Port Hudson below, were the only serious obstacles to the free navigation of the great river. But they were serious indeed.

Hurlbut was detached to watch the Memphis and Charleston Railroad while Sherman and McClernand moved to Young's Point, and McPherson was ordered soon to follow.

From here Grant would have preferred to work around the city by the north, but the Yazoo lowlands were quite under water, and all reconnoissances pointed to grave difficulties in the way of such an operation.

It will be remembered that Vicksburg is situated at the bight of a great loop made by the Mississippi. Across the loop, at its narrowest point, does not much exceed a mile. Before reaching the ground Grant had given orders to construct another canal across this loop, as Williams had done a year before, but when, February. towards early spring, he arrived and (McClernand protesting) assumed command, he discovered the uselessness of such an attempt. Work on the canal, however, was kept up by the troops for six weeks, when a heavy freshet washed away the embankments and utterly destroyed it. It is improbable that as a water-way it March 7. could ever have been utilized, for it was not in such a location as to allow the current of the river to flow freely into it.

During this period the monotony of the canal work was enlivened by various naval exploits on the river. Admiral Porter, who commanded the fleet coöperating with Grant, sent several of his vessels down past the Vicksburg batteries. Among these was prominent the feat of Colonel Ellet, already noted for much excellent work with the flotilla. In the Queen of the West he ran below the town, attacked and all but destroyed the rebel ram, City of Vicksburg. Being unable to return he proceeded down the river, and after numerous adventures, joined the forces under Banks.

Grant's task was one full of contingencies. Strangely

enough, he seems to have had no settled plan at this time. But he set on foot various projects for weakening the approaches to Vicksburg, or for opening a water-course around so as to isolate it.   He dug a canal from the Mississippi to Providence Lake, hoping to make a practicable channel through the Tensas, Black, Red and Atchafalaya rivers to a point below Port Hudson.   He opened another channel from the river to Moon Lake, purposing to run light-draught boats down the Tallahatchie and Yazoo.   For not only was there a shipyard at Yazoo city, where some vessels were building, but it was a considerable depot of stores.

The latter route, if practicable, not only afforded an opportunity of destroying this depot, but would also enable Grant to take Haines' Bluff in reverse, and capture the hills which are the key to Vicksburg.   A demonstration by land forces as well as the navy was made in connection with this scheme.   But all these attempts, which con-

March and April.

sumed over two months, resulted fruitlessly. The enemy was able to check each movement in its turn.

XXVIII.

GRANT TURNS PEMBERTON'S LEFT.

PEMBERTON had at Vicksburg some twenty-two thousand men, stationed from Haines' Bluff above, to Grand Gulf below; at Grenada, eleven thousand; at Jackson, Miss., five thousand. Johnston, though in supreme command of the forces west of the Alleghanies, was personally at Chattanooga, deeming that field of most importance to the fortunes of the Confederacy; and Van Dorn, with his cavalry, had likewise joined Bragg.

Having fruitlessly attempted all methods of approach to Vicksburg from the north and west, Grant now determined to place his army below the fortress and to turn Pemberton's left. His position was a trying one. The fickle public was all but ready to tire of him also, as it had on less pretext of so many of his brother soldiers. Since Donelson, he had fought only the battle of Shiloh, — a most questionable triumph. Iuka and Corinth had been quite forgotten, or such credit as a minor victory yields had been ascribed to Rosecrans. For a year Grant had been floundering about with no substantial success to show. Something was demanded of him.

Grant must look the matter squarely in the face. Assault

promised ill-success from any point, while involving the
certainty of heavy losses. To go back and try the really

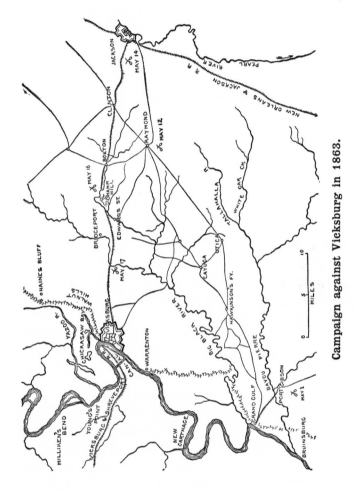

most feasible route, along the Mobile and Ohio Railroad,
seemed like failure acknowledged, and would therefore be

politically ruinous, though strategically sound. To turn
Pemberton's left was a desperate undertaking. Its only
merit lay in that it showed no sign of turning back, for,
while to do the unexpected is a sound maxim of war, this
plan in no sense partook of the nature of a surprise. Supplies must come by a most circuitous route, liable to fatal
interruption, and the fleet must run the Vicksburg batteries.
Choice was difficult. But with his usual disregard of obstacles Grant adopted the latter plan. He could face a difficult
problem rather than a simple one. His courage grew with
opposition. He could assume any risk. In this case it proved
a virtue ; but not so a year later, in Virginia. This type
of courage often lacks the tempering element of caution.

Part of Sherman's corps was sent up the river to make
a diversion which might take Haines' Bluff in reverse.
This was ably done, as was all work this
general had in hand. McClernand was
ordered to New Carthage, below Vicksburg.
March 14–27.
March 29.
Communication with Milliken's Bend, from which place
Grant drew his supplies, was kept up by flat-boats along
the innumerable bayous, and a haul overland of some
twenty-five miles. The transports and gun-boats needed
for operations below were safely run past the batteries.

Towards the end of the month, after infinite trouble with
the roads, Grant joined McClernand at New Carthage and
from there marched to a point opposite Grand
Gulf, twenty miles south of Vicksburg, at
April 24, 1863.
the mouth of the Big Black. Grand Gulf had been fortified,
though not with the strength of Haines' Bluff, for Pemberton was vastly more concerned for his right than his left

flank, and, having no cavalry, was much in the dark as to the plans of his opponent.

But the passage of the fleet revealed Grant's purpose, and reinforcements which had been ordered to Bragg, on the supposition that Grant would not soon attack, were at once recalled.

As a means of diverting attention from his movements, and to disturb the enemy's line of supplies from the east, Grierson had been despatched on a raid from Lagrange southward, with a cavalry brigade of one thousand seven hundred men. This enterprising officer, starting in light order, made his way along roads some twenty miles east of the Mobile and Ohio Railroad, detailing parties right and left to destroy tracks and telegraph, stores and munitions of war, and by his clever devices kept the enemy utterly in the dark as to his direction and purposes.

April 17.

He finally turned up at Baton Rouge, having marched six hundred miles in sixteen days, and having created vast confusion, of no little assistance to Grant in safely crossing the Mississippi.

May 2.

The presence of the Federals opposite Grand Gulf, as well as on his right, made a problem which Pemberton was not soldier enough to solve. Though he seems to have known all about Grant's manœuvre, he was incapable of action that met the conditions confronting him.

The fortifications of Grand Gulf were incomplete, but Porter could not destroy the works from his gun-boats. Unable to get over, owing to their fire, Grant dropped down a few miles further to Bruinsburg, where by crossing he could take Grand Gulf in reverse.

First McClernand with eighteen thousand
men is ferried over and marches towards
April 30.
Port Gibson.   Pemberton promptly puts in an appearance
and arrests his advance four miles this side
of the place.   Without waiting for Mc-
May 1.
Pherson, who is coming up, McClernand attacks.   We
have already twenty-four thousand men on the field, the
Confederates but eight thousand five hundred.   But they
make none the less a stubborn defense.   The ground is
very broken and difficult for the troops.   Despite his
numbers, McClernand makes small headway for hours,
when McPherson arrives and the Confederate right is
turned.   Thus thrust back, the enemy retires beyond and
burns the bridges over Bayou Pierre.   The loss on each
side is not far from eight hundred.

Next day our forces enter Port Gibson,
and repair and rebuild the bridges burned
May 2.
by Pemberton.   The enemy is now obliged to evacuate
Grand Gulf, which Porter speedily occupies.

Sherman had been left behind as rear guard.   While Mc-
Clernand and McPherson were marching on Port Gibson,
he had been making a still more noisy demonstration at Haines' Bluff.   Pemberton was
May 1.
thus kept from sending reinforcements from the city.

Matters were now much facilitated by all-water communication with the base of supplies.   This had been
laboriously opened by the engineers from Milliken's Bend
to New Carthage and thence to Grand Gulf.

Grant had at the beginning of his campaign been led to
believe that Banks would before now be in position to

coöperate with him from below. But Banks was delayed
by operations at Port Hudson ; and Grant, seeing that to
wait would only allow the enemy to accumulate as much in
reinforcements as Banks' presence would afford to himself,
concluded to push matters to an issue.

XXIX.

GRANT DRIVES PEMBERTON INTO VICKSBURG.

PEMBERTON had now got out seventeen thousand men to thwart Grant's further progress. But he found himself compelled to place the Big Black between his army and the Federals. Meanwhile McPherson and McClernand went into bivouac to wait for Sherman.

Grant was once more on dry ground, and had actually turned Pemberton's left. But this was only a beginning. He must strike hard and fast to secure the fruits of his bold manœuvre. Numbers were practically equal, but the local advantages were all on the Confederate side. They were within their own territory, near their supplies, on the defensive. Grant was obliged to get his supplies over seventy miles of treacherous country. But on the other hand Grant had a navy at his back, and above all good lieutenants, while Pemberton's military ability never proved equal to heavy strain.

Grant now advanced from Hawkinson's Ferry along the Big Black, keeping to the May 7. east of the river and cutting loose from his base at Grand Gulf. He supplied the troops with five days' rations, trusting to reëstablish himself within no great time on a new base by defeating the enemy. Until then he must sustain himself largely on the country, which could furnish him beeves and some corn.

The enemy was posted at Jackson as well as Vicksburg, and Grant calculated to thrust himself between the two bodies of the enemy at these places. McPherson commanded the right wing, Sherman, who had come up, the centre, McClernand the left. The advance was more or less irregular according to the opposition encountered and the roads pursued. McPherson pushed for May 12.˙ Raymond, and after a smart combat, in which we lost four hundred men, took possession of the place.

Grant now made up his mind to secure the town of Jackson before the enemy could erect defences about it. This would give him a point from which to threaten the rear of Vicksburg and to protect his own.

It was learned about this time that Joe Johnston was on his way with reinforcements to assume personal command. He could not be allowed possession of Jackson. Grant promptly moved Sherman and McPherson on that point while Pemberton was concentrated at Edwards' Depot, expecting him to attack there.

Jackson was readily captured with a loss of three hundred men, and Johnston, thus forestalled, May 14. was obliged on his arrival to move round by the north to seek to join forces with Pemberton.

Johnston, who was really in supreme command, had peremptorily ordered Pemberton to come out of Vicksburg and attack Grant's flank at Clinton. But Pemberton did not seem to feel that Johnston held over him exactly the

authority of a commanding-officer, and considered it the
best policy to hold on to Vicksburg, not seeing, as Johnston did, that to beat Grant was the only means to retain
possession of it. But a few days later, and too late, he
made up his mind to attack as suggested. Strangely
enough he conceived the plan of moving away from Johnston, to demonstrate against Grant's rear. Here then we
have the spectacle of two armies, of equal resources, one
solid and compact, the other split into several detachments,
in Vicksburg, under Johnston, and under Pemberton. No
military problem has ever been more often solved. Without serious blunder or mishap the concentrated army must
win.

Pemberton, soon made aware of his mistake, endeavored
to retrace his steps. But Grant was already upon him.

The enemy takes up position at Champion's Hill (Confederate "Baker's Creek"),
May 16.
between Vicksburg and Jackson. Grant moves upon him
along the three roads from Raymond and Bolton. The
divisions of Hovey, Logan, and Crocker assault his left
posted on the hill. Pemberton brings forces from his right
to sustain this key position, but forgets that a vigorous
movement along the two Raymond roads could brush away
this depleted wing and seize the fords over Baker's Creek
in his rear. The battle wavers over the hill-slopes all day,
with alternate success. Meanwhile McClernand, on our
left, in lieu of pushing through Loring's division and thus
helping Grant surround the enemy, wastes the day in mere
skirmishing, with a loss of barely one hundred and fifty men.
Towards night Pemberton is driven from the hill.

Had the victory on the right been less complete, he might not have retired, and could still perhaps have been cooped up. But to be driven back upon the fords before McClernand has seized them is his one element of safety.

Our loss was two thousand four hundred. The Confederates lost an equal number in prisoners alone, fourteen hundred killed and wounded, and twenty-four guns.

Pemberton escaped in confusion beyond the Big Black, where, at all the principal passages, he had already constructed bridge-heads. Grant in pursuit arrived at some of the crossings as soon as Pemberton, but the latter secured the railroad bridge.

Loring's division had been entirely cut off from Pemberton at Champion's Hill, and after some days joined Johnston by a circuitous march. Pemberton had charged Loring with the duty of defending the railroad bridge-head in case of need, and in the perplexities of retreat, Loring being absent, there was some confusion in supplying his place.

May 17. Sherman moved up to Bridgeport to turn the enemy's new left, and effected a crossing there. Everything was at sixes and sevens in the Confederate army. Pemberton's defences at the railroad bridge were maladroitly placed nearly a mile in advance of the crossing, without supports, and with an open plain behind the works. For troops to pass this plain under fire would prove certain destruction. The soldiers were well aware of

May 17. the fact and made but a sorry resistance, finally dwindling away with an unnecessarily heavy loss, our own being but three hundred. They burned the railroad bridge behind them.

Twenty-four hours were consumed in rebuilding the bridges. During this time, Pemberton had fallen back within his Vicksburg defences. Here he reassembled barely twenty thousand men of the force he had led out.

Thus in two weeks, Grant had driven his antagonist into Vicksburg, with a loss of over five thousand men, not counting Loring's division; had prevented the enemy from reuniting his forces, and held the key of the situation. And this on five days' rations. A splendid record!

Pemberton found that he must abandon the bluffs north of the city. These Sherman occupied, thus reaching once more the Yazoo river, but this

May 19.

time on the bluffs, and not at the foot of them. Pemberton had notified Johnston that he could not continue to hold these bluffs. Johnston replied that in that event he had much better leave Vicksburg to its fate, — for Walnut Hills was the key to the city, — and join forces with him. But Pemberton was already cooped up. Vicksburg had been invested.

On the same day Sherman gained the ridge beyond Fort Hill, and rested his right on the Mississippi. On his left stretched McPherson's line. Beyond him McClernand. The city was now besieged from the east, after the Federals had made its complete circuit by the west and south.

Altogether it has been a strange military manœuvre, which success will justify; failure utterly condemn. But it has exhibited on Grant's part exceptional self-reliance and knowledge of his opponent.

XXX.

SIEGE OF VICKSBURG.

THE logistic situation was now simplified by a change of Grant's base to the Yazoo. And, about these days, Porter found that time was ripe for an expedition up to Yazoo City, where he finally got at and destroyed the stores and the vessels building and being armed for river warfare, as well as the means of replacing them.

No sooner had the city been invested than, relying upon the demoralization of the Confederate troops, Grant determined upon an immediate assault. Preparations were yet far from complete, and to Sherman's share May 19. alone fell any severe fighting. McClernand and McPherson had not yet moved near enough to coöperate efficiently with him. And though these generals were enabled to seize an advanced position, the works proved everywhere too strong to be carried.

The troops in Vicksburg were hardened veterans, who had acquired the peculiar instinct of the soldier. In the recent conflicts in the field they had felt the want of that strong leadership without which the lives of the men are always at stake, and had behaved accordingly. But arrived behind good defences, where each man's intelligence and experience under fire came into play, they fought with their accustomed nerve, and no impression could be made upon them. Our loss was nearly a thousand men.

Grant's success, like not a few of Napoleon's, had been aided by his opponent's incapacity. Had Lee and Jackson been in his front, his triumph would have been earned at the expense of much harder blows, if at all. Later on in Virginia, with only half Grant's effective strength, Lee was able to hold him at bay for a full year, despite courage which laid in front of Lee's field-works as many dead and wounded Federals as the entire Army of Northern Virginia had under the colors.

The assault has failed, but Grant is not made of stuff to recognize defeat. A second assault is ordered. He feels confident that the works can be carried. The troops are eager for it, and are unwilling to settle down to the spade, until they have again tried the bayonet. Johnston may do something which will oblige Grant to raise the siege. The investment is not yet quite complete on the south. Every reason seems to demand prompt action, and Grant's tendency is always towards hard blows.

Two or three brigades form the storming party from each corps front, backed up by substantially the entire force. The first rush fails, though individual soldiers reach the parapet and plant their colors upon it. The men are withdrawn. At this moment Grant May 22. receives a misleading message from McClernand to the effect that he has made a lodgment in the works in his front, and asking Sherman's and McPherson's help by a renewed effort. McClernand has really only got posses-

sion of an outwork, which he can not retain.   But Grant,
supposing him to know what he asserts, orders the men in
again with the hope of sustaining him.   This second
assault adds to the loss of life to no effect.   Our casualties
have been over three thousand ; the enemy's barely five
hundred.   But the failure has caused no loss of *morale.*

Grant found himself driven to regular siege operations.
The topography of Vicksburg is singularly cut up.   The
country is full of ravines.   The Confederate line lay along
ridges surrounding the town.   The fortifications were skilfully constructed and well armed and manned.   Everything
indicated that starvation alone would reduce the town.
Our engineers got speedily to work and some twelve miles
of trenches and nearly an hundred batteries were in due
time constructed.

Within the city Pemberton was soon obliged to econo-
mize victuals, and then cut down to half and quarter rations.
The firing from our lines and the fleet was continuous.
Many thousand shot and shell were daily thrown into the
city.   In Vicksburg ammunition had necessarily to be
more sparingly used.

May 26.   Johnston now took the field, and Grant,
obliged to hold the lines of the Big Black
and the Yazoo for the safety of his rear and flank, detailed
Blair with six brigades to operate against him.

Reinforcements began to arrive from Memphis, and from
Burnside and Schofield, and swelled our force to seventy
thousand men and two hundred and fifty guns.   This
enabled Grant to complete the investment at all points.

With every day Johnston's chance of successful diversion

was disappearing. He had thirty-one thousand men "for duty," but he made no active attempt to aid Pemberton, despite constant pressure from Richmond, and appeals from his comrades within the walls of Vicksburg.

A momentary scare was created at this time by an expedition from Arkansas against our base of supplies at Milliken's Bend. But no result of value was accomplished by the enemy.

June 6 to 8.

McClernand had never been satisfied with his loss of command on the Mississippi, and at times gave cause for serious complaint by his erratic conduct. At last, on the occurrence of an act of actual insubordination, Grant summarily relieved him, and appointed Ord to his place.

One of the forts on the north-east front had been mined, and, hoping for a practicable breach, was blown up. But the enemy's countermine weakened the explosion and their loss was not severe. Our subsequent assault was met with the usual stubborn courage and shared the same failure as the others.

June 25.

Mining operations were vigorously carried on. Countermining by the enemy was almost uniformly unsuccessful. Starvation was fast approaching. The end must speedily come unless Johnston could accomplish something substantial.

Towards the end of June, Johnston did get ready to attack. He was lying in the vicinity of Canton and Jackson. Grant sent Sherman with twenty-four thousand men to watch his movements, with instructions to attack him at once if the next assault on Vicksburg, which he set for July 6, should eventuate in success. But Johnston attempted nothing which proved helpful towards raising the siege.

The garrison by the end of June was much reduced by lack of victuals.

In May, Johnston urged evacuation so as to save the army ; in June he promised aid and suggested a sortie. But the men were in no condition to cut their way through well-fed troops. They had in fact circulated a petition for surrender. Mutiny was feared. All Pemberton's officers advised capitulation, and Johnston finally notified Pemberton that he saw no chance to afford him relief. There being no alternative, Pemberton, after some interchange of letters with Grant, surrendered with thirty-seven thousand men as prisoners of war.

July 4.

His total loss during this campaign was thus above fifty thousand. Ours, in the movement from Port Gibson on, some eight thousand men.

Sherman's force was at once increased to forty-nine thousand men. He crossed the Big Black and marched on Johnston, who retired into Jackson. Here Sherman sat down before him and destroyed the railroads north and south of the town.

July 9.

Owing to Grant having laid waste the entire country around Vicksburg for fifty miles, as a means of self-protection, Johnston was unable long to maintain himself. No provision had been made for a siege. Johnston indulged hopes that Sherman would assault ; but finding him disinclined to do so, he quietly slipped away towards the east, and Grant withdrew Sherman from pursuit. The loss of each in this subsidiary campaign had been about one thousand men.

July 16.

Johnston's conduct during these hostilities was not

marked with vigor. He arrived at Jackson, as he tele-
graphed the Richmond authorities, "too late" to retrieve
the campaign; but it was quite within his power to join his
forces to Pemberton's, or failing this, to make a stout effort
to raise the siege.

Johnston, with all his ability, was never distinguished as a
fighter. His tendency was dilatory rather than active, the
very reverse of Grant's. He was never quite ready to attack. Compare this inactivity with any of the campaigns
of the Army of Northern Virginia. At Chancellorsville
Lee had but about two men to five of Hooker's. For all
that, his very audacity gained him one of the most brilliant
successes of the war. Here Johnston had all but the same
force as Grant; yet he made no active attempt whatever
to solve the problem. To be sure, Pemberton's obstinate
hold on Vicksburg did not coincide with Johnston's views;
but it was consistent with the Confederate programme. And
Pemberton's feeling that Johnston had no more than a right
to advise as to his movements, and not to give him orders,
resulted in a disastrous lack of coöperation. None the less
Johnston owed more assistance to the troops within the
walls than he rendered; and he had it in his power very
seriously to hamper Grant's operations.

Grant had won the great success of the war. And he
received his well-earned reward in the plaudits of the
people.

Thus ends the drama of Vicksburg, fit companion for the
glorious victory at Gettysburg! Both triumphs occurred
on our national holiday.

XXXI.

BANKS AND PORT HUDSON.

VERY early in the war it was determined to open some of the ports on the Gulf to serve as bases for operations extending into the interior. New Orleans was the most important of these, and its possession was of great use in wresting the control of the Mississippi river from the enemy. It was expected that Mobile would shortly after fall into our possession, and sundry efforts were made to capture it. But until near the close of the war we did not enter the city.

Mobile was the point of next military importance to New Orleans. From here an advance on the line of the Mobile and Ohio Railroad could have been made by a strong force towards the armies operating from the Tennessee river. The capture or destruction of the railroad centre at Meridian from this base would have seriously affected the ability of the enemy to detain our forces at Vicksburg; or indeed an advance in force towards Montgomery would more than once have weakened the conduct of the Confederate campaigns in Tennessee and Kentucky. And as after we had broken the Memphis and Charleston Railroad there was no all-rail route east and west except *via* Mobile, the importance of a lodgment here is apparent.

But up to this date, none of the operations on the Gulf-coast, excepting notably those of the navy under Farragut, had been conducted with such vigor as to accomplish results. The utmost that was done was to obtain a foot-hold at sundry points, which was made useful only to prevent supplies from entering the enemy's territory from abroad, and the shipment of cotton in return. All this was of course helpful to the Union cause, but it was negative helpfulness only.

Towards the close of 1862 Banks had sailed from New York with an army of twenty thousand men, and had relieved Butler at New Orleans. Some results were expected from his activity. He had at once despatched Grover with ten thousand men Dec. 14-17. to Baton Rouge. Banks had, including the troops already at this station, a total effective of thirty thousand; the whole force being consolidated into the Nineteenth army corps. But after he had made details from his troops for necessary garrisons, only fifteen thousand remained with which to operate against Port Hudson, which was his immediate objective. This force being deemed insufficient for direct attack, Banks formed a plan to cut off supplies from the place by tapping the Red river, down which the bulk of them was received.

The Confederates held Brashear City, and various points along the Atchafalaya river, to Alex-andria. Two expeditions were sent out, Jan.-Feb., 1863. one under Weitzel to move up Bayou Teche and one under Emory up the Atchafalaya. Both came to naught.

March.

Banks himself then moved to Baton Rouge, and Grover, with twelve thousand men, started for Port Hudson. He was to create a diversion while Farragut could run the Port Hudson batteries, so as to be able to patrol the river above and intercept supplies. Farragut made the attempt

March 14.

with seven ships. Owing to various mishaps only two contrived to pass above, while the rest, barring the Mississippi, which was blown up, were disabled and fell below. Still with these two, Farragut was able to blockade the Red river.

Banks projected a new expedition along the Atchafalaya. This time he was more successful. The army moved by the railroad west to Brashear City. Three

April 9–11.

days later Fort Bisland was taken. In another week we occupied Opelousas, and later, with Admiral Porter's coöperation, captured Alex-

May 7.

andria, at a loss all told of not exceeding six hundred men.

Halleck found fault with Banks for pushing his Red River schemes in lieu of coöperating with Grant in the reduction of Vicksburg. But Banks was in the right. General Taylor was not far from New Orleans in some force, and had not Banks taken measures to keep him at a distance as well as to garrison this city with sufficient troops, it might easily have fallen into the hands of the enemy. This, even temporarily, for of course it could have been recaptured, would have been a sad blow to

Federal *prestige*. As it was, no sooner had Banks left the vicinity of New Orleans than Taylor appeared upon the ground and blockaded the river below Port Hudson for quite a period. Not until the fall of that place was Banks enabled to get rid of him.

The correspondence between Banks and Grant during this campaign was conducted by couriers up and down the river. It proved very misleading, for the intervals between despatches were considerable. Each at one time had reasonable ground to expect that the other would supplement his efforts in his own special task ; and each continued to count upon the other after the changed conditions had made coöperation impossible.

Banks finally concentrated at Port Hudson, bringing from the Red River country   May 23.
the divisions of Grover, Emory, and Weitzel, and passing around the city by the north, while Augur and T. W. Sherman moved up from Baton Rouge. The works were strong and ably defended. Gardner had recently been in command of some seventeen thousand men, but Pemberton, in whose department he was, had withdrawn reinforcements and left him only four thousand effectives. Indeed, at the moment Banks completed his investment, Johnston had ordered Gardner to evacuate the place, intending that he should reinforce his own command at Jackson.

No sooner on the ground than Banks orders an assault all along the line. But,   May 27.
despite good conduct, failure results. The loss is two thousand men.

A second assault has no better fortune.
June 14.
But the issue in gaining an advanced line may have been worth the further loss of eighteen hundred men. The investment is continued, and the monotony of regular siege operations is the order of the day.

In this condition matters remain for a month. News of the surrender of Vicksburg comes to hand, and Gardner
July 8.
capitulates, on similar terms, with a large number of prisoners.

The loss by sickness had been enormous, exceeding vastly the casualties of the siege. The army left to General Banks after the surrender mustered barely one third "for duty" which had appeared on the rolls two months before.

Just prior to the surrender of Port Hudson, Confederate General Holmes, with nine thousand troops, arrived before Helena, Ark., held by Prentiss with half the num-
July 4.
ber. Holmes trusted to capture the garrison and to erect a new citadel there. But his project came to naught, with a loss of nearly two thousand men.

Very shortly after this event the steamer
July.
Imperial from St. Louis arrived at New Orleans, with a load of freight. The Great River could be said to be fairly emancipated from its bonds.

During the remainder of the war only partisan hostilities were waged upon the Mississippi.

XXXII.

SPARRING FOR A HOLD. — MINE RUN.

LEE retired from his defeat at Gettysburg, by way of the Shenandoah Valley. Meade crossed the Potomac and marched along the route followed by McClellan in 1862, east of the Blue Ridge. July 17-18. The pursuit was begun late, but once afoot it was expeditious enough to have enabled Meade to strike Lee's flank by debouching through Manassas Gap. This he attempted to do, but, owing to the delay of French's corps, the opportunity was lost. Lee retired to Culpeper. Meade advanced to the line of the Rappahannock.

Not anticipating any immediate demonstration by Meade, Lee sent Longstreet to help out Bragg, who apparently was overmatched by Rosecrans in Tennessee. Meade, however, was preparing for an active campaign, and shortly put the army across the Rappahannock. But the battle of Chickamauga, in which Bragg turned the tables on Rosecrans, alarmed the War Department, and Hooker with the Eleventh and Twelfth corps was taken from the Army of the Potomac and hurried out to Chattanooga. Meade was thus reduced to the strict defensive.

Overestimating Meade's depletion, Lee resolved to try

on the Army of the Potomac a manœuvre similar to the one practised on Pope the year before, and to seize the Orange and Alexandria Railroad in its rear. He accordingly put across the river by the upper fords. So soon as Meade fully learned this fact, he in turn withdrew across the Rappahannock.

October 9.

October 11.

In lieu of retreat, by a bold stroke Meade might have fallen upon Lee's rear, and thus have caught him in the execution of his manœuvre, — a moment always critical, because the troops are not so well in hand. But Meade was a sound rather than a bold soldier; he deemed it best to retire. Upon which, and not until then, Lee forged rapidly ahead, feeling safe for his own communications. He had won a point.

Meade assumed that Lee had abandoned his purpose and was still at Culpeper. Anxious to bring him to a general engagement if he could force it upon favorable ground, the Army of the Potomac was again put across the Rappahannock. But no sooner over than the appearance of Stuart on his right laid bare the facts, and he promptly retraced his steps.

Now follows a race for the possession of the Orange and Alexandria Railroad. Lee aims for Bristoe Station. He has the longer road, but also the clearer purpose. Meade, not understanding his intention, must divine if he would anticipate it.

Warren acts as rear guard. Meade reaches and passes Bristoe *en route* to Centreville. Warren arrives there only to find himself alone in presence of Lee's entire force.

As the boldest is often the best means of extricating one's self from peril, he smartly attacks Hill, who is in his immediate front.   A brilliant combat results in Warren's favor.   Under cover of this demonstration he retires in safety to join the army.   October 14.

Meade is now too strongly posted at Centreville for Lee to push him further.   The Confederate chieftain's efforts have been foiled.   But throwing out a curtain of troops along Bull Run he destroys the railroad south from that point and leisurely retires.   Meade follows, repairing as he goes.   Reaching the Rappahannock, he crosses, after being obliged to force the passage.   Lee at once puts the Rapidan between himself and the Army of the Potomac.   October 18.   November 7.

This unsatisfactory manœuvring served to demonstrate that if Meade was not always ready to take advantage of Lee's openings, neither could Lee make him lose his head, as he had done Pope.

The country still demanded action.   Meade appreciated the fact and sought opportunity again to try conclusions with Lee.   The latter had put his troops into cantonments for the winter over a considerable area of country.   A number of the lower fords of the Rapidan were left open, but Lee had defended his right flank by a line of intrenchments facing Mine Run, at right angles to that river.

Meade deems it possible to turn this position, and seriously cripple Lee in detail by a sudden blow before he can call in his scattered forces.   Time and distance are carefully computed.   The Army of the Potomac is to cut loose from its base with ten days' rations for a flying campaign. The several corps are simultaneously to cross

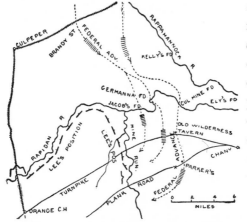

Mine Run. November 26-30, 1863.

at the various fords. The strict execution of marching orders seems to promise success. But success can be compassed by nothing short of minute accuracy.

It is never well to risk too much upon mathematical compliance with the order of march. In an ancient country, where turnpikes and bridges provide easy marching, such calculations **may** be made. On such *terrain* as was covered by our campaigns, abundant leeway was always essential. Here, however, the estimates appear liberal, and the movement is simple.

But again French is at fault. He is three hours late. And the pontoon train has been prepared without accurately estimating the depth of the stream. From the start ill-luck attends a well-conceived plan.

November 26.

Lee catches the alarm, and hastily concentrates. Meade gets into position two days later than he calculated to do. The army is not ready

November 28.

for attack till the fourth day.   Lee has made his position impregnable.

Recognizing failure, Meade ruefully withdraws.   Each army resumes its old location, and the troops go into winter quarters.

XXXIII.

ROSECRANS MOVES UPON BRAGG.

FOR full six months the Army of the Cumberland lay quietly in and near Murfreesborough, still facing Bragg. None but minor operations were undertaken. An occasional raid was made by the cavalry of either combatant. The Union horse, under Stanley, had begun to give a better account of itself than heretofore.

January to July, 1863.

Among other such operations was one by Forrest and Wheeler against Fort Donelson in which these brilliant troopers came nigh to snatching a marked success, but as the event turned, suffered defeat. And the most remarkable cavalry raid of the war was undertaken during the early summer of this year by J. H. Morgan, the Confederate partisan. With some three to four thousand mounted men this officer ranged at large through the States of Kentucky, Indiana, and Ohio, for about a month, destroying and capturing property wholesale. He was finally corralled and taken prisoner with his whole force. The consternation of the districts through which he rode was beyond anything which occurred in the North, except during the Gettysburg campaign.

Feb. 3.

June 27 to July 26.

The Army of the Cumberland was in good condition to take the field. Halleck had been urging Rosecrans to open the campaign. The latter in turn advised that "two great and decisive battles should not be risked at the same time," meaning by Grant's army on the Mississippi and by his own. This was scarcely a fair interpretation of a maxim often applicable to the operations of a single body of troops.

Grant was particularly anxious to have Rosecrans attack Bragg so as to prevent his detaching reinforcements to Vicksburg. Rosecrans, however, insisted that the sounder policy was merely to threaten Bragg. He was positive that this course would retain him in force in his own front. Bragg pursued the same policy. Each appeared to dread the struggle which sooner or later must come.

Towards midsummer Rosecrans was finally constrained to move upon the enemy. He had seventy thousand men ; Bragg lay at Shelbyville with some forty-seven thousand. Rosecrans feinted with his right against Bragg's position, in front of which some considerable skirmishing was done, to enable Thomas, whose route lay through Hoover's Gap, to move upon Manchester and thus turn Bragg's right. On Thomas' arrival at Manchester, after tedious marching over heavy roads, Bragg, who had been watching his front and had forgotten his flanks, was obliged hurriedly to retire from his well-fortified works at Shelbyville. Hereupon Thomas again marched around Bragg's right, cutting his communications at Decherd, and the Confederate found that it would be prudent to

June 23.

June 28.

June 30.

evacuate Tullahoma, which had been his depot of supplies, and move his head-quarters to Chattanooga.

July 7.

The casualties in this short campaign, in which Rosecrans fairly manœuvred Bragg out of positions which might
have cost great loss by direct assault, were not much over
five hundred men.   The operation had been skilfully
conducted and reflects credit upon the commanding general,
as well as upon Thomas, whose pertinent advice and stanch
methods always figured as an important factor in the
success of the Army of the Cumberland.

During the summer Burnside, with the forces which were
now called the Army of the Ohio, had advanced from Kentucky across the mountains into the Valley
of East Tennessee.   Buckner was in command of this Valley, but retired towards Bragg on the
approach of Burnside, who thereupon occupied Knoxville.   He was now in position
to afford protection to the left of the forces operating
against Chattanooga, and his position cut Lee off from his
easiest route to the Western armies.

August.

September 2.

Rosecrans had before him the task of flanking Bragg out
of Chattanooga.   A glance at the map will show the impossibility of taking the city from the front short of a pro-
tracted siege.   An attempt to turn Bragg's right would
necessitate a long and tedious march away from our railroad
communications, and through a country beset with difficulties.   He would have to move some seventy-five miles
up the Tennessee river before he could cross.   This was,
however, the way Bragg expected the attack, on account of

Burnside's presence at Knoxville. And it was on cogent grounds that he assumed that Rosecrans would attempt to join those forces to his own before attacking him in his stronghold.

But Rosecrans was planning a different manœuvre. He guessed that Bragg would count on his moving by his left, and knew that to do what your enemy does not expect is to half accomplish your purpose. He proposed to himself to cross the Tennessee west of Chattanooga, pass the mountain ranges below the city, and take Bragg in reverse from an unexpected quarter.

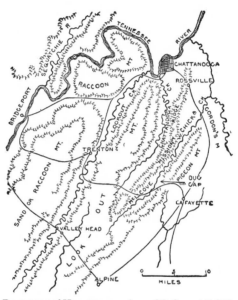

Rosecrans' Manœuvre. Aug. 20-Sep. 17, '63.

This was no easy problem. He had before him a wide river and several parallel ranges of rugged mountains traversed only by the roughest of roads. He was provided with poor transportation. Yet he must calculate on foraging his beasts, and feeding his men for at least three weeks, and must provide ammunition for several encounters, if not one or more pitched battles.

Still this seemed to him, all things considered, the preferable route.   He accordingly sent Crittenden
August 16.
with the left wing up the Sequatchie Valley
to make a demonstration on Bragg's right, to confirm the
latter in his theory that this was the real point of attack,
while himself with Thomas and McCook made ready to march
towards the most available crossing-places of the Tennessee
near Bridgeport.   He was about to place himself in the
enemy's country, with insecure means of retreat in case of
disaster, insufficient supplies, and a treacherous knowledge
of the *terrain;* while the conditions prescribed a march in
several columns.   A bold but hardly a prudent scheme.

Bragg had just been reinforced from Mississippi, and
expected Longstreet from Virginia.   He was quite intent
on watching Crittenden's movement toward his right.

September 4.
Rosecrans was unopposed in crossing the
Tennessee, and in putting Thomas and Mc-
Cook over the Raccoon range into Lookout Valley.   There
being but three practicable wagon roads, he ordered Thomas
by way of Trenton over Lookout Mountain and Missionary
Ridge into McLemore's Cove, while McCook moved by way
of Valley Head into the open country beyond Lookout
Mountain, and south of Chattanooga.

This eccentric route separated McCook by nearly three
days' march from Thomas.   Crittenden, meanwhile, had
returned and had followed Thomas across the river.

On reaching Alpine, McCook threw out a reconnoitring
party, but without encountering the enemy
September 10.
in force.   To reach McCook, Thomas must
pass through one of the gaps in Pigeon Mountain.   In

attempting Dug Gap his van was attacked, and he drew back, as he must force the defile in order to advance, — always a delicate operation, — and was in the dark as to McCook's whereabouts. September 11.

So soon as Thomas and McCook had reached Lookout Valley, Bragg had seen the necessity of evacuating Chattanooga. Hereupon Crittenden moved up the river, took possession of the town, and advanced twelve miles south to Gordon's Mills. But the situation was scarcely bettered. Rosecrans' army was still divided into three parts, each separated from the others by a serious distance in the presence of the enemy.

From Chattanooga Bragg had moved to LaFayette from whence he at once sent out detachments to hold the Pigeon Mountain Gaps. It was one of these which Thomas' head of column had encountered.

Rosecrans' position was perilous in the extreme; Bragg was afterwards severely blamed by many for not taking summary advantage of it. But the game of war is not based on mathematical exactness. What appears feasible on paper is often far from practicable in the field. Nor are all good soldiers great strategists. The heavy work of the world has to be done by the average abilities. And even brilliant genius does not always compass the most useful ends. *In medio tutissimus.*

The lack of maps and his unfamiliarity with the country was Rosecrans' only excuse for having placed himself in such jeopardy. He had got his right wing separated from his centre by three marches, September 14. and these through a long and dangerous defile. His left was equally distant from the centre. Thomas could not go to either wing without endangering the other. He must wait for each of them to rally upon him. If Bragg could but overwhelm Thomas singly, he could at once turn upon Crittenden with good assurance of crushing him, and still have ample time to retrace his steps and to cut McCook off from retreat across the river.

To have done this would have stamped Bragg as the equal of Lee. And while McCook or Crittenden would have stood a sorry chance against Bragg single-handed, it is much easier to talk of crushing Thomas than it ever proved to do it. If Bragg had undertaken this operation, so obvious to his critics, he might have fallen far short of its performance. Though indeed it was the thing to attempt, for any action would have compromised Rosecrans still further. But Bragg did not act, and Rosecrans escaped from his peril.

By a long and arduous march, McCook joined Thomas, and Crittenden soon after came within hail. Bragg must now fight the Army of the Cumberland as one body.

Sept. 17–18.

The position of Rosecrans lies facing Chickamauga Creek from a point in advance of Rossville Gap in Missionary Ridge, through which passes the road to Chattanooga, southerly past Gordon's Mill towards Dug Gap. He has finally manœuvred himself in front of the captured city. But he must fight for its preservation. And Bragg proposes to make him fight *au fond*.

September 18.

XXXIV.

CHICKAMAUGA.

LONGSTREET is now approaching the field. Bragg marshals his forces on the east bank of Chickamauga Creek. His purpose is to cross on the morrow, crush our left, seize the Rossville road, and thus cut us off from both retreat and Chattanooga. But Thomas has anticipated this probability and firmly covers Rossville. Rosecrans awaits attack.

Bragg crosses Chickamauga Creek a day later than intended, and falls upon Thomas, whom circumstances have placed in control of the left of the army. The fighting is stubborn, and during the day Thomas is somewhat thrust back; but by nightfall he regains his old position. Bragg's tactics have now become quite intelligible to him, and he re-forms during the night in such wise as to protect more securely the Rossville road, the enemy's evident goal.

September 19.

Next day Polk commands on the enemy's right, Longstreet on the left. In the forenoon Polk forces the fighting. Thomas exhibits a staying quality of the highest order, and though repeatedly thrust back, shows no symptom of weakening. Towards midday

September 20.

a serious breach is made in our line on the right of the centre, by the removal of Wood's division, through mistaken orders.   Into this cleft quickly pours a stream of

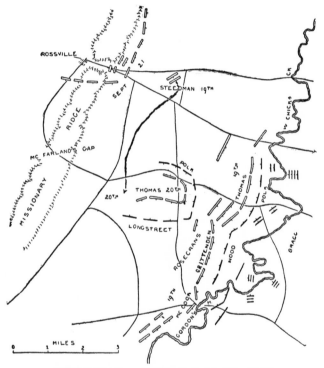

Chickamauga.   September 19-20, 1863.

Southern regiments.   The right under McCook is isolated, taken in reverse and, as at Murfreesborough, speedily huddled into shapeless masses.

The absence of the instinct of command is apparent. Thomas' flank is completely turned.   The fate of the battle hangs by a hair. No aid can now come from the right. Thomas re-forms by a retrograde movement upon Horse Shoe Ridge. Granger's divisions advance opportunely from Rossville Gap, which Longstreet might have seized, thus forces the latter back, and occupies a ridge on Thomas' right. Ammunition is getting low. Cold steel is used. The enemy is unremitting in his blows: his onslaught is redolent of success. As at Stone's River, everything seems lost. The entire right of the army, with Rosecrans and his staff, is driven from the field in utter rout. But, unknown even to the commanding general, Thomas, the Rock of Chickamauga, stands there at bay, surrounded, facing two to one. Heedless of the wreck of one-half the army, he knows not how to yield. No more splendid spectacle appears in the annals of war than this heroic stand of Thomas in the midst of a routed army, and in the face of an enemy the power of whose blows is doubled by the exultation of victory. Slowly riding up and down the lines, with unruffled countenance and cheery word, it is his own invincible soul which inspires his men for the work they have to do. It is on his courage that every soldier leans.

Rosecrans' frantic efforts to rally the right are wasted. The rout is complete, disgraceful. The panic-stricken regiments pour by, heedless of entreaty or command. Reaching Rossville, in the belief that Thomas too has been routed, Rosecrans sends Garfield, his chief of staff, to hunt him up and bid him to protect the rear with whatever force he can collect. He himself rides back to Chattanooga, thinking there to rally and re-form his troops

to meet the pursuing foe. Unhappy day for Rosecrans'
fame !

Night supervened. Bragg had torn his columns into useless shreds by dashing them against immovable Thomas.
Nor was he able to follow Thomas up, when, with broken
but undaunted ranks, this silent hero led back his men to
Rossville. Here he re-formed at his leisure. And before
morning he was joined, after a weary circuit over the hills,
by Sheridan, who had been cut off in Rosecrans' disordered
retreat, but who had kept his troops together, and was still
in condition and temper to do efficient service.

Sept. 21.
Sept. 22.
    Next day Bragg could do no more than
observe our movements with his cavalry,
and thirty-six hours later, the Army of the
Cumberland was concentrated at Chattanooga, and in fair
shape for service.

Rosecrans had been badly worsted on the field of battle.
Chickamauga was one of the direst mishaps of the war.
But the result of the campaign was that he had manœuvred
Bragg out of his key-position, and Thomas' stanch de-
fense had so weakened him that he could not, for some time
at least, undertake the offensive. On the other hand, Bragg
had practically got Rosecrans cooped up in Chattanooga.
Honors were easy between them.

Rosecrans ascribed his unfortunate division of forces to
the failure of his subordinates to obey orders. Both Mc-
Cook and Crittenden were relieved from command till a
Court of Inquiry could make disposition of their cases.

In this bloody battle, the Army of the Cumberland lost
sixteen thousand out of sixty-two thousand men on the

field, thirty-six guns and much material. Bragg's loss was over eighteen thousand out of a considerably larger effective.

There is no doubt much difference of opinion as to Rosecrans' ability. He also belongs to that large number of excellent generals upon whom Fortune did not smile. Without being a great soldier, he possessed many of the qualities of one. He was tried in the balance and found wanting. But was the balance itself true? "It was inevitable that the first leaders should be sacrificed to the nation's ignorance of war." At that time our public would not exhibit the patience which became necessary in after days if success was to be enticed to our banners.

The Army of the Cumberland in Chattanooga was really in a state of siege. The Confederate Army held the south bank of the Tennessee, and from the end of the railroad which supplied our troops, at Bridgeport, around the long bend here made by the river, was a haul of sixty miles. This distance was over roads axle-deep in mud, and daily liable to interruption by cavalry raids. Rations began speedily to fall short. The situation was grave.

Under these circumstances, the arrival of Hooker with fifteen thousand men from the Army of the Potomac was by no means an unmixed gain; but Rosecrans soon found use for his corps in an operation designed to open communications across the loop of the river, *via* Brown's Ferry.

XXXV.

THE BATTLE OF CHATTANOOGA.

THE Departments of the Ohio and the Cumberland were now merged into the Military Division of the Mississippi under Grant. Rosecrans was relieved and Thomas became commander of the Army of the Cumberland.

Oct. 16–20.

The advantage of opening the Brown's Ferry road was manifest, and with the coöperation of Hooker, the left bank of the Tennessee opposite Bridgeport was seized by a *coup de main*, and his command, consisting of the Eleventh and Twelfth corps, was posted on the spot.

October 27.

The enemy had been unable to interrupt the movement, though made under his very eyes; but loth to have the city so easily revictualled, Longstreet got together his troops and assailed Hooker in force. He must be driven from his ground, or starvation in Chattanooga would no longer be the Confederates' ally. A short and sharp action at Wauhatchie ensued; Hooker drove Longstreet back; the road was finished, and the siege of Chattanooga was raised.

Oct. 28–29.

Bragg now despatched Longstreet into East Tennessee

to dispose of Burnside, who was still in the vicinity of Knoxville, where he was a constant threat to Bragg's right. Grant ordered Sherman to join him at Chattanooga with the Fifteenth army corps. The other three corps of the army which captured Vicksburg remained on the Mississippi. While his enemy's forces were depleted was the time for Grant to push home with his sixty thousand men.

How to drive Bragg's army from our front was the immediate problem before him, and Grant's restless activity would not allow him to sit down and wait.

Bragg's right lay substantially along Missionary Ridge, its advance strongly entrenched at Tunnel Hill; his centre across Chattanooga Valley; his left holding the supposed inaccessible heights of Lookout Mountain. In whichever direction the eye was cast formidable defenses had to be pierced, and these were manned by forty thousand muskets.

The battles of Chattanooga, Lookout Mountain, and Missionary Ridge, which shortly came about, may be considered as parts of one single engagement, having for object to drive Bragg from the position he had chosen. The plan of action was as follows: Sherman was to move up the river on the north side with four divisions, cross near the mouth of Chickamauga Creek, under cover of artillery, on a pontoon-bridge to be thrown for the purpose, attack and capture the north end of Mission Ridge, and advance along it. Thomas was to concentrate in Chattanooga Valley and feel the enemy strongly to hold him there in force; while Hooker's share was to patrol Lookout Valley and make a diversion to assist Sherman. For on the latter Grant supposed the main task was to fall and desired that it should.

Knowing Sherman's method better than that of his newer lieutenants, Grant felt that he could rely on the work being done as it should be if entrusted to him.

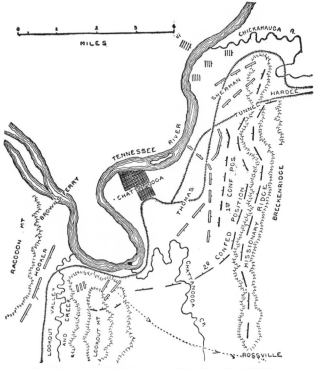

Chattanooga. November 23, 24, 25, 1863.

Some delay occurred in Sherman's crossing, but two days later than ordered he put over his command and drove the enemy from the north end of the ridge. The entire range had been supposed to be continuous; but Sherman found a deep gap which must be

November 24.

passed before he could arrive at Tunnel Hill, and his purpose was summarily arrested by this unexpected physical obstacle, of which the enemy had taken full advantage for defense.

Meanwhile Thomas makes a reconnoissance in force in the Valley, which develops the enemy in his front, and succeeds in advancing his line some distance, while Hooker pushes round the end of Lookout Mountain and fights his eccentric Battle above the November 24. Clouds, driving the enemy from every position. Next day Hooker operates towards Rossville on Bragg's left, while Sherman makes another heavy onslaught on the enemy in his front. Being met with stubborn opposition from Hardee's troops, Thomas is ordered November 25. to attack seriously all along the defenses in his front.

This attack is meant by Grant to be merely in the nature of a diversion to lighten Sherman's task. But the Army of the Cumberland, eager to show that lack of stomach did not lose the fight of Chickamauga, as well as jealous of the glory to be won, assails the field-works at the foot of Mission Ridge and captures them at the point of the bayonet. Breckenridge is quite unable to hold head against them. After which triumph, the troops, emulating each other's ardor, and without orders, press gallantly on up the ridge in full view of both armies, with deafening cheers, heedless of the deadly fire belched into their very faces, and overrun the works at the summit like a torrent, capturing thirty-five guns and prisoners wholesale. It has all been the work of an hour, and so completely has it flanked the line opposing Sherman, that he is at once re-lieved of opposition.

In this triple action Sherman's loss was fifteen hundred; Thomas' nearly four thousand; Hooker's not great. Bragg, thus worsted at every point, found it necessary to withdraw to Ringgold with a loss of sixty-six hundred men.

Granger, with fifteen thousand men, was now sent to Burnside's assistance. Longstreet was besieging the Army of the Ohio in Knoxville, and had made a very heavy assault on the place. Alarming reports com-
November 29.
ing from thence, especially as to the want of provisions, Sherman was also despatched to his aid. But as Longstreet retired towards Virginia on his approach, Sherman shortly returned to Chattanooga. He had not found Burnside in so great a strait as reported.

During the succeeding winter months minor operations alone were undertaken.

February, 1864.
Early next year Schofield succeeded to the command of the Army of the Ohio. Transportation being difficult, the troops had suffered bit-terly from lack of victuals during the winter. As spring approached Longstreet was withdrawn to the more im-portant field of operations in Virginia, and Schofield became free to join Sherman.

March, 1864.
That *beau sabreur*, Forrest, about these days made another of his chronic raids, notorious on account of the Massacre at Fort Pillow. The furthest point reached by him was Paducah, where a stub-born resistance rendered threats and attacks alike vain. On the return march, he visited Fort Pillow, garrisoned by

negro troops. Here he at first met a stout rebuff; but during a subsequent parley for surrender of the garrison on honorable terms, the Confederates advanced their lines while hostilities had ceased, and, thus surrounded, the fort was surprised and captured. It is April 12, 1864. not probable that Forrest personally had anything to do with the events which followed. But his troops, maddened by the sight of their ancient slaves in arms, began butchering wholesale after surrender had been made. It is a black page in the story of the war, and one to be quickly turned.

XXXVI.

FURTHER OUTSKIRT OPERATIONS.

NO more than a bare mention can be made of a few of the numerous small expeditions which were undertaken on the outskirts of the Confederacy.

For about a year from the beginning of the war, the town of Norfolk was held by the enemy. But shortly after the fight of the Merrimac and Monitor it again fell into our hands, completing for us the possession of the mouth of the Chesapeake.

May–Oct., 1862.

After the capture of Fort Sumter the enemy held undisputed possession of Charleston for a twelvemonth. It was then deemed advisable in Washington to make some attempt to recover possession of this politically, if not strategically, important city. Admiral Dupont and General Hunter first tried their hand at the work, but made no headway; and Hunter was relieved by Mitchel. The latter soon after died, and Hunter resumed command of the Department of the South. Three months thereafter Hunter made a further attempt upon the city, which again had no result, and Gilmore superseded him so far as the operations against Charleston were concerned.

May, 1862.

January, 1863.
April 7.

June 12.

During the next month, Gilmore made a lodgment, with Dahlgren's assistance, on July 10. Morris Island in Charleston Harbor, and Fort Wagner — a strong work there situated — was attacked. July 11–18. Failure followed two assaults with a loss of some eighteen hundred men.   Fort Sumter was demolished by the fire of the fleet, and though a naval assault on it failed, the enemy evacuated Aug. 23–Sept. 9. Morris Island.   Further operations were then suspended, and the city of Charleston remained in the possession of the enemy until Sherman marched through the Carolinas nearly two years later.

General Foster made a raid from his base at New Berne on Goldsborough, N.C., but Dec. 11–20, 1862. accomplished no result which proved to be of permanent value.

A minor campaign between Generals Blunt and Hindman in Missouri took place at the close of the second year.   Blunt had marched some December, 1862. seven thousand Union troops from Missouri into Arkansas, driving the Confederate horseman Marmaduke before him. Hindman, who was in general command, deeming it essential to arrest his progress, advanced and confronted Blunt, whom a body under Herron was on the way to reinforce.   Hindman was held in check for two days.   The Confederate then feinted on the Union front, stole by its left and attacked Herron at Prairie Grove; but being held up for three hours, Blunt reached his rear, and the two, in a sharp action, in which over one thousand men were lost by each combatant, forced December 7.

Hindman to permanently withdraw south of the Arkansas river.

September, 1863.   Steele occupies Little Rock, Arkansas.

September.   An expedition from New Orleans against Sabine Pass, Louisiana, fails.

September.   Blunt and Cabell indulge in a skirmishing campaign in Arkansas.

The guerilla Quantrell assails Lawrence, Kansas, but

August 21.   is driven off after creating great confusion among the settlers.

November 6.   Banks sends out an expedition which takes Brownsville, at the mouth of the Rio Grande.

Gilmore despatches Seymour and six thousand men to Jacksonville, Florida.   From here an advance is made

Feb. 20, 1864.   into the country, and at Olustee an engagement with the enemy results disastrously for our arms, with a loss of one-quarter the effective force. But Jacksonville is held.

October, 1862.
Jan. 1, 1863.   Galveston had early been occupied by the Union forces; but Magruder recaptured it somewhat later, and it was thenceforth held by the Confederates.

An attempt to release our prisoners at Libby Prison,

Feb. 28 to
March 3, 1864.   Richmond, was made by the cavalry general, Kilpatrick.   But this operation, made noteworthy at the time by the death of Colonel Dahlgren, fell short of success.

The Red River expedition deserves perhaps a larger treatment.   But as it had no influence upon the great strategic fields, a passing notice must suffice.

As the third year began General Banks conceived the idea that the trade of Western Louisiana could be opened by the medium of the Red   1864. river, and projected an expedition to take possession of the country adjacent to its course.   This river is open for navigation by larger vessels, only during the high water of March and April.   Porter was to command the fleet of twenty of the finest vessels on the Mississippi, and Sherman was persuaded to lend some of his troops for the purpose. A. J. Smith was to start from Vicksburg with ten thousand men, while Banks would proceed up river from New Orleans, with Franklin's division.   Steele from Little Rock was to operate towards Shreveport to join the main army.

Kirby Smith was in command of the enemy's forces in Shreveport; Taylor led an army in the field.

The fleet started up the Red River in company with the transports carrying A. J. Smith's column.   March 14. Fort De Russy was captured, the enemy retiring before our troops, and Alexandria and   March 16. Natchitoches fell into our hands as the joint   April 2. force advanced.   Banks put in an appearance a week later.   There was more or less skirmishing with the enemy's horse and outposts along the entire route; and near Mansfield, at Sabine Cross-Roads, the vanguard met the enemy in force.   Sufficient care had not   April 8. been taken to keep the several bodies concentrated.   Taylor fell smartly on Franklin, defeated and drove him back with a loss of three thousand out of eight thousand engaged.   Emory stopped the Confederates, but

we fell back on our supports.   At Pleasant Hill, A. J.
Smith made a stand for the possession of what had been so

April 9.

far gained, but despite stanch fighting the
result could not be changed.   An immedi-
ate retreat was made, without waiting to bury the dead.
The casualties now numbered about four thousand men.
The situation was threatening.

Mid-April.

April 26.

The fleet meanwhile had reached Grand
Ecore.   High water was coming to an end,
and Porter was obliged to return down river,
to Alexandria.   Here it was found that most of the vessels
were of too heavy draught to pass the falls below the town ;
and the loss of most of them would have been certain, but
for a dam and water-way ably constructed by Colonel

May 12-13.

Bailey, an engineer remarkably fertile in ex-
pedients.   By means of this device the fleet
was safely floated over.

On the retreat, Alexandria was burned by accident,

May 15.

traceable to no particular cause, though, naturally enough, laid by the Confederates to
our spirit of revenge.

The failure of this expedition came near to fatally compromising the force of General Steele, who had begun his
march down from Little Rock, and to whom no word of our
disaster could be conveyed.   But with good luck his small
army was eventually withdrawn in safety, though with the
loss of much material.

The harbor of Mobile was protected by three works,
Forts Gaines, Morgan, and Powell.   It was determined to
make a joint land and naval attack upon them, to break up

the illicit commerce of the city and, if possible, to reduce the place. Farragut's fleet was increased by the addition of some monitors, and he rendezvoused in the harbor with Gordon Granger, selected by Canby to command the land forces for this purpose. Farragut proposed to employ his old tactics of isolating the forts by running by them in column. This was done, — the gallant Admiral in command of the flag-ship Hartford, — with the loss of only one vessel. The Confederate ram Tennessee made a brave resistance, but was captured. Fort Gaines surrendered to Granger; Fort Powell was abandoned; and Fort Morgan surrendered later. But the city itself, though cut off from the outside world, maintained itself against Granger's efforts, and was not reduced till the close of the war. It then surrendered to Canby.

August 5.

August 5, 23.

April 11, 1865.

Price makes an extensive raid into Missouri and penetrates to within less than one hundred miles of St. Louis. Curtis defeats him and drives him from the State.

September and October, 1864.

A noteworthy combat between the Confederate cruiser Alabama and the United States ship Kearsarge occurred off Cherbourg, France. Among the vessels depredating on our commerce three English-built cruisers had been preëminent, the Alabama, Florida, and Georgia. The two last were captured respectively in Bahia Harbor and at sea.

June 19.

The Alabama, under command of Captain Semmes, had been sought by the Kearsarge, Captain Winslow, and sailed out of Cherbourg to accept her challenge. The

tonnage and crews of each were about equal. The armament of each was what the English and we considered
the best for war vessels of that size. They were typical
craft. The Alabama was an English vessel, mounting
English guns and carrying an English crew; the Kearsage
an American vessel, with American guns, and out of one
hundred and sixty officers and men all but eleven were
American-born citizens. Both were wooden vessels, but
the Kearsarge hung her chain cables over the sides to protect
her engines.

It was a fair fight, but of short duration. The fire of
the Kearsage was the more deliberate and proved very
destructive. The Alabama surrendered within an hour in
a sinking condition. Semmes was picked up in the water
by an English vessel, and escaped capture. The loss of
the Alabama was about forty men. On the Kearsarge,
which was but slightly injured by her opponent's fire, only
three men were wounded.

XXXVII.

THE WILDERNESS.

FOR three long years the operations of our armies had
been conducted without united effort. The campaigns
of the East and West, though nominally directed by
Halleck, had really been of so isolated a character that the
enemy could at need detach troops from Virginia to Tennessee, or the reverse, according as the tide might turn on
each strategic field. The nation had now learned that war
could not be carried on by political methods alone; that
the South must be exhausted before peace could be won;
that systematic warfare was the least costly means of bringing this to pass; and that the unhampered work of one
man, in whom the confidence of all could be centred, was
essential to a successful issue.

The choice of the nation fell naturally upon General
Grant. He was commissioned Lieutenant
General and placed in supreme command. March 9, 1864.

Grant gave over the control of events in the West to
Sherman. For himself he reserved the special field of
Virginia. He knew that he left in Sherman's hands a well-
tempered weapon with which to fight.

Grant's own success on other fields not unnaturally led him

to believe that the Army of the Potomac had never been fought *au fond;* he imagined that Lee and the Army of Northern Virginia could be beaten by the same means as Pemberton and Bragg, and he set himself the task to make the rugged old army do that which he thought it never yet had done. Moreover Grant at this time openly gave his preference to hard blows over manœuvring. "Continuous hammering" was his motto. His belief seems to have been that the use of skilful tactics exhibits weakness. Other and greater soldiers have sometimes for a while been subject to this delusion. He was to discover his error in his first clash of arms, and to recognize the fact that he had never yet faced a captain such as was the man who through so many campaigns had borne the proud banner of the South on the Old Dominion soil, nor yet had led stouter hearts against more valiant foes.

Grant's objective was Lee's army. So long as Lee held to the defense of Richmond, this city was the goal. But to destroy Lee's army was the work cut out. "On to Richmond" was an empty phrase.

The Army of the Potomac lay in and about Culpeper; the Army of Northern Virginia around Orange. A movement by our right possessed the manifest advantage of more open ground, and the yet greater disadvantage of gradually lengthening our lines of communication and supply. A movement by our left gave the Army of the Potomac lines of operation easy to keep open, because the base could be constantly shifted to points on the coast in rear of the operations actually going on, but it carried the army through a country essentially unfitted for manœuvring.

Grant had in theory favored moving on Richmond from the James river. The overland route he deemed too costly in time and men. But he eventually adopted a plan savoring of both. Only his great numerical superiority could excuse his dividing his forces. Concentric operations are always weak, because the several detachments are liable to be separately overwhelmed.

The plan was this. Grant, with the Army of the Potomac under Meade, and the Ninth corps under Burnside, was to take the overland route on the east of Richmond. Butler, with thirty thousand men (the Army of the James), was to move up James River. Sigel, who was near the Potomac at the mouth of the Valley, and Crook, who was in the Kanawha region, were to operate from the debouches of the Shenandoah.

The Army of the Potomac had had five corps. These were now consolidated into three, perhaps unwisely. For the new ones became too bulky for the difficult country through which they were to operate, and the *esprit de corps* of the ancient organizations was destroyed by their disbandment and merger into the new.

There were now Hancock's Second Corps, Warren's Fifth, Sedgwick's Sixth, and Sheridan's Cavalry Corps. These, with the Ninth, numbered one hundred and twenty-two thousand men " for duty equipped " and over three hundred guns. Head-quarters were at Culpeper Court House.

Lee confronted this splendid army with the corps of Longstreet, Hill, and Ewell, not far from seventy thousand men and over two hundred guns. He was ready for the fray. But he must have anxiously watched for the first sign of the movement of his new opponent, whose set purpose he knew as well as the strength of the army he led.

Grant purposed to turn Lee's right. No time was lost. Marching orders were issued. The army was perfect in discipline, equipment, and material. One day sufficed to put the hundred thousand men across the Rapidan. Warren led, Sedgwick followed over Germanna Ford; Hancock crossed at Ely's, further east. Burnside was to remain in camp for a day later.

May 4.

Grant's route was through the Wilderness, due south. This was the same dense forest where the Army of the Potomac, just one year before, had been so nearly wrecked. Lee made no effort to dispute Grant's crossing, but purposed to strike him while traversing these dreary woods. From Orange towards the route pursued by Grant were two parallel roads, known as the Plank road and the Turnpike, which cut the north and south roads used by us at right angles to our line of march.

Meeting with no opposition in crossing the river, Grant believed that Lee had retreated to more favorable ground. He had no idea of fighting here, in the forest which had proved so nearly fatal to Hooker. On the night succeeding the passage of the Rapidan both armies camped near by each other, Grant unsuspicious of the close presence of the enemy, and far from assured that Lee would accept battle when his position was turned. But orders were issued to attack, and next day Ewell is met by Warren, who is moving by the flank through the wood roads. Grant and Meade, at Old Wilderness Tavern,

May 4–5.

May 5.

suppose this to
be the affair
of a simple rear
guard.   At
this moment,
had   Ewell
been   vigor-
ously pushed
by Warren,
he might have
been   badly
used up, for
he was unsup-
ported.   But
as the resist-
ance to Ewell
was   propor-
tioned only to
Grant's idea of
his strength,
before   Sedg-
wick   could
come up on

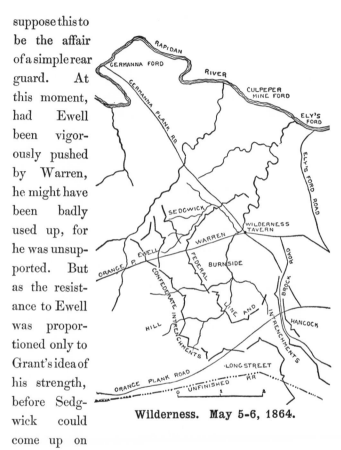

Wilderness.   May 5-6, 1864.

Warren's right, Ewell had inflicted a loss of three thousand
men upon the Fifth corps.   Still Warren clung tenaciously
to ground in advance of Old Wilderness Tavern.

Grant's eyes begin to open, but, with his usual determination, he is ready to accept the gage of battle here.
Sedgwick is ordered to join on to Warren's right.   Hancock, away off at Chancellorsville, with his head of column

at Todd's Tavern, is hurried up along the Brock road. On his arrival he promptly moves out the plank road, south of Warren, and attacks Hill. Both the Warren-Ewell and Hancock-Hill combats are isolated. No tactical connection exists between them. In fact grand-tactics are impossible on this ground. Night closes the engagement.

Both Grant and Lee determine to attack on the morrow. Burnside is ordered up to take place between Warren and Hancock. Lee awaits the arrival of Longstreet, whom he will place opposite Hancock's right.

The Wilderness is covered by a scrub growth of small trees and underbrush, so dense that one can see but a few hundred feet in the clearest places. Cavalry can not leave the roads, which are few and poor. Artillery is useless, except occasionally where a section may fire down a road. There are next to no clearings. Manœuvring is impossible. Bodies of troops have to march by the compass. Success or failure can only be guessed from the advance or recession of the infantry fire. In this blind place, familiar enough to Lee, but quite unknown to Grant, the two old enemies are again to grapple.

Grant orders an attack along the whole line at 5 A.M. Lee determines, so soon as Longstreet shall have arrived, to turn Grant's left and throw him back upon the river. To divert attention from Longstreet's absence, he strongly feels our right.

Hancock falls upon Hill at five, and drives him over a mile down the plank road. Confusion among the troops is natural in these woods. Hancock stops to rearrange the ranks. He has been cautioned to beware lest Longstreet fall upon his left along the Brock road, for Grant considers it probable that Lee may use this approach. Part of the Second corps has thus been kept there, the presence of which in the advance might have insured a larger success against Hill. While thus pausing, Longstreet comes upon the field. The suddenness of his assault takes Hancock unawares, and drives him back to his old lines on the Brock road. Here he rallies. Longstreet is wounded. The violence of the attack subsides.

Later in the afternoon, Lee again attacks Hancock. Aided by a fire in the woods, which the wind blows into our faces, he drives our line in some distance, but once more we rally and retake the ground so lost. Night again supervenes. Nothing has been decided. Grant's loss of eighteen thousand men should make him rate his own new army and his adversary's skill at a higher value than he did two days ago. Lee's loss is probably less by several thousand men.

Beyond a cavalry fight by Sheridan against Stuart there are no further operations on this ground. Both armies are exhausted. Neither has gained aught but added respect for the other's mettle.

NOTE. — Anderson succeeded Longstreet. But, for convenience, this Corps is still referred to by the name of its old commander.

XXXVIII.

SPOTSYLVANIA.

G RANT, having found that Lee is able to check any
direct advance upon his lines, concludes to resort to
manœuvring, and attempts to oust the Army of Northern

Spotsylvania. May 8-21, 1864.

Virginia from its position by a flank movement. It is
painfully apparent that no gain can be made by continuous
hammering here. He orders his trains to Chancellorsville,

and heads the left of his army for Spotsylvania Court-House. Warren is to lead and march by the Brock road upon that place; Hancock to follow; Sedgwick and Burnside to march on roads leading in the same direction from Chancellorsville.

Warren's advance was unfortunately delayed by a blockade of the roads and by some opposition of the enemy's cavalry. The trains of so large an army can not be speedily or quietly moved. Lee soon became aware that Grant was about to shift his ground and divined that it would be either towards Spotsylvania or Fredericksburg. Longstreet was ordered to protect Spotsylvania.

By a lucky accident for him Longstreet started so as to reach the place before Warren. A summary attack might have brushed him away. But our troops were weary and by no means in high spirits. So Warren waited for Sedgwick. Before the latter's arrival, night had fallen. Hancock had been kept back some hours by Meade, lest Lee should attack our rear, May 8. which Meade thought not unlikely. As a consequence of all these mishaps, Lee had managed to plant himself athwart Grant's path.

The Army of the Potomac files into line in front of Lee's position, — in order from the right, Hancock, Warren, Sedgwick, Burnside. One of the first misfortunes on this fatal ground is the death of May 9. gallant Sedgwick. Wright succeeds to the command of the Sixth corps.

Hancock is ordered to make a demonstration south of the Po, but is withdrawn without accomplishing any result. The loss is severe. Although probably too late to turn the enemy's left, the manœuvre, having been begun, should have been pushed home. Towards evening two assaults are made on a position in Warren's front. It can not be carried, even at a loss of five or six thousand men. Further on the left Upton does manage to effect a lodgment. But unsupported he can not hold it.

May 10.

Up to this moment Grant's hard blows have punished only the Army of the Potomac. Lee is neither Pemberton nor Bragg. Grant has met his match in all but material resources.

Among Grant's qualities is wonderful staying power. Up to a certain point this is one of the highest virtues of a soldier. But it can be pushed too far. Grant is altogether too blind to the advantages of combining manœuvring with direct assault. He can not believe that Lee has even greater endurance than himself; that the Army of Northern Virginia can longer resist his masses. He has yet to learn how tough is the grain of that wonderful body of men.

May 12.

An attack in force upon the centre is or-dered. Hancock, in two lines of columns of regiments, at early dawn, assaults the Confederate posi-tion, where the first line is thrown out in a salient. The troops rush over the intrenchments with a cheer, capturing four thousand prisoners and many guns. But the second line still remains. It too must be taken. The elated men, without pausing to re-form, push forward, intent upon the fruits of victory. But our loose-strung lines are met by the enemy with serried ranks, and break against their wall of steel. A countercharge hurls us back to the salient. With extreme difficulty these works are held, the Sixth corps sustaining Hancock's right.

Grant, who by this stubborn defense has got the impression that Lee has weakened his right and left to sustain his centre, orders an immediate attack by Warren and Burnside. Though stoutly made, each fails with grievous loss. Lee determines to recapture the salient at any sacrifice. Five distinct assaults are made during the day. The defences are taken and retaken again and again. The breastworks are alternately crowned by the rival flags. For twenty hours the tide has surged doubtfully to and fro. Our loss this day has been eighty-five hundred men.

Grant might readily flank the enemy out of his position. But he can not give up the contest. He will not yield to Lee. He knows him to be vastly his inferior in men, and will not believe that he can not be crushed by weight alone. For a week after he makes partial attacks at all points, shifting divisions from place to place along the line, seeking a weak point in the harness of the Army of Northern Virginia through which to thrust his weapon. Lee meets his every onset. No impression can be made.

The assailant labors under the disadvantage of attacking intrenchments. To offset this he is able secretly to mass his men and attack a single point, while his enemy must keep all portions of his line equally manned until he divines where the blow is to fall. To attack without studying your opponent's position is to throw away this manifest advantage, to refuse to add skill to mere strength of arm.

In this short campaign of little over two weeks, Grant has

lost thirty-six thousand men in casualties, nearly one in three of his " for duty " force. He has accomplished nothing which manœuvring could not have compassed, unless he has weakened the *morale* of his antagonist more than he has his own. This he has not done. The Army of Northern Virginia is elated at its successful defense. The Army of the Potomac is disheartened at its losses with so little tangible result.

But for all that, the courage and sense of duty of our brave old army are unshaken. It knows that the hopes of the nation are in its keeping, and not a weak heart beats in its ranks.

Courage is a common virtue in the soldier. That combination of physical and moral courage which enables a general to inflict and unflinchingly to resist heavy blows is the rarest and best. But this courage must be tempered with skill to be of the greatest use, and skill implies a discreet use of power. Though it was Falstaff hiding behind his shield at the battle of Shrewsbury who exclaimed that the better part of valor is discretion, yet there is, for the commanding general of a great army, a far deeper meaning in these pregnant words.

May 21. Failing to make any impression by hard blows, Grant again issues orders to move by the left — straight on Richmond.

XXXIX.

THE MINOR ARMIES.

DURING all this heavy fighting, the like of which has not been seen since Borodino, the minor armies were coöperating towards the general goal.

Sheridan, with the cavalry corps, started on a raid around to the west of Richmond. May 9. At intervals he measured swords with Stuart, with uniform success, for he largely outnumbered him. Finally after much destruction of roads, bridges, and material of war, he turned up on the James river, where Butler's army lay, and from thence rejoined the Army of the Potomac. May 25.

Butler, with his new command, moved to City Point and Bermuda Hundred, and in- May 4. trenched. His instructions were vague. When Grant, in his overland march, should reach the vicinity of Rich- mond, Butler was to coöperate from this point and move so as to lean with his left upon the James beyond the city. This plan appears weak because Butler's rear would thus be quite at the mercy of Beauregard, who was certain to approach from North Carolina, as Gilmore had been withdrawn from there to join the Army of the

James. Without the possession of Petersburg and the line of the Appomattox, there was no safety whatever in Butler's position.

But the capture of Petersburg was, strangely enough, no part of Grant's plan at this time. He perhaps thought that Lee could be annihilated before the vicinity of this city was reached. And before Butler himself saw the necessity of so protecting his rear, Beauregard had reached the place and Butler's demonstrations against it became useless.

May 7.

May 13.

Butler now moves toward Richmond. The enemy's line extends from the river at Drury's Bluff westerly. We purpose to attack. But Beauregard is again too quick. He plans to break Butler's right and seize his communications. The attack falls heavily on the centre, but meets with no success. A dense fog prevents intended combinations on both sides. A diversion from Petersburg against the Army of the James fails. But Butler is none the less compelled to withdraw, for his position is compromised.

May 16.

He has in this battle of Drury's Bluffs lost four thousand men to Beauregard's three thousand. He retires to Bermuda Hundred. Here, as Grant expresses it, he is "bottled up," and the greater part of his force is ordered to the Army of the Potomac, while the rest remains to hold a footing on the James.

The other force coöperating with the Army of the Potomac from the Valley, consisting of Crook's Kanawha Army and Sigel's troops, were under command of the latter. The work cut out for this command was to destroy the railroads in the Valley so as to cut Lee from his communications with the West by way of the East Tennessee Railroad and from his source of supplies in the Shenandoah.   Sigel lay along the Potomac;   Crook in the Kanawha region.

The latter was the first to get to work, and debouching into the Valley he and Averell did some excellent work in demolishing the railroads.

May.

Sigel moved southward about the same time, but suddenly brought up against Breckenridge at New Market.   Here he suffered a sharp defeat, and retired to the line of Cedar Creek, where he was superseded by Hunter.

May 15.

May 26.

This general again moves up the Valley, and runs across Imboden at Piedmont.   In a smart combat he defeats the enemy, capturing one thousand five hundred prisoners, and occupies Staunton.   Crook and Averell now join him, making his effective some eighteen thousand men.   Four days later he reaches Lexington, and should have at once advanced to Lynchburg.   But delays supervene and when he does leave Buchanan to march towards this key of the Valley, he finds that he is too late.

June 5.

June 8.

June 12.

June 16.

Lee can by no means afford to lose Lynchburg.   Breckenridge occupies its defences in force, and Early is hurried from Cold Harbor to strike the Valley in Hunter's rear with Jackson's old corps.

But first Early throws his troops into Lynchburg.   Hunter assaults, but is thrust back, and retires, followed by Early, who is so placed

June 18.

as to be able readily to cut off Hunter's line of retreat down the Valley. Hunter, who is entirely out of provisions, determines to retire by way of the Kanawha, where Crook has left a supply-camp at Meadow Bridge. But on reaching the place he finds that a skilful guerilla-raid has destroyed the depot. Luckily, a train of supplies reaches him at Gauley River. From here Hunter moves around the mountains to the upper Potomac. The march is full of difficulties.

June 27.

Sheridan had been sent out from the Army of the Potomac to work in unison with Hunter, but he could not successfully cope with Early, and he returned to White House, after considerable interchange of hostilities with the enemy and a loss of not far from one thousand men.

The coöperation of the Valley forces with Grant's main army had thus been summarily cut short, in part by ill luck and in part by Lee's clever dispositions.

XL.

AGAIN BY THE FLANK. — STALEMATE.

G RANT'S flank operations were uniformly well conducted. They exhibited skill in conception and execution, and commanded success which his favorite method of
hammering as uniformly failed to compass when his opponent
was his equal. The orders after Spotsylvania were for
Hancock to withdraw from the right, and,
marching behind the other corps, to push
towards Bowling Green. Lee was not slow to divine the
movement, but was too weak to attack during its prosecution.

May 20.

To meet the threatened danger, however, he started
Longstreet on the parallel turnpike in the same general
direction. When Warren followed Hancock, Ewell followed Longstreet; Wright and Burnside
brought up the rear, Hill followed suit.
As a result, the roads being somewhat shorter for Lee,
when the Army of the Potomac reached the North Anna, it
descried the Army of Northern Virginia
drawn up to welcome it on the opposite side.

May 21.

May 23.

Our left column under Hancock strikes the North Anna
near the railroad crossing; Warren, with the right, at
Jericho Ford. The latter finds his passage undisputed and

crosses some troops at once. On the other side he has a
sharp exchange with the enemy, the result of which is to
capture one thousand prisoners. Hancock finds that the
enemy occupies a bridge-head and some strong field-works,

May 24.   formerly erected, on the other side. He
forces the passage at considerable loss, and
puts his corps across.

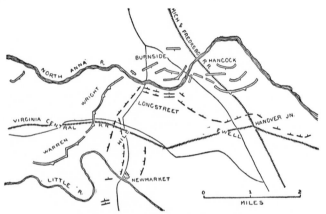

North Anna. May 23-26, 1864.

Lee's position is masterly. His centre is thrown forward
and holds the river. The wings form an obtuse angle, with
their flanks well supported on difficult natural obstacles.
Burnside attempts to force a crossing at the centre but quite
without success. Hancock is across on the left. So is
Warren on the right. But each is separated from the centre
by the river, and from the other wing by Lee's army. A
more complete stalemate can not be imagined. There
is not even a chance to hammer, unless Lee should now

assume this rôle. But Lee is wise enough to refrain. He is better suited with Grant's pursuing this policy.

The Army of the Potomac must again withdraw. At night, speedily but cautiously, the Second corps acting as rear guard, the operation is carried out. A wide easterly circuit is made to strike the Pamunkey.

May 26.

While the army was at Spotsylvania, its base had been at Fredericksburg. On moving to the North Anna, the base was transferred to Port Royal. It will now be established at White House, on the York river.

No time is lost. The order of march is systematically carried out. The entire army reaches Hanovertown next day and crosses the Pamunkey. But Lee is again on hand, facing north-easterly and covering the line of the Chickahominy.

May 27.

Grant develops his position by reconnoissances. From Hanovertown there are direct roads leading to Richmond. These Lee defends with his entire force. It is evident that only a hard struggle, or the cleverest tactics, will dislodge him. His position can not well be broken, and Grant again moves across Tolopotomoy Creek and towards Cold Harbor.

May 28.

Lee does the same, and his interior lines enable him to excel the speed of the Army of the Potomac.

Lee is of course glad to have Grant bear the brunt of attack. Grant has been steadily playing this part. But an effort can be made so to manœuvre as to make Lee attack. Opportunities are not wanting. To match Lee in skilful movements, if we can not break him down by fighting, is indeed an honor worth the seeking.

The two armies are on the old ground. Gaines' Mill is close by. Singularly enough, each army occupies the position its opponent held at the beginning of the Seven Days. But we are now the assailants. Two years ago it was Lee who forced the fighting. He had not then to husband his means so stingily. Now he can afford to fight only when pushed, or when the advantage is manifestly his.

XLI.

MORE BLOOD. — COLD HARBOR.

SHERIDAN with his cavalry has seized Cold Harbor, a centre of roads of great value. The Sixth corps is despatched from the right to this point with orders to hold it. Meanwhile General Smith, with sixteen thousand men from Butler's force, has arrived and is ordered to coöperate with Wright. Lee has divined the manœuvre and has moved Longstreet to the same cross-roads. Wright and Smith are forced to drive him out of a commanding position beyond Cold Harbor at a loss of two thousand men before they can secure the place. But the roads are held. Hancock moves to the left of the Sixth corps ; Warren remains on the right, with Burnside in support. Sheridan protects the lower fords of the Chickahominy, and the roads towards White House.

Grant is impelled to try one more blow. His faith is yet strong that he can break Lee's lines by sheer momentum. This might still be possible if he would call to his aid the resources of grand-tactics. He ought to seek the key of his enemy's position and mass his assault there. But, unlike the Army of the Potomac, he has not learned the wonderful vitality of Lee and his veterans. Orders

June 2. are once more issued to attack along the whole line at 4.30 A.M. on the morrow.

The want of definite plan is painfully apparent. Skilful manœuvring might more than once have placed Lee where he would have to be the assaulting party or forfeit his stake. New Bridge over the Chickahominy could have been seized at this very time with this result.

Grant in his despatches stated that Lee would not come out of his intrenchments to fight. But Grant had never tried the proper means to make him do so. In lieu of moving upon Lee's communications and thus compelling him to leave his works for the open, Grant had constantly hurled his men against field-works which he should have learned, by the experience he had recently been through, that he could not take. Grant's method was just what Lee preferred. He was right in not coming out of his intrenchments to fight.

Moreover an "assault all along the line" was useless. To obtain advantages from the great loss of life which was inevitable, the dominating point of the line should have been developed and the assault massed there. No reserves were apparently ready to follow up any advantages which might be gained. The extreme care in arranging details which should have been exercised was not to be seen. No picked troops were selected for the heaviest work. The orders were only for "an assault all along the line." The rank and file did not even know Cold Harbor was to be a battle. The old method of selecting your point of attack, picking your troops, and properly supporting them, is by no means obsolete. But Grant did not deem its use advisable.

Within a few moments of the appointed time this general assault takes place. Out of the grey dawn, eighty thousand men rush forward upon the enemy in his intrenched lines, meet a bloody repulse, and retire to cover themselves with such works as they can most speedily erect to hold the advanced ground which some of them have gained. The assault has failed in a brief ten minutes. All the

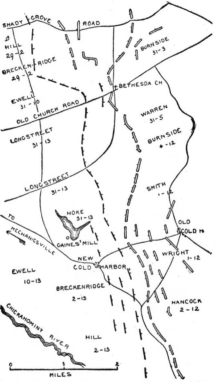

Cold Harbor. May 31-June 12, 1864.

fighting is over in less than an hour. Six thousand men have fallen. The enemy has lost but a tithe of this number.

It would have been proper on this day for Grant to ask a truce to bury the dead and care for the wounded who lay between the lines.

It was not pleasant to acknowledge defeat; but it was

the part of humanity. And no great military necessity called for the continuance of the battle for the succeeding four days. But during all this time the wounded lay upon the field. Many perished from hunger and exposure.

Grant at first proposed to himself to take the position by regular siege approaches. But he soon abandoned this idea and reverted to the old plan of a transfer of the Army to the James.

The object of Grant's overland campaign was to capture or to destroy Lee's army. He had done neither. But he had lost sixty thousand men in five weeks without inflicting corresponding loss upon the enemy. The Second corps alone had lost four hundred men a day, from the time of leaving the Rappahannock. The full significance of this is apparent when the force of each army at the inception of the campaign is called to mind. Grant had numbered one hundred and twenty-two thousand men ; Lee some seventy thousand. This fearful loss was the result of assaults in mass undertaken without the aid of that skill which Grant knew well how to employ, though he neglected to do so. Whenever Grant resorted to manœuvring, he succeeded measurably. Whenever he attacked all along the line, he failed utterly. "Turenne," says Napoleon of the campaign of 1655, "constantly observed the two maxims : first, Never attack a position in front when you can obtain it by turning it; second, Avoid doing what the enemy wishes, and that simply because he does wish it. Shun the field of battle which he has reconnoitred and studied and more particularly that in which he has fortified and in-trenched himself."

The theory has been advanced that there had to be about so much hammering, about so much loss of life, and consumption of energy and material, before we could hope to end the war; that so long as the South had any men or means, the struggle would continue. There is a groundwork of truth in this. The Confederacy was practically exhausted before it yielded.

But the corollary is likewise true. If the South would certainly succumb when exhausted, it behooved us, on merely humanitarian grounds, to fight on conditions so nearly equal as to inflict the same loss upon the enemy as we ourselves must suffer. This had not been done. And the student of this final campaign in Virginia looks in vain for the master-stroke by which our forces, numbering two to one of the enemy, could compel the surrender of the Army of Northern Virginia without losses to us greater in number than the total effective of that gallant body. Lee undoubtedly was fighting at a great advantage, on interior lines, in his own State, on the defense. But how was he overmatched in force!

Criticism can not depreciate the really great qualities or eminent services of General Grant. His task was one to tax a Bonaparte. That he was unable to put an end to the struggle by means less costly in lives and material, if not indeed by some brilliant feat of arms, can not detract from the praise actually his due for determined, unflinching courage. It rather adds to the laurels of Lee. It cannot be asserted that any other Northern general could here have accomplished more against the genius of this soldier. And it was Grant who, in the face of the gravest difficul-

ties, political and military, was able to hold the confidence
of the nation and to prevent that party at the North, which
was clamoring for peace, from wrecking our success now
all but won.   But his truest admirers, indeed he himself,
admit Cold Harbor to have been a grievous mistake.   And
all who appreciate at its solid worth Grant's ability as a
leader, regret that, in this great struggle with Lee, he
should have failed to employ the full resources he so abun-
dantly possessed.

XLII.

SHERMAN LOOKS TOWARDS ATLANTA.

WE have seen three parallel columns, west of the Alleghanies, slowly working their way southward from the Ohio river into the heart of the Confederacy. The Army of the Tennessee had hugged the Mississippi. The Army of the Cumberland had advanced with varied success and failure along the railroad from Louisville to Nashville and thence to Chattanooga, branching off for a while to Shiloh and Corinth, where its identity was merged, for the moment, in the great body there manœuvring under Halleck. The Army of the Ohio had left Eastern Kentucky by way of Cumberland Gap, and had long had its head-quarters at Knoxville. In the winter of 1863-4 these armies were commanded respectively by Sherman, Thomas and Schofield, under the supreme control of Grant.

When, towards the end of 1861, the Department of the Ohio was first created and Buell was placed in command, his forces had been known as the Army of the Ohio. A year later the Department of the Cumberland was created for Rosecrans, and Buell's old army, now advanced to Nashville, became the Army of the Cumberland. Later still, the Department of the Ohio was narrowed to Eastern Kentucky and Eastern Tennessee, and the troops in the new command received the old name of Army of the Ohio.

Opposite Thomas, at Dalton, Ga., lay Joe Johnston, now devoting himself to the personal command of Bragg's old army. For this and the army of Northern Virginia were then the sole forces on which the South could rely to save the Cause from its threatening doom, if saved it might be. Longstreet, until ordered back to the Army of Northern Virginia, confronted Schofield.

Sherman, who had rejoined McPherson and Hurlbut at Vicksburg, was commissioned to capture Meridian, in Eastern Mississippi, and destroy the railroads there centering. This work he accomplished in so thorough a manner that the State of Mississippi was rendered harmless for interference in the campaign immediately to ensue. He was severely held to task by the Southern press for what were termed his ruthless methods of warfare. But Sherman was a soldier, and when he had work to do, he did it without fear, favor, or affection. An instance of unnecessary cruelty or destruction of property by him has yet to be substantiated. After the Meridian campaign the bulk of Sherman's force was rendezvoused at Huntsville, Ala., to join in the great onset towards Atlanta.

February 3, to March 6, 1864.

Sherman assumed command of the above named three armies upon Grant's appointment as Lieutenant-General, and to McPherson fell the command of the Army of the Tennessee. Joe Johnston still lay at Dalton.

Grant and Sherman had agreed to act in concert. While the former should thrust Lee back upon Richmond, his late lieutenant was to push Johnston towards Atlanta. And Banks was to transfer his forces from New Orleans to Mobile and thence move towards and join hands with the Western armies.

Sherman devoted his earliest energies to the question of transportation and railroads. Baggage was reduced to the lowest limits, the higher officers setting the example. Actual supplies and fighting-material were alone to be carried. Luxuries were to be things of the past; comforts to be forgotten. War's stern reality was to be each one's lot. Probably no officer in such high command ever lived so entirely from hand to mouth as did Sherman and his military family during the succeeding campaigns. The entire equipment of his army head-quarters would have shamed the shabbiest regimental outfit of 1861.

Spring was to open with a general advance. It was agreed to put and keep the Confederates on the defensive by a policy of constant hammering.

May.

Bragg had been removed to satisfy public opinion in the South, but was nominally called to Richmond to act as Mr. Davis' chief-of-staff. Johnston, as commander of the Department, had personally undertaken to hold head against Sherman. But the fact that he possessed neither the President's good will nor that of his new adviser, militated much against a happy conduct of the campaign.

Sherman's forces held a front twenty miles long in advance of Ringgold, just

May 6.

south of Chattanooga. McPherson and the Army of the Tennessee was on the right with twenty-five thousand men and one hundred guns. Thomas and the Army of the Cumberland held the centre with sixty thousand men and one hundred and thirty guns. Schofield and the Army of the Ohio formed the left wing. His command was fifteen thousand men and thirty guns. This grand total of one hundred thousand men and two hundred and sixty guns formed an army of as good stuff as ever bore arms, and the confidence of the leader in his men and of the men in their leader was unbounded.

Johnston himself foresaw the necessity of a strictly defensive campaign, to which his far from sanguine character as well as his judgment as to what the existing conditions demanded, made him peculiarly suited. Counted after the same fashion as Sherman's army, Johnston had some sixty-five thousand men. Recognizing the difference in the strength of each, and knowing that Sherman must follow the railroad, Johnston was wise in adopting this Fabian policy. He could divine what Sherman's general strategy must be. The tactics of each manoeuvre he could meet as occasion offered. He was able to calculate his task, and he acted accordingly. He intrenched every step he took; he fought only when attacked; he invited battle only when the conditions were largely in his favor. Subsequent events showed how wise beyond his critics he could be.

XLIII.

SHERMAN MOVES ON ATLANTA.

SHERMAN took the measure of the intrenchments at Dalton with care, and though he outnumbered his antagonist, preferred not to hazard an engagement at such odds when he might force one on better ground. This conduct shows in strong contrast with Grant's, when the latter first met his opponent at this same moment in Virginia.

Sherman despatched McPherson towards Resaca, on the railroad in Johnston's rear, with instructions to capture the town if possible. Combined with this flanking movement, a general advance was made upon the Confederate lines, and after tactical manœuvring May 7 to 12.
of several days in front of Rocky Face Ridge, Johnston concluded to retire from his stronghold. McPherson had strangely failed to seize Resaca, though an excellent chance had offered, and at this place the Confederate army took up its new stand. Had McPherson been a trifle more bold, Johnston would have been reduced for supplies and retreat to the poor roads to the east of Dalton; and at the very outset of this campaign might, perhaps, have been seriously compromised.

This was Sherman's first earnest bout with Johnston. The former was by nature eager, sanguine, restless, and venturesome; the latter of quiet, steady nerves, unsuited to attack, unsurpassed on the defense. Yet Sherman was to beat him at his own game of patience. Nothing characterizes Sherman's versatile ability more than this.

Sherman faced his antagonist on the line of Camp Creek in front of Resaca, with his right flank resting on the Oostanaula. From this position he operated by unintermitted tapping upon Johnston's defences at constantly varying points, without, however, bringing on a general engagement. The latter, well aware that Sherman could make his position untenable by crossing the Oostanaula below, as indeed Sherman was preparing to do, evacuated Resaca and crossed the river. Sherman speedily followed.

May 15.

Sherman's uniform tactics during this campaign, varied indefinitely in details, consisted, as will be seen, in forcing the centre of the army upon Johnston's lines, while with the right or left he operated upon either flank as chance or ground best offered.

Johnston did not propose to hazard an engagement unless all conditions were in his favor. He attempted a stand at Adairsville, twenty miles south of Resaca, but shortly withdrew to Kingston and Cassville. Each captain manœuvred for a chance to fight the other at a disadvantage. Each was too wary. But either would have welcomed the other's attack in force, if only on his own chosen terms. Johnston, in fact, here issued an order looking to a general engagement, but some dissensions between himself and his lieutenants, Hardee, Hood and Polk, operated to change his mind. Both Hood and Hardee bitterly opposed Johnston's defensive policy. Its expediency appeared later.

Opportunities were not infrequent for an attack on one or other wing of the Union Army, which, from the exigencies of the manœuvring or the march, might become isolated at a distance from the rest of the army. But Sherman had abundant faith in May 18. his lieutenants, and believed that under almost any conditions either of them could hold his own long enough to enable him to bring up his other forces to their assistance. And Sherman was eager for a general action, if only it could be brought about on ground not all too favorable to his enemy. For he desired to weaken the Confederates by the attrition of battle before he forced them in retreat too far from his own base.

From Cassville, Johnston retired across the Etowah. So far this campaign had been May 20. one of manœuvres. Neither combatant had suffered material loss. Like two wrestlers, as yet ignorant of each other's strength or quickness, they were sparring for a hold. Neither would risk giving odds.

Field comforts had been very sparse, but the men had borne their privations cheerily. The example of their superiors and especially the promise of the campaign had made it easy to bear with short rations and the discomforts of the rainy season. And within the enemy's lines, the brave men were accustomed to look upon privation as a daily necessity. Though in this campaign, the Confederate army had in the fertile fields of Georgia an immediate source of supply usually much more rare.

The Union army was growing skilful.   Local difficulties, multiplied many fold by bad maps and hostile population, were overcome in considerable measure by an able corps of topographical engineers.   Their peculiar duty was to accompany the daily reconnoitring parties and furnish detailed information as to the ground on which approaching. manœuvres were apt to be conducted.

The division of engineers under Colonel Wright became singularly expert.   To the enemy fell the duty of destroying as they fell back; to us the task of reconstructing.   Bridges were uniformly burned and railroads wrecked by the retreating Confederates.   To save delays in rebuilding, so far as possible, trestles were fitted in the rear to a scale with interchangeable timbers, so that bridges could be constructed with a speed never before dreamed of.   No sooner had the Confederates put torch to a bridge, than a new one arose as by magic, and the whistle of the locomotive always followed hard upon the heels of the army.

Johnston was never in a better situation for attack than about these days.   For every mile that Sherman advanced, the Federal army was losing in numbers, by leaving detachments to protect its lengthening line of operations. Johnston, on the contrary, was gathering in his own and was daily gaining in effective strength.   If he was to fight, the occasion was good.   But Sherman would give him no opening.

XLIV

ON TO MARIETTA.

MARIETTA was Sherman's next objective. But to advance upon it along the railroad was impracticable. The Etowah river as well as Allatoona Pass lay athwart his path. He had in *ante bellum* days become familiar with this section, and had no mind to force a passage of the river and defile beyond, if he could manœuvre Johnston out of this strong defensive position. He knew that the water-shed between the Etowah and Chattahoochee offered an easier route.

Leaving to his enemy the possession of the railroad east of the Etowah, he put over his army at various points south of Kingston, and moved direct towards Dallas, intending from here to operate on Marietta. Thomas, in the centre, was the column of direction.

May 23.

Johnston accepted the change of route and shifted position to the east of Dallas on the line of Pumpkin Vine Creek. Here the rival armies closed in a struggle of more or less severity, almost rising to the dignity of a general engagement. While Hooker attacked the enemy's lines at New Hope

May 25, 27.

Church, Howard essayed to break them at Pickett's Mills.

We had not as yet been weaned from the old ideas of attack in columns of brigades. The Napoleonic theory of momentum, well suited to the short range musket and open ground, will not work against arms of precision and intrenched field-works. Neither Hooker's nor Howard's columns were able to effect a breach in the enemy's lines; and except once thereafter, at Kenesaw, this formation for assault was abandoned.

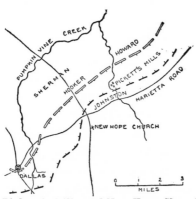

**Pickett's Mills and New Hope Church.
May 25-27, 1864.**

A single line, followed by a second one at a suitable distance, and yet another, proved to be more effective, and saved much loss. This is the origin of the successive slender lines of infantry, each able to take advantage of the accidents of the ground in moving to the assault, that were later employed against the still more accurate weapon of the day.

Our Civil War was full of suggestions as to methods of coping with the rapidly growing destructiveness of small arms and artillery, both on land and at sea. As arms of precision and heavy guns were not at that time perfected, neither did we leave perfect means to the future soldier. But nearly all the changes in the tactical forma-

tions of later European armies had their prototype in
methods adapted by us to the conditions then existing.
American ingenuity is by no means confined to the
machine-shop.

It has been said that, in this campaign, one man behind
field-works proved equal, on whichever side, to three in
attack. Two would be nearer the truth. And every mile
of ground from Dalton to Atlanta was covered with substantial works, erected whenever and wherever either army
halted in the presence of the other.

During this three days' fight along Pumpkin Vine Creek,
Sherman proved Johnston's line too strong to carry by
direct assault. He must resort to his old tactics and turn
Johnston's right. For this purpose he withdrew his own
right wing piecemeal towards his left. Johnston seized
the opportunity himself to attack during this
manœuvre. But he was repulsed in good   May 28.
style by Schofield.

For a month the troops had now been unceasingly under
fire. Nothing more nearly approaching a general engagement than New Hope Church and Pickett's Mills had been
brought on, but Sherman had suffered a loss of fifteen
hundred killed and seven thousand five hundred wounded,
and Johnston a similar loss of five thousand five hundred.
Contact with the enemy had never ceased. Skirmishing
had been severe and incessant, and the troops were kept
on the alert every minute of the time. But the health of
the army remained excellent.

By Sherman's movement towards his left, the Army of
the Cumberland and the Army of the Ohio had forced

themselves into a position in which they enfiladed a salient in Johnston's line. The latter once more deemed it expedient to retire to a new position nearer Marietta, between Lost, Pine and Brush Mountains and in advance of Kenesaw. Sherman followed him sharply up by a movement towards his left; Schofield standing fast, while Thomas and McPherson passed in his rear. The new disposition threw Schofield on the right, Thomas in the centre, and McPherson on the left. Johnston opposed it with Hardee on the left, Polk in the centre, and Hood on the right.

By this flank operation Sherman reached and reëstablished his line along the railroad; the supply-trains quickly appeared, and a new base of supplies was set up at Ackworth. Thus ended the first stage of this campaign.

June 6-9.

If Sherman had exhibited great vigor and patience in pushing Johnston back, so had Johnston shown wonderful dexterity in parrying Sherman's powerful lunges, and in preventing an antagonist of such superior strength from opening a weak spot in his harness.

The forces had been about as three to two.

XLV.

MARIETTA.

ALLATOONA is now made a secondary base from which operations against Johnston may be conducted.

During this entire campaign Sherman sought constantly to compel his antagonist to an open field engagement, sure that his heavier battalions would carry the day. With praiseworthy shrewdness Johnston as constantly declined. The open ground to the east of Marietta again tempted Sherman to move by his left in the hope of bringing Johnston to battle. But, inasmuch as an eastward movement might afford Johnston too ready an opportunity to strike at his line of communications, which such a direction would somewhat uncover, Sherman determined to forego his purpose and to operate by his right instead.

This campaign resembles a bout with the foils. Both fencers are in guard. Sherman is constantly at play with his weapon, disengaging, cutting over, beating, lunging, using every art to draw into action his antagonist. Johnston warily follows every disengagement, skilfully parries each lunge his strong-armed adversary makes, with an occasional cautious *riposte*, which in turn is invariably countered. Johnston constantly retires, Sherman as constantly advances. At every retrograde movement you expect Johnston to make a return assault. But it never comes. Nor can all Sherman's skill find the weak side of his guard, or an opening through which he can manage to plant his button squarely on his breast.

The rains had been continuous and heavy. Only those acquainted with the soil and streams of the South appreciate the full meaning of this statement. By the utmost energy only could artillery be moved, or supplies and ammunition be distributed to the troops. The lines had been laboriously advanced close to the enemy's works and a partial demonstration upon his front was begun. The situation promised serious pounding.

Sherman gives the word. Thomas throws the Army of the Cumberland upon the enemy's position ; Hooker gallantly assaults, but is foiled by the intrenchments at Pine Mountain, while Cox makes a partial lodgment in the line near Gilgal. The fire on the advanced posts is irritating in the extreme. Blair effects a breach in a part of Hood's works. The latter retires behind Noonday Creek. Again on the morrow Hardee withdraws his left to a new set of previously thrown up intrenchments, followed smartly by Sherman's right.

June 14.

June 15.

June 17.

Johnston's line is weakened by several salients which the successful issue of the partial attacks of the last few days have left. He is on the point of falling back, when Sherman launches Howard's corps upon him, and quickens his retreat. The new Con-

June 19.

federate works are nearer Marietta, with Hardee on the left,
Hood on the right, and Loring (temporary successor of
Polk) holding Kenesaw in the centre.

Since the first of the month there has been an uninter-
rupted downpour of rain.   All the streams are swollen, and
the artillery and wagon trains fairly engulfed.   Movements

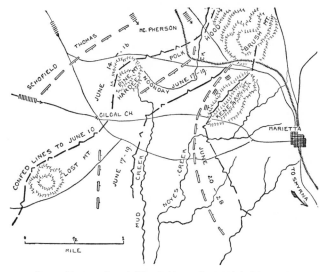

Operations about Marietta.   June 14-28, 1864.

are correspondingly slow.   The question of supplies becomes more than troublesome.   The long line of operations
is in danger of being cut.   Several Confederate raids have
already interfered with the communications, though skilful
management has quickly repaired the damage.   And it is
not feasible to cut loose from the rail, owing to the impossibility of using the country roads for heavy amounts of
transportation.

June 19.

The left is advanced, while the entire army prepares for attack, moving by the right. This manœuvre is continued to such a point as to seriously

June 20–21.

jeopardize Johnston's left.   Hood is consequently transferred from the right to the extreme left.   No sooner on the line, than, fretted with inactivity, he rushes like a hound unleashed upon Hooker and

June 22.

Schofield, in an effort to regain lost ground. But he is handsomely met.   His impetuous onslaught is repulsed with a loss of a thousand men, our own being slight.

XLVI.

KENESAW.

SHERMAN had left no stone unturned to bring on a general engagement upon favorable ground. But wily Johnston had never afforded him an opportunity to fight unless he was behind field-works too solid to promise aught but fruitless slaughter. Johnston would not be drawn into the open. Since Hood had been transferred from the right, however, the defences at Kenesaw were not so fully manned.

Inaction would not do. Sherman must choose either to move about Johnston's left, which the bad state of the roads scarcely warranted, or else to break through his lines. Failure to take some decisive action would allow Johnston time to operate seriously against our communications. Sherman decided to try once more the fortunes of assault, and selected for the attempt the bluffs of Kenesaw, as the key of the situation.

Schofield makes a heavy demonstration on the right to draw troops, if possible, away from Kenesaw. In so doing he is able to seize some advanced ground which compromises the security of Hood's

June 26.

left.   This he defends by a strong redoubt.   At the same
time an attack in force is ordered to be made on Kenesaw.
McPherson entrusts the details of his front to Logan, who
presses in with M. L. Smith and Walcutt.
June 27.
Howard pushes Newton forward in column
from his front, and Palmer sends in Davis on Newton's
right in like formation.   Hooker is in reserve.   Meanwhile,
on the right, Schofield supports this onset by pushing his
advantage against Hood to the utmost, with the railroad
south of Marietta as a goal.

The attack on Kenesaw has been preceded by general
artillery fire; and the columns advance with confidence.
But, as was demonstrated a month ago, heavy masses are
found useless against intrenched lines and rapid musketry.
Newton and Davis both fail to effect a lodgment, but with
obstinate gallantry each holds and intrenches a line within
a few hundred feet of the works from which they have
recoiled.   Smith carries and holds the skirmish pits, but is
brought up standing against the works of the line.

The enemy has quickly comprehended that the real
attack is against the key of their position at Kenesaw, and
so soon as the first rush is over, and the works still remain
theirs, the lines are at once reinforced and all chance of
success is past.

The loss has not been as great as might have been expected.   Our own adds up about three thousand men;
the enemy's barely five hundred.   Whether the works
could have been carried by a sturdier onset is uncertain.
But the days of massed columns are numbered.   Their
weakness has now been doubly proven.   The only gain

has been by Schofield on the right. The enemy has won the battle of Kenesaw Mountain.

It has been alleged that the impossible nature of the task made the assault on Kenesaw unjustifiable; and the loss of life has been characterized as mere wilful slaughter. It is difficult to answer such criticism. But if it has any weight, what can be said of Fredericksburg or of Cold Harbor? Who shall decide upon what is justifiable in war? What, indeed, becomes of the art of war itself? Must not all swords be forthwith beaten into ploughshares and all spears into pruning-hooks? The same criticism has been passed on other soldiers — notably on Gustavus Adolphus for his assault on the Alte Veste. But Gustavus was in the right, and so was Sherman.

The rainy period now came to an end. The roads again began to harden. Sherman saw that his advantage lay in moving around Johnston's left, as he could now with less danger leave the vicinity of the railroad. Johnston began to fortify Atlanta and make new lines to defend the Chattahoochee. For this purpose he employed large bodies of negroes, always fortifying positions in the rear to which he could withdraw at will. McPherson was moved to the right of the army, as the first step in a new flank march. But Johnston did not wait; he evacuated Marietta. Thomas at once advanced July 1-2. through the town, while McPherson moved on Turner's Ferry, obliging Johnston to defend the crossing.

The casualties in June had been seventy-five hundred men, of which fifty-five hundred were from the Army of the Cumberland. This meant a daily loss of some two hundred men in the constant bickering at the advanced posts.   Johnston's may have been five thousand men. The habit of both contestants had been to intrench the skirmish as well as the main line.   Every advance on either side called for the capture of field-works.

The only great physical obstacle now in Sherman's path is the Chattahoochee.   Beyond this lies Atlanta.   But his problem is a grave one.   To cross this river in face of an enemy intrenched and well equipped is no simple matter.

Johnston had spent a month on his *tête de pont* at the main Chattahoochee crossing.   But he could not presume to hold it beyond a few days, for he was exposed to being turned out of it by Sherman's putting over a part of his force above or below to move on Atlanta, while observing Johnston with the balance.

July 7.   Sherman, after some days, discovered an unused crossing above the railroad near Soap Creek, and passing over a few regiments, intrenched a bridge-head on the east bank.   Other fords above were utilized, and the cavalry kept up a constant demonstration below to distract the enemy's attention from the operations up the river.   Rousseau was despatched on a cavalry raid south of Atlanta.   Stores were accumulated at Marietta.

July 9.   Johnston now entirely withdrew from the west side of the Chattahoochee.   Sherman, after long deliberation, made ready to cross his army by the left around the north of Atlanta.   By this means he might, after seizing the railroad, intercept any reinforcements which should be sent from Virginia.   In this movement,

Thomas was to cross and establish the Army of the Cumberland as the new right, and press towards Atlanta; while McPherson was to pass in his rear and manœuvre towards the left, breaking the railroad at Decatur. Schofield was to follow and fall into line in the centre.

Some Southern historians claim this entire campaign from Dalton to Atlanta as a Confederate success. Johnston " had brought his army to Atlanta after inflicting a loss upon the enemy five times as great as his own; and he had performed the almost marvellous feat of conducting a retreat through a difficult and mountainous country more than a hundred miles in extent without the loss of material or of a single gun. Gen. Johnston held Atlanta more firmly than Lee held Richmond. Sherman was unable to invest the city, and to withdraw he would have to pass over a single road, one hundred and thirty-five miles long, traversing a wild and broken country. Johnston held him, as it were, suspended for destruction. The situation was brilliant for the Confederates." [Pollard.] It does not appear that such deductions from the facts do Johnston the justice he deserves for the very able conduct of the campaign now soon to close. To allow Sherman the credit due him for exceptional skill and vigor certainly throws Johnston's defense into higher relief.

The situation of the Confederate army was far from brilliant. The advantage was with the Federals.

XLVII.

GRANT'S CHANGE OF BASE.

WE last saw the Army of the Potomac when it was about to leave the fatal ground on which Cold Harbor had been fought. Let us return to it.

Gradually moving successive corps from the right, Grant extended his left down towards the crossings of the Chickahominy. Warren seized Long Bridge, crossed, and demon-

June 11. strated along all the roads leading towards Richmond, in order to mislead Lee. Hancock pushed his corps over the same bridge towards the James. Burnside and Wright crossed lower down and

June 12. marched to Charles City. Smith had already moved by water from White House to Bermuda Hundred, whence he was sent out to seize Petersburg

June 15. with his own and other troops.

The Army of the Potomac reached the James in two marches, and, with a day's delay, was put

June 14–15. over to the south side. Lee had not been slow to discover Grant's purpose, and, pursuing the same policy as heretofore, he followed on parallel roads and crossed the James, near Drury's Bluff, one day later than Grant put over his troops below.

The City of Petersburg acts as an advanced fortress to protect the communications of Richmond with the interior. It is a strategic point of the greatest value. No operations on the James can be secure without its possession.

But neither Hancock, who was first ordered forward from the Army of the Potomac in the direction of the place, nor indeed Meade, appears to have known that Grant intended that Petersburg should be at once captured. Specific orders had not been issued to this effect. Smith had taken the outer works, but had not followed up his success, though opposed only by militia. Hancock should at once have been sent to finish the operation; but the orders eventually issued did not reach him in season, and before he was prepared to act, Lee had already thrown some old troops into the city.

June 15.

Even then an immediate assault gave some promise of success. But Hancock's dispositions had not sufficient vigor to command a satisfactory result.

Burnside now comes upon the ground. He and Hancock twice assault the enemy's lines, with some gain of ground, but without material result. Their loss is four thousand men. A third attempt is made, but still fruitlessly. Lee retires to the interior lines. The losses in these four days aggregate eleven thousand four hundred men.

June 16–17.

June 18.

The Second and Sixth corps are now ordered to extend their lines to the left so as to gain ground well south of the town, and towards the Weldon Railroad. During this manœuvre, the Second corps, on the extreme flank and in the thickets, moves so far beyond the Sixth that it opens a gap between the two corps. Into this gap Hill,

June 22.
wide awake for a chance to check our advance, immediately thrusts a force, taking both exposed flanks in reverse, and captures a number of guns and some seventeen hundred prisoners. The extension has proven costly.

Sheridan was out on his expedition in aid of Hunter's march on Lynchburg. In his absence Wilson and Kautz, with their cavalry divisions, were ordered to operate against the Weldon and Southside railroads. These are Lee's two important lines of supply. Moving in light order these officers proceeded on their task, reached their objective and destroyed a large amount of rolling stock, track, and other property.

June 22–July 2.
Wilson on the return trip got rather roughly handled by the enemy's horse, near Reams' Station, and suffered largely in casualties and prisoners. The damage inflicted to the railroad was not of a permanent nature.

There was now no hope of carrying Petersburg by assault. The losses had reached sixteen thousand men. Regular siege operations must be resorted to.

The army was not in good condition for any severe work. It needed recuperation, if any army ever did. In a little over six weeks sixty-two thousand men, out of one hundred and twenty-two thousand with which it left the Rappahannock, had fallen in their tracks. The drain had been particularly severe in experienced officers. To be sure, these rents had been to a certain extent patched by reinforcements; but they were none the less appalling. It was no longer the proud Army of the Potomac.

Nor do these figures cover all. The casualties of the Eighteeenth corps and the Army of the James had been ten thousand men besides. The forces now about to lay siege to Petersburg had lost in battle over one-half of their effective strength in this short space of time.

Success might have justified this awful sacrifice. But there had been no success for the Army of the James. Still less had there been for the Army of the Potomac. Its every manœuvre had been checkmated; its every attack repulsed. No wonder that its confidence had begun to ebb.

But there was work in it yet if called out in the right way. All that it needed was to know that the reason was good, and it was ready for any effort. The American volunteer was too intelligent not to recognize when blood-shedding had gone too far, and too independent not to show his conviction. But his courage would not let him turn his face from work to which he had once put his hand.

XLVIII.

PETERSBURG. — THE MINE FIASCO.

PETERSBURG was not besieged. It was only observed. All its lines of communication were open. Its defences began far beyond Grant's extreme left, and extended round to the Appomattox. From the further side of this river the works continued northward so as to keep the Richmond and Petersburg Railroad safe from the attacks of Butler, who was still at Bermuda Hundred; and from a force under Foster at Deep Bottom on the north bank of the James.

Grant could operate against Richmond at pleasure, while observing Petersburg. Or he could organize a force to act as a flying column against the railroads west of the latter place. The second plan would interfere with Lee's supplies, and was the most dangerous thing both for the Army of Northern Virginia and the Confederate capital. For to procure supplies was already Lee's hardest problem.

By a variety of movements Grant could keep Lee on the *qui vive*. But meanwhile, some weeks must

July.

be spent to perfect a system of works in which the army could defend itself from sorties by the enemy.

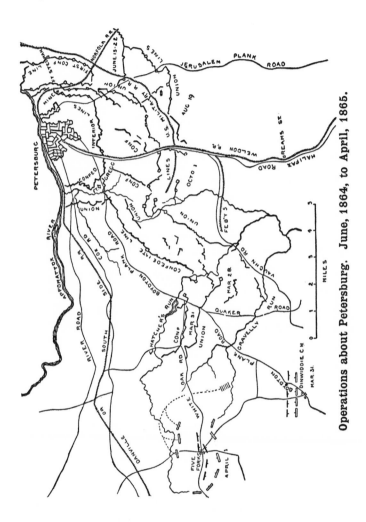

Operations about Petersburg. June, 1864, to April, 1865.

In the prosecution of this work, Burnside had run a mine under one of the Confederate forts in his front. It was determined to fire this mine and to follow the explosion by an

assault, in the hope that the crest beyond, which dominated the city, might be carried by the troops.   Hancock, with his corps and two divisions of cavalry, had been across the
James river on an expedition against the de-
July 26–29.
fences of Richmond, which, though it had failed, had drawn a large force from Petersburg to check it. The time was opportune.

But the dispositions were not careful.   The storming column, which should have been chosen from the best stuff of the army, was actually selected by lot from among the divisions in the immediate front of the mine.   These were by no means the best, and the actual column of assault contained poor material and was not well led.   No special instructions were issued.   There was no *place d'armes* on which the men could speedily deploy for the attack after filing out of their intrenchments.   No community of action was apparent.   All the preparations were wanting in skill and care.

The mine was exploded early in the morning.   Heavy
artillery fire had silenced the enemy's guns in
July 30.
the surrounding forts.   But in lieu of the storming column taking advantage of the surprise by a rapid advance, it debouched slowly from its position, and far from rushing for the crest to be captured, sought refuge in the crater made by the exploded mine !

More troops were pushed in only to make the slaughter-pen more bloody.   The enemy was not long in recovering from his astonishment and began to pour a heavy artillery fire into the crater.   A few partial charges were headed by some of the more courageous officers in the *mêlée*, but no

semblance of efficient work was done. It was purely a
case of bad management and worthless leadership. The
mass extricated itself as best it might with a loss of four
thousand men. The preparations had been such that nothing short of failure could well ensue.

XLIX.

WASHINGTON IN ALARM FOR THE LAST TIME.

THE opposing forces in front of Petersburg at this time had dwindled to much smaller proportions. They numbered about seventy-five thousand on the Union to fifty thousand on the Confederate side. But their purpose was none the less set.

Hunter's eccentric retreat had offered the enemy an excellent chance to resort to the old Washington scare, for the Valley was defended by only Sigel's small division.

July 1.   Early is accordingly instructed to force his way into Maryland. Sigel retires from his front across the Potomac at Shepherdstown. Early

July 3.   confines him to Maryland Heights, and moves around his flank to Frederick.

July 7.   Early has fifteen thousand veterans, just fitted for the work. There is nothing of any moment to withstand him, but General Lew. Wallace assembles a motley force of hundred-days' men and militia, and boldly plants himself athwart Early's path.

Ricketts arrives opportunely in Baltimore, for Grant, on

July 8.   receiving the news of the invasion, has at once hurried the Sixth corps by water to

the capital.   The Nineteenth corps, from Fortress Monroe, has taken the same direction.   Wallace, and Ricketts with two brigades, at Monocacy Junction make a
gallant stand to cover Baltimore, losing seven

July 9.

hundred men killed and wounded, and then retire to Elli-cott's Mills, to oppose Early's advance on the capital.   But the Confederates push on to the gates of
Washington without serious loss.

July 11.

At this moment Early's vanguard might easily enter the city.   For Washington has for its defense not much else than citizen-soldiery, improvised from department clerks and non-combatants.   But seeing the fortifications of the capi-tal well-manned, Early imagines that troops from the Army of the Potomac are on hand, and delays his attack to make proper disposition of his corps.   This delay is fatal. When he actually moves to the assault, the Sixth and Nine-teenth corps have put in their appearance,
and his one chance of making the most
brilliant stroke of the war has vanished.

July 12.

Early ruefully retires by way of the Valley.   Lee's di-version has not budged Grant from Petersburg, and has therefore failed of its main purpose.

Hunter reappears at Harper's Ferry before Early gets well back to the Valley.   Wright is also on his heels.   It seems as if Early might, in his turn, be trapped.   But he slips from between these corps, suffering only from a cavalry attack by Averell, while he repels
one by Thoburn.

July 15-20.

At Strasburg, Early's retreat ends.   Not so however his activity.   A few days later Crook crosses swords with

July 24.

his forces at Kernstown, on the same ground where Shields had defeated Jackson. But the result is different. Crook loses twelve hundred men and is driven back upon the Potomac.

McCausland again crosses the river with a body of Con-

July 29.

federate horse. Couch makes a show of defending Chambersburg, but McCausland occupies the town and levies a contribution of $500,000 upon it. In default of payment of this sum, which cannot be raised upon the instant, the Confederate leader deliberately puts torch to the town.

This act was utterly indefensible, for Chambersburg had committed no overt act of war.

From here McCausland escapes to West Virginia, while our infantry forces are marching purposeless hither and

August 7.

yon. At Moorfield he encounters Averell, who in a smart combat inflicts heavy loss upon him, but cannot prevent his escape.

L.

ATLANTA.

THE Richmond government had become alarmed at the results of the inaggressive policy of Johnston. Able as had been his retreat in the face of Sherman's heavier battalions, retreat was the last thing which the Confederacy and its foreign policy demanded. A bolder front and more fighting seemed strategically desirable, — politically essential. So judged at least the Southern President and his Chief of Staff, Bragg.

Mr. Davis was a West Pointer, and while he had no personal experience in war, he believed military affairs to be his strong point. He certainly interfered constantly in the conduct of the Confederate campaigns, and often with disastrous results.

Hood had all along been critical of Johnston's Fabian tactics and was *par excellence* a fighting general. He was accordingly put in command in Johnston's stead, though, it is claimed, with reluctance on his part. It was expected that he would show what aggressiveness could accomplish.

Hood was certainly a stanch soldier, but his bravery exceeded his discretion. He could not brook delay. He was impatient in method; and his whole war creed was summed up in the belief that a well-planned attack driven home can shatter any obstacle. He was the very reverse of Johnston, — every inch a fighter, but lacking Johnston's cool calculation and singular absence of flurry. The one quality necessary to oppose Sherman's restless activity was the power of waiting. This Hood had not. What made Lee so great was that he had both this quality and the added power of striking a blow often marvelous when the small weight of his army is considered.

Johnston had already prepared to fall upon our forces as they filed into line along Peach-Tree Creek. Hood, on acceding to the command, decided to carry through the plan of his late chief. Stewart's (late Polk's) corps was on the left; Hardee's in the centre, and Cheatham's (late Hood's) on the right. His line lay in a semi-circle about the north suburbs of Atlanta.

So soon as the Army of the Cumberland has passed the Chattahoochee, it falls into position as a pivot on which the rest of the army shall wheel into line, and soon gains a foothold south of Peach-Tree Creek, — a very formidable obstacle, — with three heads of column. Meanwhile Schofield and McPherson are executing their delicate manœuvre of passing Thomas' rear and filing into line on his left. Owing to the broken nature of the ground they are cautiously feeling their way to their appointed places.

July 17-18.

July 20.

Hood, whose scouts keep him well informed of all that is going on, proposes to push a column in between these two and Thomas, and to fall in force upon the latter before his

associates can come to his assistance.   The character of the
terrain separates the several detachments of the Federals
and opens a gap of dangerous proportions in the centre of

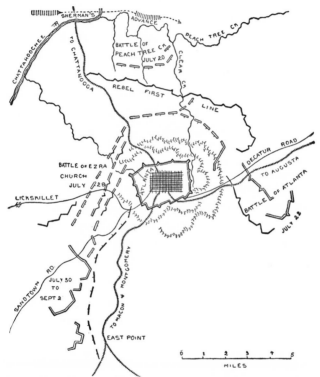

Operations about Atlanta.   July 17-September 2, 1864.

our line.   Into this gap Hood thrusts Hardee with a heavy
force.   This general falls upon Newton at
Clear Creek and on Ward, Geary and   July 20.
Williams.   His intention is to force a general engagement
while Sherman is getting into line.   This is a moment of

great danger at all times for an army in the immediate presence of the enemy.

But McPherson has marched with more expedition than
Hood expects. The sound of heavy firing between him
and Thomas quickens his stride still more. He drives his
vanguard sharply in upon Hood's right flank. To meet
this inopportune diversion, Hood is forced to call for Cle-
burne's division from Hardee's corps. So considerable a
drain cripples Hardee in his onslaught on the Army of the
Cumberland. Hood has only done the essential. Had he
paused, McPherson might have moved into Atlanta unopposed. But Hardee, thus weakened, cannot
July 20.
wrest any ground from sturdy Thomas. The
first aggressive tactics of the new general have been foiled,
with a loss of perhaps double our two thousand.

The armies of the Cumberland and Ohio now unite upon
a new line nearer Atlanta. A strong hill is seized and fortified by Leggett's division, from which the city can be plainly
seen. Hood withdraws into his main Atlanta works.
The siege begins by another advance of Thomas and Schofield, while the engineers are bridging the river, and heavy
guns are coming to the front.

McPherson has extended the extreme left around to a
point southeast of the city. Hood, still determined to carry
things with the strong hand, assigns the task of dislodging
him to Hardee. This general, familiar with the ground,
makes a circuit of McPherson's exposed flank before the
latter has fully completed his field-works, and falls upon his
rear. In the confusion McPherson is killed.
July 22.
Logan assumes command. The troops,

hardened to surprises, face steadily about and receive the
enemy from the other side of their breastworks. Cheatham again assails them upon their new rear, intending to
coöperate with Hardee. Again the breastworks are reversed and a cheerful defense offered, for the stout-hearted
troops of the Army of the Tennessee are not easily discon-
certed, even by surprises such as these.

Hardee and Cheatham are attacking at right angles to
each other and do not readily work together. Their assaults, if simultaneous, would have been fatal to the Federals. But McPherson's old soldiers, though hard put to it,
repulse each foe in turn. Our loss has been three thousand
five hundred; the Confederate, much heavier, was never
officially reported.

In after days Hood passed serious criticism upon Hardee's
conduct of this battle of Atlanta, but without justice.
Hardee had behaved with unusual discretion and skill. He
had simply met his match.

Hooker was senior to both Schofield and Thomas. He
was in a measure entitled to succeed McPherson. But his
peculiarities made Sherman fear that he would not find in
Hooker a cordial support, coupled with such deference to
his judgment as supreme control demands. Howard was
appointed to command the Army of the Tennessee. Hooker
sullenly retired and Slocum was given the Twentieth corps
Sherman thus retained lieutenants who were in warm sympathy with his plans, and able to second him in their efficient conduct.

The railroad had been finished to the rear of the Army of
the Cumberland. So far Sherman's manœuvre around

the north of Atlanta did not promise success.

July 25. He reconsidered the situation and proposed to try an operation on the west and south of the city, instead of the one now going on on the north and east. From the new side he might wrest from Hood the Macon Railroad, a manifest advantage. Stoneman was sent on a raid towards Macon, and Howard was withdrawn from the battle-field of Atlanta to the extreme right.

Hood had been placed in command to fight. He had fought — boldly and skilfully, but so far with most disastrous results. But to fight was the condition on which he held command. He determined to attack Howard on the march

July 28. over towards the right, and to repeat the tactics, topographically reversed, which he had employed against McPherson. Advancing along the Lickskillet road he fell upon Howard at Ezra Church. But again he was repulsed, with a loss much exceeding our own, which was about a thousand men.

Sherman's troops have acquired the instinct of victory. They are almost invincible. Hood's vast waste of life, without gain of any kind, goes far towards vindicating Johnston's defensive policy.

Schofield moved upon the heels of Howard and speedily got into line. Sherman's purpose was to hold the bridgehead at the Chattahoochee, and swing the entire army upon that pivot into position west and south of Atlanta. Hood began to see that his tenure of Atlanta depended on a slender tie. So far his fighting policy was barren. Good speed enabled Sherman to anticipate him in the possession of

Jonesborough, south of the city a dozen miles. Attacking at a venture, Hardee was here repulsed by the Army of the Tennessee.

Schofield was meanwhile engaged in destroying the railroad between Jonesborough and Atlanta. Hood ordered Hardee out to drive him back, as a last means of holding the city. Sherman endeavored to surround Hardee, and a serious combat resulted. The loss on each side was about two thousand, but we captured fully that number of prisoners.

September 1.

Unwilling to be cooped up, an event which he now could not but foresee, Hood reluctantly evacuated Atlanta and moved towards Macon. The Army of the Cumberland at once occupied the city, while the Army of the Tennessee remained at East Point, and the Army of the Ohio held Decatur. A season of rest and preparation for the new conflict ensued.

September 2.

It is difficult to gauge the relative losses of the opposing armies during the campaign from Chattanooga to Atlanta. The Union forces outnumbered the Confederate on the average probably as ten to seven, if the muster rolls of both are estimated in the same manner. Sherman captured thirteen thousand prisoners all told.

Hood manifestly understated his losses. He placed them at five thousand two hundred and fifty men, while Hardee claimed himself alone to have lost seven thousand during Hood's command. It is asserted that Sherman buried not far from four thousand Confederate dead during this campaign. There is some duplication here no doubt. But the War Records, which are as exact as careful comparison can make them, give the Confederate losses in killed and wounded, from May 7 to September 1, as twenty-two thousand four hundred, to which number the prisoners are to be added. The Union losses during the same period were nearly thirty-two thousand men.

LI.

A PROTRACTED SIEGE.

FOR many weary months, while Sherman was battling for Atlanta, the Army of the Potomac was detained by Lee at the portals of Petersburg. The uniform success with which he managed to check every attempt of Grant to break or turn his lines became monotonous. But these failures must be described in their proper sequence, though they had no immediate effect on the whole result. It was the gradually growing exhaustion of the resources of the Confederates which was our strongest ally.

Another diversion against the lines of Richmond, north of the James, was attempted by Hancock. Crossing as before to where Foster held his August 12-21. lodgment at Deep Bottom, he advanced out beyond Malvern Hill, in the hope of finding some favorable point of attack. But Lee reinforced the troops on the east of Richmond almost as soon as Hancock arrived, and in a combat at Bailey's Creek, followed by desultory skirmishing for several days, prevented our forces from gaining any ground which could be held. The command returned to camp with a loss of fifteen hundred men.

About the same time Warren conducts another operation

against the Weldon Railroad. A foothold is effected on this road after a smart action at Yellow Tavern, in which we lost a thousand men. Lee, unwilling to forego the use of any part of this line, makes strenuous efforts to recover its possession by a number of stout attacks, but Warren is not to be dislodged, and intrenches the position. What he has gained, however, is at a sacrifice of forty-three hundred men. The scale on which some of these operations are conducted necessitates heavy work and serious losses.

August 18–21.

On his return from his expedition north of the James Hancock pushes rapidly out to the left of Warren to supplement the latter's efforts. He destroys the railroad to Reams' Station, and the cavalry operates beyond his left towards Dinwiddie Court House. Hancock has with him Miles' and Gibbon's divisions, some eight thousand men. Lee detaches A. P. Hill against him. Hill assaults with his usual vigor, and is favored by his intimate knowledge of the ground. The conduct of all but Miles' force and the cavalry is of the weakest character, and the upshot of the entire movement is a retreat by us with a loss of twenty-seven hundred men. The whole operation has been disappointing in the extreme.

August 25.

A few weeks of rest now supervene. But Grant is not content to remain long quiet. His continuous hammering has its valuable side. His tendency is always towards great activity. An attack in force on the right is this time projected, to sustain which a diversion on the left is undertaken by Warren with

Sept. 30–Oct. 5.

Parke and Gregg. Ground is gained and intrenched beyond Peeble's Farm. Loss three thousand.

Butler meanwhile has been operating against the defences of Richmond, and has actually captured and held Fort Harrison, against a number of strong efforts to recover it. His loss has been September 28-30. heavy. Beyond this the movements on the right appear to be attended with no success and are shortly abandoned.

But before settling down to winter-quarters Grant was desirous of dealing one more serious blow to the enemy, in the hope that some permanent gain could be made with which to close the year. He again decided for a movement by the left in sufficient force to break in the Confederate right, and to seize the Southside Railroad, on which Lee depended for most of his supplies. The force consisted of the bulk of three corps. Warren and Parke (now commanding the Ninth corps) were to attack the extreme right of Lee's line in front, while Hancock should by a circuit seize the Boydton Plank Road October 25-28. and the railroad.

Warren and Parke struck Lee at Hatcher's Run. Parke assaulted in front while Warren endeavored to turn the Confederate right. Parke fell short of accomplishing his aim, upon which Meade ordered Hancock and Gregg to halt on the Boydton road so that Warren and he might coöperate. But before these two corps could reach each other, so as jointly to attack Lee's flank, the latter thrust A. P. Hill into the gap between them.

Moving through the wooded country, with the ease bred of perfect familiarity with every path, while our troops blunder about in utter ignorance of their own or the enemy's whereabouts, Hill suddenly falls upon Hancock's flank. The attack has well-nigh come to a fatal pass, when Egan changes front and pours his volleys into the rear of Hill's column. Unable to hold his own, Hill summarily withdraws.

Gregg has, meanwhile, been skirmishing on Hancock's front and left, and has made good headway against the enemy's horse. But, though our losses are seventeen hundred men, and the troops have all done creditable work, the result has been renewed failure to make any satisfactory gain of ground.

For several months to come nothing in particular was undertaken except along the regular lines. But before winter set in, Warren made one more expedition down the Weldon Railroad, of which he destroyed eighteen or twenty miles, much to the annoyance of Lee, to whose already serious difficulty in obtaining supplies this break greatly added. For it materially increased the length of his wagon-haul from the point where stores could be unloaded south of the break to the Richmond and Petersburg lines.

December 7-11.

Still another of the ineffectual manœuvres by the left was made during the winter by the Fifth corps and the Second, — now commanded by Humphreys, — accompanied by Gregg's cavalry, against the Southside Railroad. The Second corps moved upon the right of the enemy at Hatcher's Run while the Fifth marched around their flank. Next day the two corps joined hands on either side of Hatcher's Run, at Dabney's Mills, and Gregg came up from Dinwiddie.

February 5-7, 1865.

But the enemy are proof at all points.   They have spent many months in devising means to resist an attack from every imaginable quarter, and are prepared to act decisively on the spur of the moment, while our troops must grope blindfold over unknown ground.   Lee contrives to out-flank our line.   Warren loses fifteen hundred men; but we gain ground as far as Hatcher's Run.

This uniform failure of movements by the left was dis-heartening to a degree.   Lee's defences had been made impregnable to front attack and extended far to the west of Petersburg.   And his interior communications enabled him at any moment to detach heavily from his centre to check any operation against his right.

It had become evident that Petersburg could not be taken, or the enemy's hold on Richmond compromised, by a continuance of the policy pursued so far.   It is not im-probable that Grant might have made more headway by leaving a sufficient part of his army in the trenches in front of Petersburg and by moving with a heavy force far to the west upon Lee's communications; or, if it were deter-mined to capture the place *à main forte*, by making a massed attack upon some point in the centre after suitable mining operations had weakened Lee's defences and pre-pared for such an operation.

But the end was to come with opening spring.   To the far-sighted, this was no longer doubtful.   The South must succumb to the greater material resources of the North, de-spite its courage and its sacrifices.

Hancock was unable to resume command of the old Second corps.   His history is that of the Army of the

Potomac.   None of the corps-commanders in Virginia whose names are household words have earned their laurels by sounder, better work than he.   That he never rose to the command of a separate army was due solely to circumstances.   He was too necessary to the Army of the Potomac to be allowed to leave it.

Hancock was one of the most cheerful men under fire we ever had.   In the thickest of the fight, his appearance and manner infused a singular confidence in the troops.   He was an uniform favorite, rarely made a mistake, and always finished his work in good style.   His is an enviable record among the great names of the war.

LII.

SHERIDAN IN THE VALLEY.

EARLY, after the failure of his raid on Washington,
had retired into the Shenandoah Valley. His presence there was a constant threat, and it was evident that
Lee had no intention of recalling him. The Sixth and
Nineteenth corps, of which Grant had sore need at Petersburg, were thus kept from their legitimate duty for the
protection of Washington. Grant therefore determined to
make a clean sweep of the Valley and if possible prevent
further use of it by the Confederates for campaigning purposes.

The division of our forces in Northern Virginia into
petty independent commands had up to this time wrought
only mischief. Grant saw that at least one vigorous campaign must be conducted there under a
single head. He selected Sheridan for the   August 7.
task, and promised to give him sufficient force to do his
work full justice. This promise in due time took the
shape of the Army of the Shenandoah, and consisted of
forty thousand infantry and a superb body of fifteen
thousand horse.

Sheridan had never yet enjoyed a separate command.

Whatever operations had been his to conduct had shown him to possess brilliant powers. He was now entrusted with an army destined for a service of equal importance and delicacy. For some weeks he exhibited great caution, due in part to Grant's unwillingness that he should strike out beyond his depth, and in part to his own appreciation of the fact that in his front lay an old and wily tactician, who, though commanding a much smaller force, had both audacity and skill, and the keenest tools to handle.

Sheridan adopted Hunter's position at Halltown, in the angle of the Potomac and Shenandoah. Of this he resolved to retain firm hold, whatever his manœuvres. He first moved towards the line of the Opequon.

August 10.

Early retired to cover Winchester, for the reinforcements promised him by Lee were still on the way, and he must keep a clear road open for them. On his arrival at Fisher's Hill the reinforcements began to come in, under Kershaw, with Fitz-Lee's horse. These forces were commanded by Anderson, who was senior to Early by commission. Some slight friction thus engendered worked tardiness in the Confederate plans.

Grant imagined that Early's force might have been increased to forty thousand men, and advised Sheridan, who was at Cedar Creek, not to attack. In consequence the Army of the Shenandoah was retired to Berryville.

August 17.

Early followed, but could not advance further north without uncovering his rear. Some manœuvring, however, resulted in Sheridan letting go Berryville and retiring again to Halltown, while Early demonstrated on Shepherdstown as if again to cross the Potomac.

But Lee must have men, and again with- September 14. drew Anderson. Early retired behind the Opequon. Quiet reigned for a fortnight.

In all this manœuvring, during which each general was gauging the skill of his opponent, the losses had been but a few hundreds on each side, in occasional skirmishes of the outposts. Now that Early had been weakened by the loss of Anderson, was Sheridan's time to " go in," as Grant tersely formulated his orders.

Early's position along the Opequon protects Winchester and at the same time threatens an incursion into Mary- land ; while Sheridan lies in such a position Mid-September. back of the stream as to threaten Early's communications if he should move in the latter direction.

Early's first manœuvre is to operate by his left towards Martinsburg. Nothing loth, Sheridan crosses the Opequon and advances straight on Winchester, to September 19. strike Early's right while his left is at a distance. But delays often incident to the movement of troops in battle enable Early to recall his left and save him- self from a crushing blow. Sheridan has twice Early's force. It is noon before he is ready to attack. When his lines advance they meet with a warm reception. But numbers tell. Except for a temporary check on the left, due to the impetuosity of Early's attack, the Army of the Shenandoah carries everything before it. Sheridan throws his cavalry upon Early's flanks. By nightfall, despite the utmost gallantry, Early is driven from the field, in broken ranks, with a loss of thirty-six hundred men, half of which are in prisoners.   Our own loss is five thousand.

This battle of the Opequon, or "Winchester," saved Maryland and Pennsylvania from future invasion.

Early retired to Strasburg, where he could rest his flanks on the heights and the north fork of the Shenandoah.   His

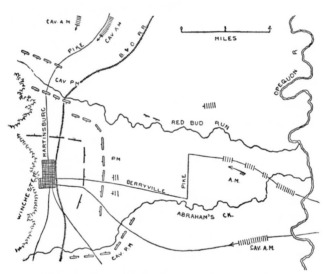

Opequon, or Winchester, Va.   September 19, 1864.

position at Fisher's Hill appeared stronger than it actually was, for these obstacles could be turned by a superior force.

September 22.   Sheridan soon put in an appearance and despatched Torbert's cavalry by Luray to Newmarket to seize the upper end of the Valley in Early's rear.   But before awaiting results he attacked the

enemy in his chosen position, throwing Crook in force
around his left.

By evening
Crook got into
place and moved
in upon Early's
flank and rear,
while the Sixth
and Nineteenth
corps assaulted
in front. Stout
resistance availed
Early naught.
He was broken,

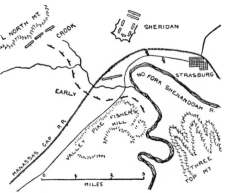

Fisher's Hill. September 22, 1864.

and retreated in much disorder. Our loss was only
five hundred men; Early's one thousand two hundred.
Torbert did not get in Early's rear, being held at Milford
by an insignificant cavalry force of the enemy.

Sheridan pursued Early up the Valley. The latter made
a stand at Mt. Jackson, but was driven from
the place and retired through Newmarket.   September 24.

Lee had ordered Kershaw back to Early, on hearing of
the disaster at the Opequon, and Early moved towards Port
Republic to join force with him. Sheridan marched to Harrisonburg. Torbert made for Staunton, where he began to
tear up the railroad, but was interrupted with
work half done by Early.   September 28.

Grant believed that Sheridan should now advance toward
Lynchburg and destroy the railroads and the James River
canal. Sheridan objected that his line of operations would

be too long, and would take a full corps to protect, and suggested, in lieu of Grant's plan, the devastation of the Valley so as to render it useless to the enemy as a campaigning ground ; after doing which he could rejoin the Army of the Potomac with the bulk of his force.

October 6.

To this suggestion Grant acceded. Sheridan commenced his return march, and while retracing his steps he utterly destroyed grain, forage, barns, agricultural tools and material of all kinds over the entire breadth of the Valley, collected and drove off the stock, and left that section a desolate waste.   Some two thousand barns and seventy mills filled with grain were thus destroyed, He then fell back and took up position along Cedar Creek.

The destruction of provisions, forage, or any supplies which could enable the enemy to protract the struggle was no doubt justifiable.   It is very questionable, however, whether the burning of barns, agricultural implements, and means of future thrift not applicable to the conduct of an immediate campaign comes under the same head.   Such destruction is not considered defensible by the best authorities.   Nor does it appear to have been essential, for a new crop could not have been raised for many months.

Sheridan did not expect to be followed up by Early ; but the latter again put his divisions afoot towards the old ground as soon as the Army of the Shenandoah retired.

On the home march, Torbert, with Merritt and Custer,

October 9.

crossed swords with the enemy at Tom's Brook, capturing eleven guns.

Early reached Strasburg, and again reëstablished himself at Fisher's Hill.   From here he pushed out a sharp reconnoissance of our position, at a loss of three hundred men.

October 13.

The Sixth corps had been recalled, and was actually on its way out of the Valley. Upon the return of Early it was again brought back. Sheridan started for Washington to consult with the authorities as to the best course to pursue, leaving Wright in command.

Early was soon out of supplies. The Valley was no longer a granary for the Confederates. He must fight for his rations or fall back. He planned a surprise of the Union Army at Cedar Creek. Crook, with the Eighth corps, lay on the left; Emory's Nineteenth corps held the centre; the Sixth corps under Ricketts, with the cavalry of Custer and Merritt, formed the right. Crook was covered by Averell's horse, but insufficiently.

Gordon cautiously moves about the Union left, under cover of the night and foggy dawn. Kershaw is to make a heavy demonstration on the Union centre along and south of the turnpike as a feint to cover Gordon's march.

Advancing with the utmost silence, even leaving canteens behind, lest their clatter

October 19.

should disturb the Federal camps, Gordon passes Cedar Creek, moves well around Crook's flank, and falls with Southern vehemence upon his left and rear. The onset is entirely unexpected. Crook's corps is at once demoralized and soon utterly broken up in confused retreat. Gordon cheerily follows up his gain and soon draws into the vortex of defeat the centre under Emory. The only sound member of the Union Army is the Sixth corps. Ricketts succeeds in making a rapid change of front and falls upon Early, checking his onset till the Eighth and Nineteenth corps can reach some place to rally.

An attempt to re-form is made at Middletown, but it is futile. A second stand, a mile and a half farther back, is more successful. Wright patches up the line upon a nucleus of Getty's division, which this gallant officer has rallied on the pike. The troops have recovered their bearings. The stampede has not quite demoralized them. Early makes no impression by a smart attack.

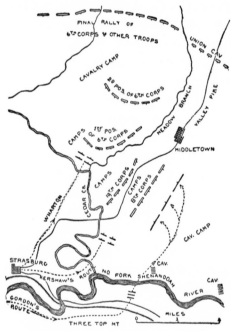

Cedar Creek. October 19, 1864.

Sheridan opportunely arrives upon the field. His magnetic presence caps the structure already built. Wright is placed on the left; Emory on the right; Crook in reserve. Merritt and Custer with their horse fall in upon the right and left flanks. It is 4 P.M.

A general advance is ordered upon the Confederates, who now approach flushed with victory, but disorganized withal. The first onset bears Early back. He has nothing to oppose to the heavy numbers of the Federals. Sheridan sweeps the field. The enemy is broken, routed, driven in as wild confusion up the Valley as we had just fled down.

Early's loss was twenty-nine hundred ; ours fifty-six hundred, including seventeen hundred prisoners, which the Confederates got quickly to the rear after the morning's surprise.

Early next turned up at Newmarket, where he remained three weeks.

October 20.

Sheridan withdrew for readier supplies to Kernstown. Early again followed, loth to acknowledge his defeat, and indulged in a needless combat with our outposts. This was the end of the drama. The bulk of both the Confederate and Union forces was ordered to Petersburg.

November 13.

The Battle of Cedar Creek finished forever the Valley campaigns. Sheridan had forces vastly outnumbering his opponent. But his handling of his troops, especially the cavalry, was handsome, and the work done was crisp and clean. The forces on either side were nearly forty thousand men under Sheridan to less than half the number under Early.

The Confederate general never recovered the *prestige* lost in this Valley campaign. And yet he had fought bravely, skilfully. But he was overmatched in numbers and found himself opposed by equal skill. Success could not well be expected.

Except some operations in Loudon County against the guerilla Mosby, no further hostilities were attempted in Northern Virginia.

Sheridan was a typical soldier. Men who love fighting are rarely the best generals. A distinguished example of this was Charles XII. The keen enjoyment of the fray does not often coexist with the power of cool calculation and of intense mental effort essential to the commander of an army. But it did in Sheridan. It is hard to say whether he was best fitted to command a cavalry corps or an army. In either capacity he excelled. Wherever Sheridan appears in the annals of the war it is in stemming an adverse tide with a vigor almost unequalled, or in leading victorious troops to certain triumph.

We cannot try him in the same balance as we try Stonewall Jackson, though he has some of the latter's traits ; for Jackson won his important successes with scant material, and almost invariably against odds, while Sheridan's means were always ample. But his methods were sharp, clear, exact; and his power over men equalled his capacity as a soldier. His is a case of *nascitur, non fit.*

LIII.

HOOD TAKES THE OFFENSIVE.

LITTLE rest was to be allowed to Sherman after his arduous labors in the capture of Atlanta. His line of operations was now one hundred and forty miles longer than it was at Chattanooga, and liable to interruption at any moment. Coöperation by Canby from Mobile had been part of the summer's programme. But Canby's forces had been depleted by details, and he had not yet been able to capture Mobile.

Sherman made his dispositions to remain in Atlanta. He contracted his lines for easier defense, and deemed it essential to remove the non-military residents. This course gave rise to a terrible outcry at the South, and some adverse criticism at the North. But the act was entirely justifiable as a military measure; and the necessity for the removal must be held to have depended upon his own sole discretion. Sherman extended all possible help to the departing inhabitants in the matter of rations and transportation.

After consultation with President Davis, Hood now planned to operate seriously against Sherman's communications. Our army had largely lost in numbers by fur-

loughs, sick and wounded, and the time was opportune.
Wheeler and Forrest were sent out to open the affair by a

Aug.–Sept.   raid upon the railroad in Sherman's rear.
But their efforts had no serious results.

Sherman cannot mistake Hood's purpose. But he does
not propose to be ousted from Atlanta. Thomas is sent
back to Nashville, and about the same time Hood
moves northward. Sherman is not to be called off his
quarry by any ordinary threat. He cautions Thomas to
keep a keen lookout for any attempt to cross the Tennessee,
and leaves Slocum to hold Atlanta. Howard still commands the Army of the Tennessee, and Cox, during the
absence on political affairs of Logan, commands the Army
of the Ohio.

Hood marches on Marietta. He has no doubt that he
will draw Sherman away from Atlanta and transfer the
seat of war to the Valley of the Tennessee.

October 4.   The Army of the Cumberland repasses
the Chattahoochee and reaches Smyrna. It
is difficult for Sherman to divine Hood's immediate purpose, but he has no idea of letting go what has cost so
much.

October 5.   A detachment of Hood's army attacks
Allatoona, but is repulsed with heavy loss.

October 12.   Sherman's forces are concentrated about
Rome. Hood pauses at Resaca, but shortly
moves to Dalton. But for the continued possession of
Atlanta it would almost seem that nothing had been gained
by the galling summer's work.

Hood's campaign does not, however, promise immediate

great results.   Sherman proposes to keep all he has won,
and no serious break has as yet been made in his communications.   He has absolute confidence in the solidity of
his position.   He asserted later that, if Hood had entered
Tennessee, he could have surrounded him and compelled
the surrender of his entire force.

The bulk of the Union army in pursuit
of Hood reaches Gaylesville, Ala.   There October 19.
are absent only the Atlanta and other garrisons along the
line of the railroad.

LIV.

HOOD MAKES FOR TENNESSEE

FOR some months Sherman had contemplated and had been urging upon Grant a march from Atlanta to the seaboard, during which he should destroy all munitions of war, cotton, crops, factories and machine-shops, tear up railroads, and render the country useless to the Confederacy as a means of continuing the struggle. It seems to be well settled that the plan was of his own conception. And he urged it many months before it secured a willing ear.

His objective would be Columbia, S.C., at which point he would be in rear of Lee at Richmond, and could throw his forces into coöperation with Grant's. But before he could march on Columbia, he must establish a new base upon the seaboard. If his manœuvre should prove successful he would, by isolating Virginia from all the Southern States except North Carolina, deal the virtual death-blow to the Confederacy.

Two general postulates only were a part of the problem. If Lee should turn upon Sherman, Grant must so follow him up as that between them they could destroy him. And Thomas on his part must use up or neutralize Hood.

It was a bold game, this marching away from Hood

while the latter was trying to lure Sherman back to the line of the Tennessee by threatening his communications. If Hood had crossed the river near Sherman's army, the latter might have been seriously compromised by failing immediately to follow him, for he was not yet ready to cut loose from his base. But when he saw that Hood kept south of the Tennessee until he reached Decatur, Sherman's mind was made up.

Schofield, Stanley, and half the horse were sent back to Thomas, and A. J. Smith, then in Missouri, was ordered to Nashville as a further reinforcement. These, with some recruits, swelled Thomas' ranks to a point enabling him successfully to cope with Hood. And Thomas was the man for the task. Somewhat too deliberate, almost indeed lacking the power of assuming the initiative, when he did move, it was with the stride of a giant; when he struck, it was the blow of a battering ram. And on the defense he had never yet met his equal.

After the capture of Atlanta, Governor Brown had furloughed the Georgia militia, which had been called out to make temporary headway against the ruthless invader. He had alleged, as a reason for thus disbanding them, the pre-eminent necessity of gathering the crops. There had been much friction between Hood and Hardee and the latter had been ordered to the coast. There was no force to oppose Sherman's march to the eastward.

Beauregard had been placed in command of the entire military division, including Hood's territory, but with a caution not to interfere with the latter's field operations. Wheeler's cavalry alone was to stay behind to watch

Sherman, while Hood retained both Forrest and Jackson as a part of his column.

Hood's effective was about fifty-four thousand men. He expected, by crossing the river at Tuscumbia or Decatur, to draw Sherman back to Nashville. His attempt to pass at Decatur was successfully resisted. He then moved on to Tuscumbia and effected a

Oct. 29–Nov. 13.

passage. But once on the north side he found himself compelled to sit down three weeks at Florence to accumulate the supplies of which he stood in urgent need. This delay, though doubtless essential, was fatal to Hood's success in this campaign.

The Confederate armies, both in the East and West, were always ready to move with less transportation than our own, partly because they possessed less material and issued rations and equipage more irregularly to the men. Certain it is that the Southern soldier did his wonderfully efficient work on a basis of victuals, clothing, and ammunition which would generally have kept a Federal force in camp, as unfit to move. But even they had sometimes to delay their march for rations.

Meanwhile Forrest raids on Jackson, Tenn., and on Fort Henry, hoping to draw Thomas

Oct. 16 to
Nov. 10.

away from Nashville. But in vain. And Hood is equally disappointed at not having decoyed Sherman from hard-won Atlanta. Beauregard spurs on Hood to a bold initiative. Hood surely needs no spur.

November 4.   Stanley's Fourth corps is concentrated at Pulaski. Schofield joins and assumes com-

mand at that place. His force consists of
the Fourth corps and Cox's division of the   November 14.
Twenty-third corps. Altogether Thomas numbers fifty-
five to sixty thousand men, including Schofield's command.

LV.

SHERMAN ASTONISHES HOOD.

IN due time Sherman cut loose from his communications. He destroyed the railroad in his rear, after
first sending back such portions of his command as would hamper in lieu of furthering
November 12.
his movements. None but the stoutest of heart and limb must follow him on the coming march.

He was now fairly launched on a great strategic manœuvre. The hardihood of this undertaking has been often overrated; its conception and its valuable results cannot be. Sherman himself "regarded the march as a shift of base, as the transfer of a strong army which had no opponent and had finished its then work, from the interior to a point on the sea-coast, from which it could achieve other important results." He "considered this march as a means to an end, and not as an essential act of war." As compared with his progress through the Carolinas, Sherman gauges this march as of but slight importance. It was the result of the entire achievement which made it what it was. The boldness lay in conceiving its far-reaching advantages; not in carrying through the mere details of the progress.

Sherman was by no means certain what point on the

seaboard he should reach; but he made his calculations to meet the Union fleet which was to be sent towards him, in the neighborhood of Ossabaw Sound. He had with him two corps of the Army of the Tennessee, under command of Howard, as his right wing, and two of the Army of the Cumberland, under Slocum, as the left. These troops numbered over sixty thousand rugged veterans, unhampered by sick or off-duty men, with twenty days' rations, plenty of beef on the hoof, about one field-gun per thousand effective, and an excellent canvas pontoon train.

Atlanta Sherman thoroughly destroyed, so far as future utility to the enemy for the creation of war material was concerned. In other respects it was left intact.

His first objective was Milledgeville, threatening both Macon and Augusta on the way. His route lay between the Ocmulgee and Oconee, both of which rivers take their source not far from Atlanta, and flow south-eastwardly towards the coast, joining to form the Altamaha.

Kilpatrick commanded Sherman's horse. His first demonstration was towards Macon, during which he encountered some opposition from Wheeler's cavalry, which was constantly hovering on Sherman's right front.

While Howard's column crossed the Ocmulgee, Slocum, whose wing Sherman personally accompanied, was engaged in destroying the railroad from Atlanta to Augusta as far as the Oconee.

November 18–20.

Beauregard did not long remain silent. The ebullition of his zeal took the form of volleys of telegrams, promises, appeals, threats, addressed alternately to Sherman and to the entire population of Georgia. Anything to destroy or impede the invader. Sherman's sole response was an order that all law-abiding citizens should be protected, but that any person caught damaging roads or engaged in any overt act of war should have his houses burned and his property destroyed as a penalty.

No engagement of serious moment occurred. Walcutt's Brigade had a sharp skirmish with the enemy near Macon,
Nov. 22-28.   suffering the loss of about one hundred men, and Kilpatrick defeated Wheeler in a smart combat at Waynesborough. But Kilpatrick's attempt to release our prisoners at Millen was foiled by their removal.

Leaving Milledgeville Sherman marched on Millen, and
December 3.   here broke up the railroad between Savannah and Augusta. His route now lay between the Ogeechee and Savannah rivers, excepting the Fifteenth corps, which marched south of the former stream. Progress was easy, and no further attack from the enemy was anticipated.

As a permanent interruption of the railroads between Richmond and the Southern States was one of the great objects of Sherman's raid, the work of destruction was accomplished in such a manner as to make it difficult to repair the damage. The rails, after being taken up, were heated in the middle upon bonfires made of the ties, and then twisted around trees or posts in such a manner as to render them useless. And as all rolling-mills were wrecked, no means of re-rolling the rails was at hand. A corps, strung along the track, could in this way utterly ruin about fifteen miles a day.

All supplies of food and forage, over a belt of country

sixty miles wide, from Atlanta to Savannah, in like manner fell a prey to this march.   Either the Confederates destroyed them to prevent their being of benefit to us, or else
we in turn used or wasted them, leaving the people only
the bare necessaries of life.   Nothing remained which could
subsist an army.

The negroes who endeavored to follow " Massa Sherman "
proved a great embarrassment.   If allowed to join the column they would have seriously jeopardized its safety.   A
few able-bodied men were carried along.   Families and
the extreme young and old could not be.

Much criticism was passed upon this method in the
North, by those who looked upon the war from a merely
political stand-point, or indeed as a war waged against
slavery, and who forgot that its conduct, to secure good
political results, must strictly conform to military usage.
As an instance, General Davis of the Fourteenth corps, from
pure necessity, to carry out his order of march, withdrew his
pontoon bridge at Ebenezer Creek before a horde of colored people could cross, who had been fully warned not to
follow his command and yet persisted in their infatuation.
Quite a number were drowned in frantic endeavors to swim
the stream.   A cry of horror arose at this " act of barba-
rism " and Davis was held up to the bitterest censure,
though absolutely in the right.   He was a soldier under
military orders ; not a humanitarian peacefully guiding the
movements of an exodus.

Probably no body of men ever so fully embodied the two-
fold purpose of fighting and foraging as Sherman's " bummers."   The work exactly suited the genius of the people

composing the army, and the natural law-abiding quality of the American checked extravagance and cruelty. It would be absurd to deny that there was some looting, and an occasional but very rare act committed in hot blood. Mayhap Kilpatrick and his men earned a somewhat bad reputation on just grounds. But no army ever enjoyed such freedom and kept within such bounds. Indeed the Southern press complained at the time more bitterly of Wheeler's cavalry for their reckless vandalism than of our troops. And with rare exceptions the collection of supplies was systematically conducted, and the men who were detailed on this duty fought and foraged with equal alacrity, good-temper and even-handedness.

It may be confidently asserted that no army ever moved through an enemy's territory with like purpose, which so scrupulously observed the humanities if not the amenities of life. The rare exceptions which occurred are quoted, multiplied ; the thousand instances of moderation are forgotten. And war is not a gentle art. Its methods necessarily partake of the horrible. But during our Civil Conflict we may truthfully claim that its terrors were almost uniformly confined to the actual field of battle.

The weather was bright, and everything tended to give the whole affair the aspect of a frolic. Certainly it was the one thoroughly enjoyable operation of the war. Without the stern duties of the field, all the pleasures of the soldier's free and hardy life were ever present; and the men and animals reached their goal in far finer condition than that in which they started.

LVI.

SHERMAN'S GOAL.

THE city of Savannah had strong defences on both
its sea and land fronts. Under Hardee's command
were some eighteen thousand men. He prepared to hold
the place, trusting to keep open his communications on the north with Charleston. December 10, 1864.

Arrived before the city, Sherman stretched out his
left in the endeavor to cut Hardee off from this source
of supply and means of retreat, but to no purpose. General Foster, from his foothold on the coast at Port Royal,
sent Hatch's division to cut the Charleston Railroad, but
for once Governor Brown's militia proved to be of use,
and Hatch's attack was repulsed with a loss of seven
hundred men.

Sherman closed in on Savannah and com-
pleted the investment, save only the above December 12.
outlet.

To open communication with Dahlgren's fleet in the
offing it became necessary to capture Fort McAllister on
the south side of the town. The detail for the assault fell
to Hazen's division and the work was sturdily
done. The fort was taken at the first rush. December 13.

Hardee continued to operate the Charleston Railroad to Hardeeville, not far from Savannah, Foster's renewed efforts to cut it having proved unsuccessful. Sherman was forced to prepare for regular siege operations against Savannah. He drained the rice-fields surrounding the city and began to mount some heavy guns. The men's rations at this time consisted largely of rice, and the animals were fed almost exclusively on rice straw.

During these preparations Sherman received Grant's orders to send the bulk of his forces to Virginia by water. For the army in front of Petersburg had been greatly depleted by the summer's campaign. While preparing to comply, though strongly urging the advantages of his own plan for a march overland, he partly lost his grip on Hardee. The latter, smelling disaster afar off,
December 20. deemed it wise to evacuate the place before his sole outlet was cut. Although he lost the chance of capturing Hardee's forces, Sherman was thus enabled to make the President a Christmas present of the city of Savannah.

LVII.

HOOD SEEKS TO CRUSH SCHOFIELD. — FRANKLIN.

WHEN Sherman unexpectedly eluded Hood, this general became doubly anxious to get at Thomas, and retrieve the standing of the Confederacy by some brilliant feat of arms. But the November storms interfered so materially with his movements, that it was not until late in the month that he pushed from Florence on towards Duck River. This November 21. stream was the first serious natural obstacle in his path, and here also lay Schofield.

Thomas occupied Nashville, shaping the somewhat discordant elements now under his command into an army which he could handle with confidence against an active enemy. This was a task of no small magnitude. His force embraced the Fourth corps under Wood, the Twenty-third under Schofield, three divisions of the Army of the Tennessee under A. J. Smith, and Wilson's cavalry, beside a motley collection of clerks, recruits, and quartermaster's employés, of questionable utility in a fight. Hood's command consisted of Lee's, Stewart's, and Cheatham's army corps, and he was ably supported by Forrest's horsemen.

Schofield's orders were to retreat when he must from before Hood, but to hold him as long as possible so that Thomas might finish his preparations. Schofield was anxious to keep south of the line of Duck River and to preserve the important bridge at Columbia. But Hood flanked him by crossing the river above, and he was obliged to retire to the north side. Wilson, though weaker numerically than Forrest, began to show himself amply able to cope with this clever trooper, and protected Schofield's movements against his sudden dashes.

November 29.

Hood's next move was to despatch Forrest around Schofield's left to his rear at Spring Hill, whither he himself soon followed, obliging Schofield to let go his hold on Columbia and retire by his left so as readily to form line to the east.

A slight interchange of hostilities took place at Spring Hill, but Hood seemed here to lack his usual strong initiative, and the advantage of his manœuvre was lost by failure to push the fighting while Schofield was on the retreat.

Schofield wisely retired to Franklin, intending to put the Harpeth river between himself and the enemy. Lack of pontoons, however, prevented his crossing at once, and he was obliged to form line south of the town, and to intrench in the usual manner. He at once set to work, however, to improve the fords, and reëstablish the bridges, by which means he managed to get his artillery across and out of danger, while it could still be used to advantage from the north side. He planted the guns on some high ground, and in a fort formerly con-

November 30.

structed on that spot.   With considerable exertion he also placed his trains beyond danger.

Hood had rather unnecessarily complained of his subordinates for what he termed their lack of enterprise at Spring Hill, and all were in high tension at the approaching opportunity to prove his strictures false.   And Hood felt justly confident that he could crush Schofield, separated as he was from the main Federal army.

Schofield had ordered the troops to begin the crossing of the Harpeth River, unless attacked, at 6 P.M.   Himself was on the north of the river, where he could best watch operations on the other side, as well as pay heed to Wilson, who was holding head against Forrest on our left.

Wagner's two brigades formed the Union rear-guard, with clear instructions to retire, slowly and without bringing on a serious combat, within the main line. This was protected by excellent parapets, and able to give a good account of itself.   The ground was open.   The advance of the Confederates could be plainly watched.

Our main line was bracing itself for the approaching conflict, expecting Wagner's men to retire in good order from their front, so as to afford a clear sweep for their fire. But, to every one's

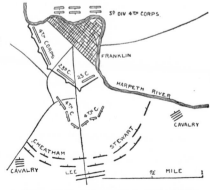

Franklin. November 30, 1864.

surprise, Wagner opened upon the approaching Confederates, and almost instantly provoked a desperate charge upon his isolated brigades.

With a yell, Wagner was brushed away, his men rushing frantically through our lines, followed by the victorious enemy, who, absolutely on the heels of Wagner's broken regiments, overran our parapets in the centre, and drove our troops back in much confusion. A countercharge by the reserves managed to recapture a portion of the breastworks, while the enemy was not to be driven from the rest. But our troops established a new line of intrenchments within twenty-five yards of the one they had just lost.

This preliminary attack was made about 5 P.M., and heavy fighting ensued all along the lines until nearly four hours after dark. The combats were isolated, but desperate and sanguinary, without advantage to either party.

Tactically Franklin was a drawn battle, but as his position could be easily turned, Schofield, at 11 P.M., ordered a withdrawal to the north side of the river. This was accomplished without loss.

Nothing better proves the enemy's determined purpose to crush Schofield's forces in this battle, than their heavy loss, especially in officers. Hood confesses to six thousand three hundred men. Our own was twenty-three hundred. This disproportion savors of inaccuracy. The forces on the field were twenty-seven thousand Federals to a slightly less number of Confederates.

Thomas now ordered Schofield to retire on Nashville.

LVIII.

HOOD BROKEN BY THOMAS. — NASHVILLE.

ACCORDING to his wont, Thomas took such time as he deemed essential to complete his preparations, despite constant, almost angry, demands for an advance from the War Office, the President and General Grant. With all just confidence in Thomas' ability, the entire North insisted on instant action, and Grant finally ordered Thomas either to move upon Hood at once or else turn over the command to Schofield.

Thomas quietly replied that he would cheerfully do the latter, if directed, but would not attack Hood until he was satisfied that the time was ripe. He desired both favorable weather and to increase his force of mounted men.

But the enemy was devastating a considerable part of Tennessee and was forcing all the young men into their ranks ; and every one was fearful of a repetition of Bragg's march to the Ohio in 1862. Logan was finally ordered to Nashville to supplant Thomas. But before he could reach the ground, Thomas had struck his blow.

His preparations had been two weeks before substantially completed. Small detachments were at Murfreesborough, Chattanooga, and along the railroad. This latter had

been, however, interrupted by Hood for a number of days.
A heavy storm of sleet and ice had made the country
almost impassable and would render the operations of the
attacking party uncertain.   Thomas had made up his mind
December 15.   to wait for clearing weather.   Finally came
sunshine, and with it Thomas' advance.

Hood lay in his front, with Stewart on his left, Lee in

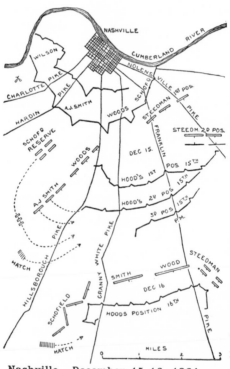

the centre and
Cheatham on the
right, while a
portion of For-
rest's cavalry
was operating
out upon his
right. He had
some forty-four
thousand men,
but his check
and heavy losses
at Franklin had
seriously impair-
ed the *morale*
of his army as
well as thinned
his ranks. Hood
could, however,
not retreat. He
was committed
to a death-

Nashville. December 15-16, 1864.

struggle with Thomas.   It was his last chance as a soldier.

Thomas had placed A. J. Smith on his right, Woods in the centre, and Schofield and Steedman on the left. He advanced on Hood, bearing heavily with his right, while sharply demonstrating with his left. The position of the Confederate Army had placed A. J. Smith's corps obliquely to their general line of battle, an advantage not to be neglected. Smith pushed in, later supported by Schofield, and successively capturing the fieldworks erected by the enemy's main line and reserves, disastrously crushed and turned Hood's left flank.

Meanwhile Wood was making all but equal headway against Hood's centre, and the first day closed with remarkable success for the amount of loss sustained. Still this was not victory. The morrow might bring reverse. Hood's fight promised to be with clenched teeth.

Hood seriously missed Forrest, whom he had detached on a raiding excursion and without whose cavalry his flanks were naked. Cheatham he moved during the night over from the right to sustain his left, which had proved the weaker wing. On the morning of the next day he lay intrenched upon the hills back of his former line, with either flank somewhat refused.

December 16.

Thomas sent Wilson with his cavalry to work his way unobserved around the extreme left flank thus thrown back.

At 3 P.M. a general assault was made all along the line. Upon our left, Wood and Steedman met with no success. On the right, however, A. J. Smith's onset, concentrated at the salient of Hood's left centre, proved heavy enough to break down the Confederate defense. Sharply following up his successes, allowing no breathing time to the exultant troops, Smith pushed well home, and overcoming all resistance, drove the enemy in wild confusion from the field.   Meanwhile Wilson's troopers, dismounted, fell upon the Confederate flank and rear and increased the wreck tenfold.   Reaching Granny White Pike, they cut the enemy from this outlet.   Wood and Steedman charged again, broke through, and with renewed joint effort the rout of the enemy became overwhelming.   Almost all organization was lost in Hood's army as it fled across the country towards Franklin.

Pursuit was promptly undertaken, but though seriously harassed, Hood saved himself beyond the Tennessee River with the remnants of his army.

December 27

Thomas' losses were three thousand men.   Hood's were never officially given, but our trophies included forty-five hundred prisoners and fifty-three guns.

Thomas had settled all adverse speculation upon his slowness in attacking Hood by the next to annihilation he wrought when he actually moved upon him.   No army was so completely overthrown during our war.   Nothing succeeds like success, and we may be content, perhaps, to leave the grand old soldier his full triumph.   Criticism may be well laid aside.

But as a pure matter of curious study, it might with some justice be claimed that Thomas was at any time strong enough to meet Hood on the line of Duck River ; and that with Schofield's force, reinforced by what he himself had, he might then and there have overwhelmed him as he did later before Nashville.

Thomas was a Virginian.   In 1861 he had been seeking a college position in his native State, and some unnecessarily feared his loyalty. Man was never born more true. He was essentially cast in a large mould, in mind and body; so modest that he shrank from command, to which he was peculiarly fitted; with courage of the stamp that ignores self; possessing steadfastness in greater measure than audacity, he yet lacked none of that ability which can deal heavy blows; while no antagonist was ever able to shake his foothold. Honesty in thought, word, and deed was constitutional with him. A thorough military training, added to a passionate love of his profession, and great natural powers, made him peer of any soldier. Sedate in mind, and physically slow in movement, he yet aroused great enthusiasm among his men, as well as earned their warm affection. Uniformly successful in all he undertook, from Mill Springs to Nashville, he has left a memorable name and an untarnished reputation. He perhaps falls as little short of the model soldier as any man produced by this country.

LIX.

SHERMAN MOVES THROUGH THE CAROLINAS.

GRANT'S general plan for a final campaign had included a march by Thomas, after he should have used up Hood, on a similar scale to Sherman's, to a new base which Canby at Mobile should open for him, destroying in his path all the munitions of war, factories and mills. But Thomas considered it unsafe to leave Tennessee, and preferred to operate only with his cavalry. A. J. Smith was consequently sent to Canby, while Schofield was ordered to the Atlantic seaboard.

Schofield moved by way of the Ohio and Washington, with the Twenty-third corps under Cox, to join forces with the Tenth corps under Terry, then on the coast of North Carolina. Here he would be ready to coöperate with Sherman as the latter moved northward.

Fort Fisher protected the harbor of Wilmington, N.C., the last of the ports open to blockade runners, Savannah, Charleston, and Mobile having been closed by our naval and land forces. It was of importance to neutralize this asylum also. Admiral Porter had prepared a fleet of seventy vessels for the expedition, and Grant had selected Weitzel as the officer to accompany him, with some sixty-five hundred men.

As ill luck would have it, Butler had become greatly exercised over a scheme for blowing up the magazine of Fort Fisher by exploding a powder-boat near by, and not only did he accompany the expedition, but he undertook, without orders, claiming this right as senior officer present, to control its operations.

On arrival of the forces three thousand men were landed, the guns of the fort having been silenced by a bombardment of the fleet. The explosion of the powder-boat was a complete *fiasco*, exciting only curiosity among the enemy at the moment, and laughter afterwards. The land forces advanced, and might well have captured the place, but Butler saw fit to recall them, alleging that Fort Fisher was so strong that it could not be taken, and that he was unwilling to sacrifice the lives of the men.

Dec. 24-25, '64.

The folly of this course was shown within a month. Terry joined Porter in Butler's stead, and with about the same force, after a gallant assault, captured the fort at a loss of seven hundred men. The navy lost some three hundred more.

January 15, '65.

The Twenty-third corps having reached Fort Fisher, Schofield assumed command of the joint forces and soon after captured Wilmington. From here Cox was ordered to New Berne to make a new base for future movements and later the bulk of Schofield's forces entered Goldsborough.

February 22.

March 21.

No sooner fairly in Savannah than Sherman, glad enough to leave political and commercial questions to be settled by the civil authorities, put his army afoot for Columbia, which had been his ultimate objective when he left Atlanta. He purposed to feint on Charleston and Augusta, and to march through Columbia to Goldsborough, while Grant, by extending his left west of Petersburg, would prevent Lee from turning against him. The projected route followed the water-shed between the Combahee and the Savannah rivers, as it was necessary to cross the intervening streams near their sources, where they were not wide. At this time of year, even small rivers in this section become swollen and impassable.

January, '65

Charleston, dear to the Confederate heart, was held too long — Sherman's advance from Savannah not being expected in the month of January — to enable the enemy to concentrate in Sherman's front. Beauregard and Hardee had calculated to oppose the further advance of the Federal Army in February with some thirty-three thousand men, but Sherman was well ahead of them before they awoke to the reality.

The rains had been persistent and heavy. There was greater difficulty than usual in bridging streams. The soil was so treacherous that in order to pull through the artillery and trains, nearly the entire distance marched had to be corduroyed. It required exceptional energy and vast labor to push an army through such a country. Joe Johnston has complimented Sherman's veterans as being the toughest and most ready men since Julius Cæsar commanded his

Gallic legions. And indeed, as Romans in courage and endurance, and as Yankees in inventiveness and adaptability, Cæsar's legionaries were a fair prototype of Sherman's bummers.

The army reached Columbia after an arduous march. Before entering the town February 17 Sherman ordered all public property and factories c pable of making munitions of war to be destroyed; all private and educational property to be left unmolested. Not the slightest desire to injure the town was manifest, for no such intention existed. But a fire was accidentally started, and before it could be got under control had made such headway that the greater part of the city was consumed.

The crimination and recrimination which has been indulged in about the burning of Columbia probably resolves itself into the simple fact that a fire of cotton bales, started by the retiring Confederates, extended beyond control. There is abundant proof that everything possible was done to extinguish the flames, but to no avail. And after the calamity Sherman did all that man could do to help the citizens to food and shelter. There may have been some drunkenness and rioting among the men. Under such circumstances, when are they absent? But the testimony before and the decision of the Mixed Commission on American and British Claims, in the matter of cotton then destroyed, settles the responsibility beyond further argument. That body, as able as disinterested, attached no blame to the Federal army.

Sherman almost immediately continued his march. Skirmishing was now incessant with the enemy in his front, but the loss of life was small. Hardee, finding Charleston of no further strategic value and hoping still to effect something against Sherman in the field, evacuated the city, upon which Dahlgren and Foster occupied it.

March 2.   The Confederates concentrated at Cheraw to oppose our advance, but by pushing forward Slocum's left wing, they were manœuvred out of their position. Hampton's cavalry was very active in Sherman's front. On one occasion he surprised Kilpatrick, who had become somewhat careless about his outpost service, and came near to putting a term to the latter's usefulness ; but this slight success eventuated in no gain to the Confederates.

When Lee found that Hardee was making no headway against Sherman's progress, he assumed the March.   prerogative of commander-in-chief, and assigned Joe Johnston to command the forces, some twenty-six thousand men, in front of his late antagonist.

March 16.   Johnston at once took the reins in hand, and began to harass Sherman's van. In the small affair at Averasborough, Sherman gained an unimportant success, but at Bentonville came near a grievous check.

The army, partly owing to the bad roads and partly to the necessity of foraging on the country, has got much strung out. Johnston, well aware of this, and hid behind a curtain of Hampton's cavalry, concentrates at Bentonville, hoping to strike a heavy blow at Sherman before he can effect a junction with Schofield.

Sherman himself is with the right wing, so as all the sooner to open communication with his lieutenant. Davis' division, leading the left wing, stumbles upon Hampton in a manner indicating the proximity of other troops. Sherman is duly notified, but makes up his mind — rather hastily it appears — that it is only a cavalry force, little suspecting that Johnston, with twenty-two thousand men, lies massed behind it, ready to fall upon Slocum, whose entire force within a day's march is dangerously small.

March 19-20.

The blow falls. At first it staggers Davis, whose men fall back in confusion, but without panic rally and reform. Slocum speeds back messengers to bring up Williams' army corps, next in rear. Morgan and Carlin handle their divisions to great advantage, and yield no ground to the attacks of double their number of the enemy. Sherman's bummers are unfamiliar with defeat. In this picturesque combat, which wavers fiercely to and fro from morn till dark, our troops are called on several times to fight on opposite sides of the same breastworks, so completely are they surrounded by the Confederates. But they hold their ground without loss of courage.

During the night, reinforcements arrive from the right wing, and the rear of the left wing comes up. Johnston retires foiled. But he has been nearer success than he has guessed. His loss somewhat exceeded two thousand three hundred men; ours was over sixteen hundred. This was his last chance in the Carolinas. And he had lost it.

Stoneman, accompanied by the Fourth Corps, had been

March and April. ordered into the Valley from Nashville to destroy the railroad from Virginia to Tennessee. This was designed to cut off from Lee this means of retreat from Virginia, and source of supply from such part of Tennessee as was still in the enemy's hands. The raid was successfully accomplished and had no small effect upon the *morale* of the Virginia forces. Stoneman made his way as far as Salisbury, N.C., where he destroyed a vast depot of reserve stores.

Wilson led a cavalry expedition into Alabama. His progress was opposed by Forrest. Wilson drove this noted partisan into Selma, stormed and carried the town.
April 2. Forrest escaped, but only to fall somewhat later into the hands of a detachment of our horsemen. Wilson won great credit by thus ending the career of this doughty champion of the Confederacy.

Sherman was duly joined at Goldsborough by Schofield and Terry. This ran his force up to ninety thousand men. He occupied Raleigh without opposition. The end of the Confederacy had come within sight.

Sherman's active field-work ends here. What has been said about his Atlanta campaign sufficiently stamps the man and the soldier. No praise can add to, no blame detract from, Sherman's splendid reputation and services. He, if any one, showed during our Civil War the divine military spark.

In his 1864 campaign he was pitted against the strongest of the Confederates, always excepting Lee; and he wrote his own strength upon every page of its history. It would have furnished an interesting study to have seen him at the

head of the splendid force which started from the Rappahannock when he himself started from Chattanooga.   For
Sherman's work never taxed him beyond his powers.   It
is difficult to say what he still held in reserve.

LX.

THE FINAL CAMPAIGN.

THE marvellous gallantry of the South had availed it nothing. The toils of its stronger opponent were drawing closer and tighter. Never had nation fought more nobly for what it believed to be right. No race can harbor a more just pride in its achievements than the American Anglo-Saxon may do in the splendid resistance of the South. Happy our Northern homes that we were not called on to endure to such a bitter end!

Sherman, in his march through the Carolinas, has drawn a line of steel from the Appalachians to the Atlantic. Grant holds Lee fast in his stronghold. The end must speedily come.

Sheridan's Valley command has been broken up, and the Sixth and Nineteenth corps have returned to the army before Petersburg.

Sheridan himself, with ten thousand sabres, is ordered to operate against Lee's communications at Danville. This is the plan Grant has been urging on him for six months. He moves to Staunton and from there to Charlottesville, March 2. crossing swords with the enemy at Waynesboro. But he is unable to cross the James

on account of high water. Foregoing his purpose of destroying the Danville Railroad he breaks up the James River
Canal and the Lynchburg Railroad and strikes
across country for White House on the York		March 19
river, from which place he joins the Army of the Potomac.

Lee could not expect further reinforcements. There
were still men to be had; but the population of the
South was growing tired of the manner in which the
politicians were conducting the war. And there was not
a house in which there was not one dead. The people
saw the end if the politicians would not. The starving wife and children called from his duty under the
colors many a brave man who had for four years risked his
life for the cause which he now saw was beyond saving.
These deserters were all but impossible to capture. They
were shielded wholesale from the provost-marshals. The
commissariat, too, was in a condition of collapse. Only
the despairing courage of the leaders remained, and their
dwindling retinue. The means of carrying on the struggle
had been exhausted. The last ditch had been reached.

Lee had little over sixty thousand effectives. Grant
surrounded him with more than twice the number. The
return of the Valley troops and reinforcements had again
placed Grant in overwhelming strength. He had one
hundred and twenty-five thousand men. No doubt as the
time approached for the opening of what all saw must be
the last campaign, Lee had fully determined to forsake Richmond, and, joining to his own the forces of Johnston, to
retreat to the mountains, where, if he could not prolong
the war, he might, at least, command better terms of

peace for the Confederacy. He accumulated a supply of rations at Amelia Court House, west of Richmond, ready to take with him when he should retire along the Danville Railroad.

In order to be able to retire, as he desires, by the south side of the Appomattox river, Lee must drive Grant from his hold on the Boydton road. And to make the operation of disengaging himself from Richmond and Petersburg safe, he plans to attack Grant as a diversion. Selecting Fort Stedman, on Grant's centre, as the most available point, he vigorously assaults the place in three columns of selected troops.

March 25.

Negligently guarded, Fort Stedman is captured by a *coup de main*, causing the abandonment of some adjacent batteries. But the assaulting force is not promptly supported, and Lee is forced to retire under the concentric fire of other batteries commanding Fort Stedman, — (Confederate, " Hare's Hill "). His casualties amount to twenty-five hundred men and two thousand prisoners, — a loss he can ill afford.

Grant can not well mistake Lee's purpose. He knows that the attack on Fort Stedman is but a cover for some other operation, presumably retreat, for the prisoners recently captured have told a sorry tale of the condition of the Army of Northern Virginia. Grant therefore once more adopts his ancient tactics of a move by the left. But this time he leaves a small body only in front of Petersburg, and makes his turning force solid and strong.

Sheridan is on the extreme left, moving towards Dinwiddie. Warren, with Humphreys on his right, first finds the enemy as he pushes for the White Oak road.   A combat, with loss of four hundred men, results in Warren's favor.

March 29.

The Union line stretches out from the Appomattox River to Dinwiddie Court House, in order Parke, Wright, Ord, Humphreys, Warren, Sheridan.   With not much over fifty thousand muskets, Lee has thirty-five miles of intrenchments to hold.   Longstreet is in the Richmond defences; Mahone at Bermuda Hundred.   In Petersburg are Wilcox, Pickett, Bushrod Johnson, Heth, and Gordon.

Starved as he is for men, Lee still clings to his old and daring tactics.   Stripping the lines to the barest, he collects fifteen thousand men, and once again essays his so often successful assault upon our right.   A heavy storm supervenes.   Grant arrests the movement of the Army of the Potomac.   Lee completes his preparations.

March 30.

Warren has formed his divisions in *echelon*.   The habit of moving forward in line enables an opponent who can effect a breach in one place to bear back the whole body. The disposition in *echelon* allows easy support of one portion of the line by another, while not subject to the weakness mentioned.   Ayres is sent forward to seize the White Oak road.

March 31.

Lee once more makes a sudden swoop upon Warren's left.   Ayres and Crawford are driven in; but Griffin holds on, and Humphreys thrusts Miles forward upon Warren's right.   Lee fails, but we lose two thousand men.

Sheridan with his horse moves forward to Five Forks.

Lee, whose safety demands that he shall hold this point, advances an equal number of foot upon him, and drives him back towards Dinwiddie.

Grant and Meade become solicitous for Sheridan's safety, and send Warren to his succor. Warren throws Ayres forward towards Dinwiddie. Ayres is stopped for a few hours by a broken bridge. But in reality Sheridan is in no degree compromised. Lee cannot afford to leave so many men at Dinwiddie, and withdraws them to Five Forks.

April 1.   Sheridan again follows up Lee to that place. He is in command of the joint cavalry and infantry forces. Masking the Fifth corps with his cavalry, and attacking smartly on the right of Lee's line to divert his attention, he sends a body of horse up the White Oak road towards Richmond to arrest any reinforcements which may chance to come from that direction. Warren forms his corps with Ayres on the left, Crawford on the right, and Griffin in rear of Crawford as reserve.

Ayres and Crawford have each two brigades in front, each brigade in two lines of battle, and a third brigade in similar formation in rear of the two advance brigades. Griffin is in columns by battalion.

The march is directed by the sun, which is to be kept over the left shoulder. The line of advance is to be upon and around the left flank of the enemy, thus taking him in reverse. As in all such cases, in wooded country, there is some delay in the advance, due to no particular neglect.

April 1.   The cavalry attack in front, the foot falls upon the enemy in flank and rear. The enemy struggles with all his old nerve, changes front in good style, and fights manfully; but outnumbered and outmanœuvred, he can make no headway. His line is broken. Part fly westward, five thousand are captured. Our loss is less than one thousand men.

After the battle of Five Forks was over, Warren was relieved by Sheridan from command of his corps, and Griffin was placed in his stead. It can not be denied that Sheridan had the right to do this. But it was a hard blow to one of the most gallant men of the Army of the Potomac, who had ever made a brilliant record in all that he had done. To say that a Court of Inquiry found no want of activity or of intelligent effort in Warren's conduct affords little consolation. But Warren's history is written. Few can boast so clear and bright a fame.

After this battle Grant opens on Peters-   April 2. burg a heavy artillery fire, and Parke with the Ninth corps goes in on the right of the line. He carries the outer defences, but the inner works are stubbornly held by a mere handful of the enemy. Wright with the Sixth corps carries everything in his front and marches down the Boydton Plank Road towards Petersburg. Humphreys does the same.

Opposite Ord is Fort Gregg. Here some two hundred and fifty Confederate marksmen place five hundred of our men *hors de combat*. Longstreet brings what reinforcements he can from Richmond to Lee at Petersburg.

Lee nobly meets our vigorous attack.   April 2. None of the fire which in days of high emprise and brilliant hopes blazed in his assault, was now found wanting. But gallantry can no more avail. And brave A. P. Hill, whose name is written upon every page of the history of the Army of Northern Virginia, falls in this last attack. Our loss is thirty-four hundred men.

April 2–3. During the night, silently, unperceived, Lee retreats from both Richmond and Petersburg. With twenty-five thousand men, he marches sixteen miles west from Petersburg along the north side of the Appomattox. In the morning the Union forces enter both the cities which they have so long and so arduously labored to capture.

Little caring for these empty prizes, Grant pursues by the south side of the river. Lee hurries along towards the Danville Railroad, still hoping to push beyond his enemy to a point where he can join to himself the forces of Johnston. Either Lynchburg or Danville may compass this end.

A train of supplies has been ordered to remain at Amelia Court House. Lee proposes to ration his men, cut loose from any base, and push boldly for the foot-hills of the Alleghanies. His is the courage which does not forsake him. There is yet work to be done.

It is difficult to picture Lee's utter consternation, — despair, when on reaching Amelia, he discovers that, under mistaken orders from the capital, this train of victuals, which is all that stands between him and sheer starvation, has been run on to Richmond. The authorities had wanted the cars on which to load the archives and valuables of the Confederate Government, intending that the rations should be left for Lee. The rations had

not been unloaded, and the cars had been forwarded to
the capital.   Lee's twenty thousand men have not a
mouthful to eat save what they can gather in little driblets
along the road.

April 4.

Sheridan with the Second, Fifth and Sixth
Corps pushes remorselessly onward.   Both he and Lee aim
for Burkeville, but Sheridan is the fleeter of foot and
reaches that place first.

Lee dares not halt.   He now has Union columns pressing hard upon his left, upon his rear.   Sheridan's cavalry
hurries far ahead to cut him off in the advance.

A running fight is kept up between the armies all the
way.   Despite gallant defense, the day generally goes
against the enemy.   At Sailor's Creek

April 6.

Ewell's eight thousand men are cut off and
captured.   Our loss is twelve hundred.

The Confederates are literally starving.   For four days
they have had nothing to eat save the crumbs of their last
issue of rations.   Even the buds of the trees are put to use
for food.   Those who are best off have but a few handfuls
of corn.   And yet 'they cling fondly to their chief and
trust that all may yet be well.

Lee crosses the Appomattox at Farmville and fires the
bridges.   Humphreys comes up barely in

April 7.

time to save one of them.   On this he
crosses and attacks the Confederate rear.   But the gallant
fellows have lost none of their soldier's pride, and repulse
the onset handsomely, with a loss to us of six hundred men.

Lee must escape, if at all, over the narrow neck of land
between the James and Appomattox rivers to the west

of his present position. But Sheridan's horse is nimbler-footed. He reaches the ground first and closes this last outlet also.

Lee is trapped. Like his old self, he promptly decides

April 8. to cut his way through. But Sheridan anticipates him in his attack. The brave Army of Northern Virginia comes to the end of its glorious career, and its faithful commander can do no more. After a short correspondence, the chieftains meet, terms

April 9. are agreed upon, arms are stacked by the troops, and, at Appomattox Court House, Lee surrenders to Grant's armies some twenty-nine thousand men, bearing, it has been said, but ten thousand muskets.

The first act, upon capitulation having been made, is to ration the starving Confederates. Lee takes leave of the tearful veterans who have seconded his purpose so nobly, and whose very rags are a shining honor, in a few heart-felt words : —

"Men, we have fought through the war together. I have done the best I could for you."

The Union loss in these closing operations was about ten thousand men.

General Meade had remained in command of the Army of the Potomac till the close. Grant had directed the larger operations, but had left Meade the immediate control. Meade was a ripe, sound soldier. He fell short of greatness, perhaps, but few equalled him in precision and steady-going capacity. Under him the Army of the Potomac saw its greatest triumph, and its greatest humiliation. Gettysburg was Meade's victory ;

Cold Harbor was not Meade's defeat. While he was in command the army was always in safe hands; its discipline was excellent; its *esprit de corps* high. All his subordinates held him in great esteem.

In minor stations Meade obeyed with alacrity; in supreme control he commanded with discretion. His qualities are not salient; but he was well rounded both as a soldier and as a man.

Johnston surrendered to Sherman towards the close of the month. There was some friction be-   April 26. tween Sherman and the Secretary of War as to the terms granted to Johnston, but the capitulation was eventually completed. And gradually, so soon as the news had spread, the smaller armies of the Confederacy surrendered upon similar conditions. These were substantially the giving up of all material of war, and the signing by all Confederate soldiers of a parole not to take up arms again against the United States, and to return at once to their homes. Transportation and rations were furnished them so far as could be.

Anger, on the one side, was swallowed up in gladness for the happy outcome of the war; regrets on the other disappeared in the cessation of the unavailing strife.

The men composing the vast armies on either side soon peacefully dispersed to their homes and were speedily engrossed in their ancient occupations or in new pursuits. No act of lawlessness is on record to stain their proud repute as soldiers and Americans. This remarkable fact is the most splendid of tributes to the value of the liberties of the New World. It would be impossible elsewhere.

LXI.

A FEW STRAY ITEMS.

THE theory of the North that no State could leave the Union by its own sole act had been maintained. The seceding States were still part and parcel of the nation. But the inhabitants of this section had waged war upon the United States, and had thereby forfeited their civil and property rights. Something must be done to restore the *status quo ante bellum*.

May 29, 1865.

Within a month after the close of hostilities the President issued a proclamation of amnesty to all who had participated in rebellion, excepting only certain prominent classes, on condition that each person taking the benefit of the proclamation should subscribe an oath of allegiance to the United States and accept the results of the war. This would restore to such affiant his rights as a citizen and his rights of property; but the oath itself, as well as the proclamation, expressly sustained the emancipation of the slaves.

The great bulk of the Southern population accepted the amnesty thus offered, and gradually thereafter those persons who were excepted in the first proclamation were readmitted to their citizenship upon promise of future loyalty to the laws and constitution of the United States. Legally speaking, the Union was once more what it had been, profoundly at peace, and without any stain of discord upon its garments.

To trace the history of Reconstruction in the South; of the bestowal of Civil Rights upon the former slaves; of the vast frauds committed by the "carpet-bag" administrations of the several Southern States, and the unnecessary hardships arising from this vicious system; of the turbulence thereby excited, and the cruel and sometimes bloody attempts to cow the negro population into its ancient servility; and of the gradual renewal of good feeling and concord, is beyond the scope of this little work. The actual war for the Union had ended; the Union and the Constitution had been maintained; and, as a result not anticipated at the outset, freedom had been given to the slave. The price paid in blood and treasure had been vast. But the gain for future generations had been equally vast. North and South now recognized each other's strength, and each other's readiness to battle for the right. Slavery was buried. And the Southerner had learned that honest labor is not only the duty, but the privilege, of every man who values the heritage of our common country.

A few stray statistics must close. These come mainly from the War Department records and the tables of the Treasury Department and Pension Office. Any inaccuracy in approximation is traceable to paucity of Southern records.

The average population of the North and South from 1861 to 1864 was thirty-five millions, including four million slaves.

In the North and South alike the first troops were raised by volunteering. But within a year, in the South, conscription acts were passed and thereafter kept in force. In the North, volunteering obtained until late in the third year of the war, when the draft also went into effect in most of the States.

Northern troops were furnished for various terms of service, from three months to "three years or the war." The actual enlistments were two million seven hundred and eighty thousand men for the armies and navies, or, reduced to a three years' term, *i.e.*, counting three one-year men as one three-years' man, and, estimating as a full man only one who enlisted for a term which could have lasted three full years (men who enlisted in January, 1865, for three years could actually serve only four months, and would count as one-ninth of one man each), there were furnished in the North about one million seven hundred thousand men. In the South, counting in the same manner (a man who enlisted for four years was a man and a third), there were furnished about nine hundred thousand men. These forces came from a military population, according to the census of 1861, of four million six hundred thousand in the North and one million and sixty-five thousand in the South. Of these, about one-fifth were, as usual in every country, exempts. Thus, in the North, about four men in every nine served three years; in the South, exemption being much rarer, nine out of ten did so.

The regular army of the United States was never large. Only some sixty-seven thousand regulars served through the war. The bulk of the forces were called volunteer troops, though few regulars in any country were ever better soldiers. But the prominent general officers, and many of the minor ones, were men whom the government had educated at West Point. This applied equally to the South.

In the North over two-thirds of all the men who served were American-born. In the South all but a small percentage were so. Among the foreign-born soldiers the greater part were naturalized citizens.

Much to the credit of our colored fellow-citizens, there were one hundred and eighty thousand negro soldiers.

In the North the troops served in twenty-five Army Corps, consecutively numbered, and one Cavalry Corps. In the South the corps bore the names of their commanders.

The following was the strength of the United States' and the Confederate States' forces at various dates, present and absent. The Southern figures are from accurate data. If anything they are understated : —

	U.S.	C.S. About
Jan. 1, 1861	16,367	
July 1, 1861	186,751	98,000
Jan. 1, 1862	575,917	350,000
March 31, 1862	637,126	353,000
Jan. 1, 1863	918,191	441,000
Jan. 1, 1864	860,737	471,000
Jan. 1, 1865	959,460	418,000
March 31, 1865	980,086	175,000
May 1, 1865	1,000,516	

This gave the North, on the average, about double the force of the South (17 to 9) ; but owing to the larger amount of garrison duty done by the invading force, in the field the numbers stood, up to 1865, as not far from three to two.

Of every thousand men there were, in the North, on the average, seventy-three men sick, and two hundred and thirty-four men absent for various reasons, leaving six hundred and ninety-three under the colors.

In the South, except towards the close of the war, when desertions became frequent, the average with the colors was somewhat higher, as furloughs were much more rare.

The deaths during the war, in the North, were as follows : —

Killed or died of wounds	110,070
Died of disease (two-thirds due to service exposure)	199,720
In Confederate prisons	24,866
Accidents	9,371
Murders and suicides	1,015
Military executions	331
Other causes	14,155
	359,528

In the South, the losses in killed or died of their wounds were 94,000 men; those dying of disease are unknown. The sacrifices of the Confederates were appalling. South Carolina (*e.g.*) lost in killed or mortally wounded one-quarter of her military population — a record probably unequalled in any war.

The above table of Northern losses does not include the

great number who were discharged for disability during the war, and who died at home from the results of exposure, wounds, or disease contracted in the line of duty, and other causes. Counting all losses directly due to the war, it would be safe to say that half a million men were lost in the North, and close upon the same number in the South.

There are buried in the national cemeteries three hundred and twenty-five thousand Union soldiers.

At least seven hundred men a day were victims of the four years' war; and there was, in battle, during this period, a daily loss in killed and wounded of over four hundred men.

These casualties occurred in some two thousand four hundred actions of sufficient importance to be identified by name; in eighteen hundred and eighty-two of which a regiment or more was engaged. This is nearly two for each day. There were one hundred and twelve of these actions in which the loss exceeded five hundred men. All this tale makes no count of the innumerable small affairs on the picket-line and outpost service, and in scouting and reconnoitring duty.

At the outset of the war no prisoners were exchanged between North and South. But, later on, better counsels prevailed and a system of exchange was inaugurated. The exchanges covered several hundred thousand men, and were made on equal terms. Retaliatory measures on prisoners were, except in isolated cases, not resorted to.

The medical service and the ambulance system of the Northern armies were more efficient than had ever before existed. The Sanitary and Christian Commissions rendered

services never to be forgotten. Scores of thousands of
men to-day owe their lives to the fidelity and skill of these
ministers of mercy. Numberless surgeons and their attendants lost their lives on the field of battle in pursuit of their
humane duties. In the South scant means prevented the
same lavish outlay for this purpose.

At the close of the war one hundred and seventy-five
thousand Confederates surrendered.

The South raised its means for carrying on the war by
internal revenue and by loans of various kinds at home and
abroad. Some of these had the cotton-crops pledged to
secure the bonds issued. None of the debt created by the
South has been or ever can be paid.

The North raised its moneys from loans similarly placed.
The United States debt was, substantially,

June 30, 1861	$65,000,000
June 30, 1865	2,682,000,000
Increase of debt	**$2,617,000,000**
There was raised by customs, etc., in addition to the above, and spent on the war, some	783,000,000
making the whole cost of the war . .	$3,400,000,000

or nearly two and a half millions a day, as a rough calculation, during the entire struggle.

Republics are said to be ungrateful. But the United
States has paid to its soldiers, in addition to larger emolu-
ments than any nation ever gave its troops, three hundred

millions in bounties, and has already paid two thousand millions in pensions. Add to this the pensions which will continue to be paid until the pensioners gradually drop off the rolls, and we reach a total of probably four thousand million dollars. This is about eight thousand dollars for each man who died in service, or who was discharged for disability and died at home, in addition to his pay, rations, and clothing while in the service. This does not look like ingratitude. The like of it has never been known.

GLOSSARY.

Abatis. — Trees cut down and having the branches stripped and their ends sharpened and pointed towards the enemy in front of intrenchments. Abatis delays the attacking party and keeps it longer under fire.

Act of War. — Any act which is incompatible with the friendly relations which exist among nations at peace with each other is an act of war, unless immediate reparation is made. War usually follows such an act among nations of equal strength.

Ambulance. — A vehicle specially adapted to carrying wounded men. Sometimes used, in a broader sense, as the hospital system of an army.

Affair. — A small engagement or action between forces which are not very numerous. A skirmish.

A main forte. — " *With a strong hand.*" By a sudden or overwhelming attack or movement to capture a place or do any work is to do it *a main forte.*

Arms of Precision. — The breach-loading small-arms of to-day, which are very precise in their fire.

Au fond. "*To the bottom.*" A force is said to fight or to charge *au fond,* when it does its work thoroughly, with a will, or to the bitter end.

Base (of operations). — The country, city, depot or locality from which an army starts on its campaign, and on which it relies for victuals, men and material. The *line* of operations starts from the *base* of operations, and reaches out to the army. Along this line supplies are carried. The line may be a railroad, a river, or a road; or several such.

Battle. — A serious engagement between rival armies which is apt to lead to decisive results. An action of large proportions.

Belligerents. — Legally, only those nations which are recognized by other nations as independent, and which are deemed to have the rights of independent powers, such as the right of carrying on war. Colloquially, any fighting forces.

Bivouac. — A temporary encampment. Sometimes used when no tents are on hand, and the men shelter themselves as best they may.

Blockade. — The closing of a port by an enemy's fleet or by other means, to prevent ingress or egress. The object is to keep the nation whose ports are blockaded from receiving contraband of war or from exporting its own commodities. To be respected by other nations, a blockade must be strictly kept up.

Campaign. — A series of operations covering some period of time, or beginning with a definite plan and ending with its accomplishment or with failure.

Cantonments. — Quarters occupied by troops for a considerable time, in villages or in more or less permanent barracks, huts or shelters. Winter quarters are often cantonments.

Cashier. — An officer is cashiered when he is (by sentence of a Court-martial) dismissed from the service, and forever incapacitated from holding any office of trust or emolument under the United States.

Casus Belli. — That act which is the immediate cause of war, or which is alleged to be the reason for a declaration of war.

Charge. — An advance to the assault.

Close Order. — Massed in column.

Column. — Troops in close, compact order, many files deep. A mass of troops. There are many kinds of tactical means of forming column.

Column by Battalion. — A brigade will be in column by battalion, when the battalions composing it are each in line and in rear of each other.

Combat. — An engagement of no great length or dimensions. But it may be sharp and bloody.

Commissariat. — The force employed to accumulate and distribute rations to armies. Colloquially applied to the supply of food on hand.

Commission. — A permission granted by a government to a ship to go on a cruise or to do some definite act of war. The letter appointing an officer to his rank.

Communications. — The line of operations. (*See* Base.) The route by which an army communicates with its depot of supplies. An army must keep its communications open, or else live off the country; this latter is always difficult for a large force.

Concentric. — Towards a common centre; towards the same objective from different places. The movements of the Army of the Potomac, the Army of the James, and the Valley Armies on Richmond, in 1864, were concentric operations.

Conscription. — A forcible method of raising troops. Every citizen capable of bearing arms is enrolled (*i.e.*, put on a list) in his own district, and drawings by lot are made from the list for the number of men apportioned to that district when a call for troops is made.

Contraband of War. — Any stores or arms or goods of any kind whats-ever which will enable a military power or force to carry on or prolong a war; such as powder, medicines, rations, ship-timber. Almost any article may be contraband of war, according to the circumstances, and the use for which it is destined, or the amount of it on hand, etc., etc. Such articles may legally be seized by either belligerent wherever found.

Corduroy. — To mend a road which is deep in mud, by laying across it small trunks of trees, or rails, and filling the same in with dirt or brush. This is sometimes done very carefully and a substantial road produced.

Corral. — A large enclosure into which wild horses or cattle are driven and captured. A stock-yard. A trap. To entrap.

Counter. — To meet a blow by a blow, or an attack by an attack.

Court of Inquiry. — Military tribunals may be Courts-martial or Courts of Inquiry. The former try officers or soldiers for crimes or offences against military law. Courts of Inquiry inquire into any matter, the facts of which are in dispute. They may find the facts such as to warrant the calling of a Court-martial.

Counter-charge. — A charge made by the army or body of troops which is on the defensive upon another which is advancing upon it, in order to break up the onset of the latter. A charge from intrenchments upon a body of troops, which has attacked and recoiled from them, in order to disperse the assailants more effectually.

Counter-march. — When marching in one direction, to face to, and march in substantially the opposite. To retrace one's steps. There are tactical manœuvres specifically called counter-marches.

Coup de grâce. — The death stroke. So called because it may put a suffering creature out of its agony. The finishing stroke.

Coup de main. — A quick, sudden attack by which any place is seized or any object accomplished. A surprise.

Cul de sac. — "The bottom of a bag." A blind alley. Any place having but one means of entrance or exit. A trap.

Cut. — To interrupt or sever, as a road or other means of retreat or advance.

Debouch. — Any place from which you can unobserved fall upon the enemy, or so move as to compromise him. To debouch is to fall upon the enemy or to move from such a place. Troops may debouch from a bridge, a town, a pass in the mountains.

Declaration of War. — A formal notice by one nation to another that it considers its friendly relations with the latter at an end. It is usual to give it before opening a war.

De facto — Absolutely done or accomplished, whether rightfully or wrongfully. A *de facto* government is the one actually in power, whether legally or not.

Defile. — A long narrow pass which obliges troops to march through it in very extended order, as a bridge, or a gap in the mountains. To pass a defile is a delicate operation, because the troops are not in such order, at the moment of passing, as to be ready to meet an attack. To force a defile is difficult because only a few men can move through it abreast, and the enemy can do great damage to the long line of troops by firing on them as they march through.

De jure. — A de jure right is a legal right to do or to be anything whether you assert it or not. One man might be *de jure* (*i.e.*, rightful) governor of a place while another might, by usurpation, be *de facto* governor.

Deploy. — If troops are in column or close order they deploy into line or open order. If in line or open order, they ploy into column or close order. Troops fight in line, as a rule. They used to charge in column. They camp generally in more or less close order, but taking up more space than if drawn up for manœuvres.

Demonstrate. — To operate against or to attack in order to ascertain the condition or position of the enemy, or to blind him as to what you intend to do. To demonstrate is to make a diversion, *q. v.*

Detail. — A selection of men for any purpose from a larger body. Such as a detail for picket duty from each company of a regiment. The detail may be regular, *i.e.*, from all the men by rote, or it may be a special detail of reliable men for a work requiring intelligence or courage.

Develop. — To adopt means, as by a reconnoissance or by a slight attack, to ascertain all about the force opposing you. To do any act which makes the enemy develop his strength or position.

Direction, Column of. — That body by whose movements the rest of an army has to govern its line of march.

Diversion. — Any attack, large or small, which will divert the enemy's attention from the main object you have in view and enable you to carry out your plans. A diversion often draws the enemy's troops away from the main point where you intend to attack.

Draft. — Conscription. The actual drawing by lot of a required number from the enrolled men of a district.

Eccentric. — Out of the central line on which military movements should be conducted, in order to protect the base of operations. If an army retreats along any except its line of operations, it makes an *eccentric* retreat, which may be disastrous to it unless it has another base to fall back upon. Even then, it leaves its old base open to the attack of the enemy.

Echelon. — A line of columns or bodies of troops in which each successive column or body is placed a trifle in rear of the line of the one next on its right or left, — like a ladder (*échelle*), or more like the tread of a pair of stairs. The bodies do not lap, or stand behind each other, but only stand in line, each one further to the rear.

Effective. — That portion of a body of troops which is " for duty," *i.e.,* ready to do effective duty; which will be able to fight. Every army has many non-combatants, often not reckoned as a part of the effective.

Elan. — Dash. That vigor or spirit which carries troops forward with a rush.

Enfilade. — To fire, with artillery or musketry, along a line of troops, *i.e.,* from a position on their flanks. Such a fire is very destructive and demoralizing.

Engagement. — A smaller battle.

Entrenchment. — (*See* Intrenchment.)

Esprit de corps. — When companies, regiments, and brigades have served beside each other for so long a time that they have learned to know and to have confidence in the courage and energy of each other, a *spirit* of pride and reliance animates the whole *body*, which is of the greatest value in a military sense.

Fall in. — To take one's place in line, or column.

Field-works. Intrenchments thrown up on the field out of the most available means on hand. Fortifications not of a permanent nature.

File. — A file is the depth of a body of troops from front to rear, with one man front. Rank is the length from right to left. Thus, in a company of eighty men in two ranks, the file will be two deep, — the rank will consist of forty men. To *file* out of a place generally means to march out of it by the flank, for when a line faces to either flank, its then front has the width only of the depth of a file, and it marches *by file.* Tactical formations, however, for ease of marching, generally double these files, so that a body in two ranks marching by the flank, has four men abreast.

Flank. — Troops in line of battle have a front, a rear, and two flanks. The flanks are the ends of a line of troops. Troops can only fight towards their direct, or slightly oblique, front. If attacked in the flank they must change front in whole or in part towards the attacking party. This is more or less difficult. If attacked in rear they can face about; but troops cannot fight with equal confidence faced to the rear.

Flankers. — Small bodies of troops marching in the same direction as the main column, but at a distance on either side of it, to protect its flanks from sudden attack. The distance varies according to the size of the columns and the nature of the ground.

Flank March. — Troops march in action by the front; for short distances by the rear; when not in presence of the enemy by the right or left flank. A flank march sometimes means a march with either flank leading; but as generally used, it means a march around the flank of an enemy; a circuitous march to reach and attack the enemy in flank or rear.

Flying Wing. — A body of troops out on the right or left of an army, and at some distance, but under independent control and command as to all but its general operations. It acts in a larger way as flankers do.

Flying Column. — A body of troops cut loose from its base to do some special work, and meanwhile to live on the country or on the rations it starts with.

Forage. — Food for the beasts which form part of an army. To forage is to go out for, capture, and bring in any kind of food or feed for man or beast. Foraging parties detailed for the purpose generally do this work.

Forced Marches. — Twelve to twenty miles a day is good marching for a column. If the troops are forced they can do much more than this amount for awhile, but not keep it up. Forced marches are made to reach a place where the troops are much needed, with the utmost despatch.

Forlorn Hope. — A body selected to capture by assault a very dangerous position. So called because the hope which each man has of surviving the attempt is a forlorn one. A forlorn hope, if it makes a breach in the enemy's defences, is followed up by reserves, so as to hold what the forlorn hope has seized.

Furlough. — A permission to a soldier to be absent for a definite period.

Garrison. — A body of men holding or defending a town or fort or other place.

General Engagement. — A battle.

Grand-tactics. — The art of moving large bodies of men on the field of battle. "Tactics" is also used to express the art of handling arms and performing manœuvres by soldiers or small bodies of troops, as companies and regiments.— *See* Strategy *and* Tactics.

Guerillas. — Irregular troops which conduct irregular warfare. Land pirates. Unorganized forces. "Peaceful farmers" when they are not making raids or shooting from behind trees and hedges. Troops which are raised for a sudden incursion, and then disappear into the population. The word means *petty war* in Spanish. Guerilla warfare is not considered legitimate. War is supposed to be conducted only by organized bodies of troops under recognized leaders. For organization alone can control the actions of the individual soldiers.

Honors of War. — When your enemy has made a gallant defense of a citadel, and you find you cannot easily reduce it, he may still perhaps agree to surrender it to you, if its importance has ceased, or if he thinks he cannot hold it much longer, on condition that you will allow him to march out with colors flying, drums beating, and such parade as to show that he has not been vanquished. Such a body so marching out is entitled to be saluted by you. These courtesies and parade are called the "honors of war." Surrender of the place alone is usually made, and not of the troops as prisoners of war. In an ordinary surrender the troops give up their arms and become prisoners.

Hors de (or du) Combat. — "Out of the fight"; killed, wounded or missing men are said to be placed *hors de combat*.

Incursions. — Attacks across the border, and into the enemy's territory; or into territory occupied by him.

Intrenchments. — Defensive works thrown up to help troops to hold a position. The simplest form is a ditch the dirt from which is piled up in an embankment behind which the defenders stand. Abatis, and various kinds of entanglements, are erected in front, when time allows, to keep the enemy long under fire from the intrenchments.

Itinerary. — Order of march. Instructions or minutes showing when and on what roads each portion of an army is to march.

Key of a Position. — That point of a battle-field which stands in such relation to the enemy's position that if captured it will oblige him to retreat or will compromise him in some way. A hill overlooking or enfilading his line may be the key to a battle-field.

Left (by the). — A body of troops moves by its left when it moves with its left flank in advance. An army must be so marched as most readily to face towards the enemy, and may be marched by its right or left for this purpose.

Letters of Marque. — Permission given by a government to private individuals to equip vessels and prey upon the commerce of the enemy.

Line. — The length of a body of troops from right to left. Troops used in ancient days to be fought in masses, with files many men deep. This depth has been gradually decreasing. In the last century the file was of eight, six and four men. In this it has come down to three and two. A line of battle of a regiment now consists of two ranks. But a number of regiments may each be in column and the whole army or part of it may be in line of such columns.

Line of Columns by Battalion. — A common form in action for making a heavy line. Each battalion or regiment is ployed into column.

Line of Defense. — A line along which troops are posted across the path of the enemy to resist his further advance. Such a line may be near our base, or out beyond it and connected with it by our line of operations. A river, or a chain of hills, or other natural obstacle is desirable as a line of defense. Such a line is generally intrenched, often with permanent fortifications.

Line of Operations. — (*See* Base.) The line along which an army is advancing or retiring and by which it is victualled.
and such columns stand in line, with suitable intervals.

Lodgment. — A foothold in the enemy's territory, or position, or works.

Logistics. — Originally the art of lodging troops. (*Logis.*) Now the art of supplying troops with rations, material of war, transportation, camp and garrison equipage, and of marching it from place to place. In short, the art of doing everything for an army except manœuvring or fighting it.

Lunge. — The fencer's thrust, to which he gives strength by a quick forward step so as to add to the thrust the weight of his moving body.

Manœuvre. — Any movement of a body of troops intended to accomplish a tactical or a strategic result.

Material of War. — Anything in the nature of arms, ammunition or supplies which pertains to the conduct of war or the support of an army. The word *matériel* is often used to convey a larger meaning than the English word.

Mélée. — A mixed fight, in which the troops on either side are huddled together in a mass, neither party yielding.

Morale. — That cheerful confidence in itself, or its situation, or its leaders, which makes an army full of courage and readiness to encounter danger. The converse of demoralization.

Munitions of War. — Generally applied to ammunition, ordnance and fighting-material of any kind. It may be used in a larger meaning.

Muster. — To bring together a number of men. To enrol men. Specifically, to swear into the U. S. service. A volunteer or drafted man only became entitled to pay and allowances when he was sworn into the U. S. service, or mustered. It might be weeks or months after enlistment before he was mustered. In raising a regiment, the men were enlisted singly, and the regiment, or its companies, when full, were mustered.

Non-combatants. Any one in the military service whose duties do not oblige him to bear arms or to take an active part in battle. Such are surgeons, quarter-masters, their assistants and camp-followers.

Objective. — That place or goal to reach or capture which is the object of the movement going on.

Observe. — To keep watch of a place with a body of troops, so as to hold an enemy in it, or to prevent his attacking you from it.

Offensive-Defensive. — In offensive warfare we attack the enemy to destroy him. In defensive warfare we repel his attack. In offensive-defensive warfare we are on the defense but we attack the enemy to keep him busy so that he shall not invade our territory, or attack us at a disadvantage.

Open Order. — Extended in line.

Outpost. — A small body posted out beyond an army in camp to give timely notice of danger, and to hold the enemy in check until the main body can form to resist his attack. An army in camp is surrounded by a circle of such outposts.

Overslaugh. — When a senior officer has a junior promoted over his head he is said to be overslaughed.

Overt Act of War. — Communities on whose territory the operations of war are being conducted are by the law of nations entitled to protection from harm if they remain peaceful, unless grave public necessity requires the destruction of what may be contraband of war within their limits, or the taking of provisions and supplies for the armies. But any community whose inhabitants interfere with these operations (as by burning bridges, obstructing roads or taking any part in the strife) is liable to be treated as part of the enemy's forces and to be visited with punishment by fire and sword.

Parade Order. — With the steadiness of troops on parade. In action troops rarely preserve anything like such order.

Parapet. — A breastwork. Part of an intrenchment.

Parley. — A communication between enemies for which a temporary cessation of hostilities is made, in order to arrange terms for surrender, or attend to the burial of the dead, care of the wounded, etc., etc. During a parley it is understood that neither party shall alter its position, or take advantage of the situation.

Parole. — The promise on honor given by a prisoner that he will not take up arms again to serve against his captors. Prisoners of war are often paroled when they cannot well be kept and are then set at liberty. They are thereafter exchanged as if still prisoners of war.

Patrol. — A force which moves to and fro to keep watch of a certain point, or which moves around from place to place inspecting the condition of affairs. The force which moves among the outposts of a camp to see that everything is in order.

Picket. — Substantially the same as outposts. The picket-line is generally understood to mean the line of individual sentinels furthest out; the outposts are small bodies acting as reserves to the picket-line.

Place d'armes. — An open spot on which troops can form in proper order as the successive bodies arrive. A parade-ground. It is difficult to deploy troops and start them on their work quickly and in good order, without suitable ground to do it on. Such ground is an essential point in the calculations of any general planning a manœuvre.

Ploy. — To form close-order from open. (*See* Deploy.)

Pontoon. — A portable boat used to bridge rivers. Several pontoons anchored in line at suitable distances with their length up and down stream, and joined by timbers, form a pontoon bridge. Pontoons and their timbers are transported in wagons. The whole is a pontoon-train.

Prestige. — The credit attached to having accomplished success, or to having acted with conspicuous gallantry.

Provost-marshal. — An officer whose duty it is to arrest and hold deserters, spies, etc., and substantially to do the police work of an army or military post.

Raid. — A sudden operation; generally upon the communications of the enemy, or into the enemy's territory. Cavalry, because it moves more swiftly, is used, as a rule. A raid which cuts an enemy's communications with his base seriously compromises his safety, unless he can at once repair damages.

Raise a Siege. — To withdraw from besieging a fortress.

Rank. — A line of men standing shoulder to shoulder; a file is a line of men standing one behind another. " Rank and file " form any body of troops, and is applied to include all but officers.

Rear-guard. — A portion of an army following at a suitable distance to protect it from attack. On the retreat the rear guard is large and important.

Reconnoissance. — The operation of a body sent out to reconnoitre, or discover the whereabouts and force and probable intentions of the enemy. Reconnoissances often end in heavy combats, and sometimes rise to the dignity of battles. A reconnoissance in force is one on a large scale, ready to do heavy fighting if it becomes essential.

Reduce. — To capture a place.

Refused. — When one flank of a line is bent back in crochet-form it is said to be *refused.* This is often done to protect the line from a probable flank attack.

Retire upon. — To move towards, so as to derive support from a depot or citadel or friendly force.

Right (*by the*). — A body of troops moves by its right when it moves with its right flank in advance.

Riposte. — A return lunge in fencing, after a parry.

Salient. — A salient is an outward angle thrown out from a line of troops or fortifications. Its weakness consists in the fact that there is a point in its front from which the enemy can enfilade its sides. Still, a salient is sometimes useful, for if strongly held and protected it can flank an enemy attacking the line on its left or right.

Sally-port. — A gate by which a force can make a dash from a fortress upon the besiegers.

Scout. — A man or a party sent out to discover the enemy and his condition. Also used as a verb.

Siege batteries. — Batteries of heavy guns which cannot be readily moved with an army, as batteries of field-guns are. Siege guns are kept at the rear until wanted. They are generally mounted on specially prepared foundations.

Sit down before. — A besieging or observing force *sits down* before a fortress or strong place.

Skirmish. — A scattering engagement of no great moment. It often precedes more serious work.

Sortie. — A sudden attack from a strong place upon its besiegers, in order to interrupt their plans or break up their lines of approach.

Strategy. — The art of making war on the map. The movement of armies out of sight of each other, after the opening of the campaign. The manœuvres or marches by which a general seeks to place the enemy in such a position that he can fight him at a disadvantage. Strategy is the art of so moving your army that you may in some manner compromise or weaken the enemy's army before you fight it. (*See* Tactics and Grand-tactics.)

Tactics. — In its lesser meaning, the instruction of the soldier or squad or company or regiment in bearing arms and moving as one body. In its larger meaning, the art of moving bodies of troops on the field of battle or in the immediate presence of the enemy. (*See* Strategy.) Having been brought upon the field of battle by such *strategic* movements that your enemy is less well placed than you are (with regard to retreat if he is beaten, or in respect to the ground he actually occupies, or numbers, or in any other way), it still behooves you so to manœuvre *tactically* that you shall defeat him by actual fighting. *E.g.*, a movement of an army or part of an army so as to threaten its enemy's line of operations, if at a distance, would be be a strategic movement. Such was Jackson's march through Thoroughfare Gap, in Pope's campaign. The same movement on the field of battle would be a tactical manœuvre. Such was Jackson's march about Hooker's left flank at Chancellorsville. Again, Lee threw Longstreet upon Meade's left and Early upon his right at Gettysburg on July 2d, and Pickett next day upon Meade's centre, as tactical manœuvres; but the operations by which the Army of Northern Virginia and the Army of the Potomac moved away from and towards each other, starting at Fredericksburg and moving until they reached Gettysburg, were strategic. Tactics often trench on the domain of strategy, and *vice versa.* Many soldiers would call Jackson's manœuvre at Chancellorsville a strategic one; but it **was** constantly in the presence of the enemy.

Take in reverse. — To attack an enemy in his rear or well back of his flank.

Terrain. — The actual ground on which manœuvres or marches are conducted. Generally used in a topographical sense; *i.e.*, with reference to the surface of the land, whether flat, rolling, sandy, much cut up by ravines or streams, or covered with forests, etc., etc.

Threaten. — So to place your army as to be able, unless your enemy alters his position, to attack some weak spot in his defense.

Transports. — Vessels used for transporting troops.

Turn an enemy out of a place. — To oblige an enemy to evacuate a position by moving around his flank and threatening him from this quarter.

Turn the right or left. — To march around the right or left flank of an enemy so as to oblige him to change front or move in retreat.

Uncover. — An army uncovers its line or base or communications when it so moves that the enemy is nearer to them than itself is. Though not directly in front of its base an army may still cover it.

Vanguard. — A smaller force preceding an army by a distance varying according to the numbers and ground, to protect it from sudden attack.

Wing. — An army has a centre and a right and left wing. These three parts may be substantially equal, or either may be larger, according to the lay of the land, the position of the enemy, the work to be accomplished, etc., etc.

Works. — Fortifications or intrenchments of any kind.

INDEX.

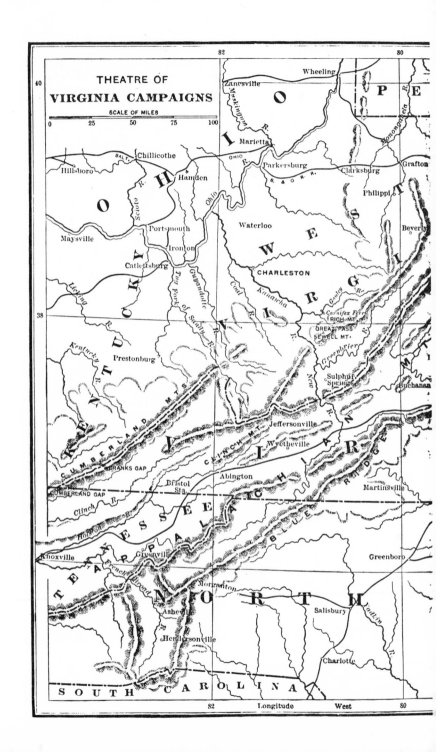

THEATRE OF
VIRGINIA CAMPAIGNS
SCALE OF MILES
0   25   50   75   100

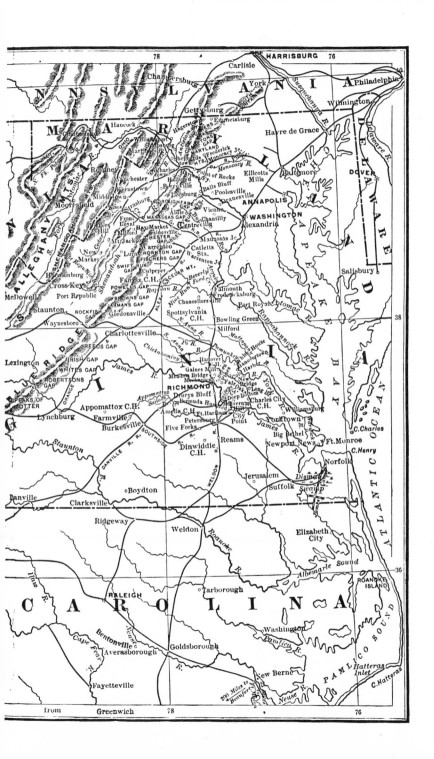

Other titles of interest

A DIARY OF BATTLE
The Personal Journals of
Colonel Charles S. Wainwright,
1861–1865
Edited by Allan Nevins
New foreword by Stephen W.
Sears
584 pp., 11 maps
80846-3 $17.95

THE JEWEL OF LIBERTY
Abraham Lincoln's Re-election
and the End of Slavery
David E. Long
410 pp., 40 illus.
80788-2 $15.95

**THE LIFE OF GENERAL
ALBERT SIDNEY JOHNSTON**
His Services in the Armies of the
United States, the Republic of
Texas, and the Confederate States
Colonel William Preston Johnston
New introd. by T. Michael Parrish
807 pp., 9 illus., 9 maps
80791-2 $19.95

CAESAR
Theodore Ayrault Dodge
816 pp., 253 illus.
80787-4 $22.50

ALEXANDER
Theodore Ayrault Dodge
723 pp., 234 illus., maps, and
charts
80690-8 $19.95

HANNIBAL
Theodore Ayrault Dodge
702 pp., 227 charts, maps, plans,
and illus.
80654-1 $19.95

ABRAHAM LINCOLN
His Speeches and Writings
Edited by Roy P. Basler
Preface by Carl Sandburg
888 pp., 6 illus.
80404-2 $19.95

**THE ANNALS OF THE
CIVIL WAR**
Written by Leading Participants
North and South
New introd. by Gary W. Gallagher
808 pp., 56 illus.
80606-1 $21.50

**THE ANTIETAM AND
FREDERICKSBURG**
General Francis W. Palfrey
New introduction by
Stephen W. Sears
244 pp., 4 maps
80691-6 $13.95

**BATTLE-PIECES AND
ASPECTS OF THE WAR**
Herman Melville
New introd. by Lee Rust Brown
282 pp.
80655-X $13.95